Television by Stream

Also of Interest
and from McFarland

The Netflix Vision of Horror: A Narrative Structural Analysis of Original Series (by Sotiris Petridis, 2021)

Anatomy of the Slasher Film: A Theoretical Analysis (by Sotiris Petridis, 2019)

Television by Stream

Essays on Marketing, Content and Audience Worldwide

Edited by Christina Adamou *and* Sotiris Petridis

McFarland & Company, Inc., Publishers
Jefferson, North Carolina

This book has undergone peer review.

LIBRARY OF CONGRESS CATALOGUING-IN-PUBLICATION DATA

Names: Adamou, Christina, 1977– editor. | Petridis, Sotiris, 1990– editor.
Title: Television by stream : essays on marketing, content and audience worldwide / edited by Christina Adamou and Sotiris Petridis.
Description: Jefferson, North Carolina : McFarland & Company, Inc., Publishers, 2023 | Includes bibliographical references and index.
Identifiers: LCCN 2023009359 | ISBN 9781476685915 (paperback : acid free paper) ∞ ISBN 9781476648330 (ebook)
Subjects: LCSH: Streaming video. | Digital television. | Internet television. | Television viewers.
Classification: LCC HD9697.V542 T45 2023 | DDC 006.7/876—dc23/edtf/20230306
LC record available at https://lccn.loc.gov/2023009359

BRITISH LIBRARY CATALOGUING DATA ARE AVAILABLE

ISBN (print) 978-1-4766-8591-5
ISBN (ebook) 978-1-4766-4833-0

Printed in the United States of America

McFarland & Company, Inc., Publishers
Box 611, Jefferson, North Carolina 28640
www.mcfarlandpub.com

Table of Contents

Part 3—Case Studies and Narrative Representations

Introduction

Christina Adamou
and Sotiris Petridis

Television content has expanded to new and different ways of distribution and screening enabled by the evolution of technology and the advent of new media. The diversity of production and distribution models can be divided into three general categories: broadcast networks (such as ABC, NBC, CBS etc.), cable networks (such as HBO, Showtime, AMC etc.), and online subscription services that provide their content via streaming (such as Netflix, Amazon, Hulu, Apple TV+, Disney+, HBO Max etc.)

The question that emerges is whether online television platforms constitute an evolution or a revolution, in relation to the production, distribution and interaction with audiences. Although the death of television has too often and prematurely been announced, television has proved to be resilient and quick to adapt. Television has been in transition for a long time: the industry has been undergoing important changes, although forms of traditional television production and broadcasting are persisting. Television content is both re-distributed on subscription internet platforms and produced for them. As audiences, we are able to customize and personalize our viewing.

Subscription video on demand (SVOD) platforms are similar to traditional TV packages that allow users to consume as much content as they desire at a flat fee per month. Unlike the economic model of conventional broadcast networks, which is primarily dependent on revenue provided by advertisers in exchange for a network's inclusion of advertisements within their programming broadcasts, the subscription model is based on a direct economic relationship between the institution and its subscribers who pay a fee in exchange for access to programming. Netflix is a pioneer in this field, but numerous other production companies, like Disney, Apple, and WarnerMedia, have created subscription video on demand (SVOD) platforms to host their content. The market is booming and audiences seem to welcome this new relationship to television content.

Apart from giving new life to older audiovisual works by making them accessible to the wide public through an alternative way of consumption, SVOD platforms are producing original content that is meant to be consumed exclusively via online means. Industry changes also affect the content: Significantly, some popular series produced for or by SVOD platforms are interactive, thus forging a more personalized and direct relation to the viewer. Conventional television practices are now largely replaced by the technological evolution of the medium, which has drastically changed the landscape of the audiovisual industry.

Audiences have also evolved in opposing yet interlinked ways: the globalization of the audience is unprecedented but so is its fragmentation. Personalized viewing and viewing on demand have resulted in audience fragmentation, solitary watching and binge-watching. Although cable networks had already started these shifts in how audiences and their relations to content are constituted, the shifts have become more dramatic and more attention has recently been called to them. Television as a mass medium often seems to be a thing of the past, as mass audiences largely seem to have been replaced by niche audiences and/or solitary watching. Yet, content addressed to mass audiences such as news and sport are missed and retain their importance, while solitary viewing is more than often dependent on which programs are trending. Audiences have become more complex as our viewing experiences have evolved.

Content has also evolved in complex ways that reflect both changes in industry and viewing habits. Narrative complexity and emphasis on aesthetics, which were initially linked to cable television, have gained more importance and are most prominent on SVOD platforms. They aim to retain viewer interest while binge-watching as well as build quality connotations for the internet television platforms. Genre hybridity and the re-invention of TV genres also characterize a lot of the new content, which aims to renew the interest of audiences and/or create niche audiences. Yet, renewed genres, complex narratives and "quality" aesthetics co-exist with old genres and/or programs, forming a very complex televisual landscape.

This edited collection will focus on this turning point of the medium and the fundamental changes that it has brought, as well as any continuities noted. It will cover aspects of the globalized markets and their relationship with audiences, focusing both on the globalization and second-tier SVODs, while it will include in depth analyzes of case studies and representations.

In order to achieve these goals, the book is divided into three major parts. The first part is dedicated to Netflix and its responses to globalized markets and audiences. Here, in their essay "On Netflix's Alleged Distinction and the Future of Television," Mayka Castellano and Melina

Meimaridis investigate Netflix's current status, calling into question the expectations created after the streaming service was introduced to the global television market.

In "Streaming Audience Data, Ratings, and the Future of 'Popular' Television," Michael L. Wayne uses a variety of publicly available secondary data from sources including trade press articles, press releases, trade and popular press interviews to construct a history of the industrial discourses surrounding Netflix's audience metrics. These discourses are then compared to those related to Nielsen ratings as the traditional metric for U.S. commercial television.

Ahngeli Shivam in "A New Age of Diversity and Visibility" examines three distinct but linked medial entities that uniquely interrogate dominant paradigms of power, creativity, and collaboration that influence each other and the larger media landscape [mediascape]: the executive level, the writers' room, and the "Matrix Stage." These entities illustrate a certain function and importance for the representation for and by transpacific cultural producers and also highlight the limitations they face with the current, albeit changing, state of affairs.

The last essay in the first part of the book, "Contemplating the 'Original' in an Age of Branded Content, Branded Networks, Branded Genres and Branded Adaptations," by Katerina Marazi, centers around a guiding question: What is an "original" in a branded context unlike that of an adaptation context? While the answer may appear self-evident and simple, it prompts an array of numerous inter-related questions that can be examined from various perspectives as the effects of such clashes do trickle towards multiple directions be that branded storytelling, branded marketing, industrial intertextuality, branded experiences and even reconfiguring or branding terms such as "original." The Netflix branding practice of "original" is examined in connection with the recent Disney brand practices related to *The Jungle Book* (Benson 2020) as well as to the Marvel/ Netflix superhero productions so as to examine the multiple layers of the term "original."

The second part of this book is called "Beyond Netflix: Globalization and Second-Tier SVODs." This part starts with the essay of Daniel Keyes called "Encore+: Orphaned Canadian Content in the Age of Digital Abundance," in which he explores how the ad revenue model of YouTube provides a path for reviving and preserving access to Canadian content that has fallen through the cracks of SVOD that characteristically provides abundance defined by the newest and latest while ignoring older content.

Alexa Scarlata and Andrew Lynch in their essay, "Opting Out of the Streaming Wars: Second and Third Tier SVODs," explore multinational second-tier players hayu (reality TV) and Acorn TV (British drama), and third-tier services MUBI (rotating arthouse and auteurs) and Full Moon Features (exploitation and horror), that have largely escaped academic inquiry, despite their strategic diversity and surprising commercial resilience making them worthwhile objects of investigation. They have been able to carve out a viable place in the larger streaming ecosystem, where they are complementary to the first tier SVODs rather than competitive.

The last essay of the second part of the book is Jason Scott's "Disney+: Legacy Media Strikes Back," in which he develops the significance of Disney+, to the conglomerate but also the evolving and contested streaming market. For Disney this encompasses the major change to the conglomerate's business model, with its reorganization emphasizing this new focus on the direct-to-consumer global market, but also includes continuities with its economic history. Disney+ brings to streaming a combination of the legacy media focus on content (particularly branded and franchised) coupled with distributor power, and the digital business model focused on data that enables personalization, aggregating taste cultures through an intuitive interface.

The third and last part of the book is dedicated to "Case Studies and Narrative Representations." Here, in "Coherence Effects in Digital TV: The Case of Anthology Series," Patrick Gill tracks the arc of the narratological development of TV series from network TV via box sets to streaming services and investigates different forms of coherence favored in different media contexts. This essay discusses the boom of supposedly serial sitcoms in the first decade of the 21st century and the devices they used to suggest coherence and teleology. With this exemplar of a purported need for seriality over episodicity as its backdrop, this essay then moves on to the second decade of the 21st century and new forms of coherence established in anthology shows such as Black Mirror and Fargo.

Despoina Triantafyllidou in "Joshua Marston's *Come Sunday* (2018): Biopic in the Streaming Era" examines a biographical film about the true story of Carlton Pearson, an Evangelical Bishop who was expelled from his church for heretical opinions. The analysis focuses on a "contextual" and "textual" approach of the film, while examining whether this biopic, produced and distributed by Netflix, is constructed according to its classical origins.

In "The Binge-Watch Experience and the Three-Act Structure: A Narrative Analysis of *Stranger Things*," Sotiris Petridis analyzes the overarching story of the series and argues that the structure of the narrative works more like a long-form film, rather than a TV series. In order to prove this argument, he compares the narrative structure of the first season of *Stranger Things* with the structure of *Stand by Me* and proves that both audiovisual works are created based on the norms of the three-act model of narration.

In their essay "Repackaging the Past: Commodification, Nostalgia and Feminist/Queer Politics in Netflix Originals *GLOW* (2017–2019) and *Hollywood* (2020)," Spyridon Chairetis and Georgia Aitaki contribute to the emerging debate on the potentialities and specificities of original content of SVOD platforms by focusing on two Netflix Original dramas: *GLOW* (2017–2019) and *Hollywood* (2020). Against the background of the post–me too era and with reference to the notion of "woke TV," as well as drawing from Netflix's use of nostalgia as a strategy to engage with multiple audiences, they argue that these cases offer complex and insightful entry points into the status of gender/queer politics in contemporary television through various uses of the past.

In Jossalyn G. Larson's essay, "Cats and True Crime: Empathetic Responses and Moral Consequences in On-Demand Docuseries," there is an examination of cat-centric true crime through the lens of moral psychology in order to consider the manner in which the new and intense consumption behaviors enabled by SVOD platforms expediates the articulation of new moral standards, of protagonists and antagonists, and situates the viewer as a flawed crime fighter.

Finally, in "Super-Heroines to the Rescue (of Feminism): *She-Ra and the Princesses of Power*," Christina Adamou focuses on three popular children's programs available on Netflix that feature super-heroines: *PJ Masks*, *Miraculous: Tales of Ladybug & Cat Noir* and *She-Ra and the Princesses of Power*. She takes into account the age and gender of target-audiences and analyze the narrative structures (typical of episodes as well as over-arching narratives), choice and design of characters, super-powers and sexuality as well as intertextual relations (to super-heroes and princesses) in order to link them to performances of gender, third-wave feminism and queer theory.

This edited collection is dedicated to the study of the SVOD platforms and the future of television. We feel that an important contribution to the field is that the edited collection expands beyond Netflix, in order to analyze a complex global phenomenon and take into account contemporary evolutions in the industry and the SVOD market. The book also aims to re-contextualize notions such as originality and popularity in television studies as well as trace aesthetic and narrative trends. Representations and ideological characteristics of audiovisual texts are also studied, since content is considered an important and ever-evolving part of popular culture. Based on a plethora of carefully organized and similarly structured essays, this book enriches the bibliography regarding the future of television and thoroughly studies the effects of the new media in the television landscape with regard to institutions, audiences and content.

Part 1

Netflix Responds to Globalized Markets and Audience

On Netflix's Alleged Distinction and the Future of Television

Mayka Castellano
and Melina Meimaridis

In 2020 the U.S. television industry produced over 490 scripted shows.[1] Other prominent markets have also seen an increase in TV exports, as Brazil, Spain, and South Korea. Given the recent technological advancements, the contemporary television landscape has an overwhelming quantity of available products and intense consumption of fictional serialized narratives. In this context, Netflix established itself as an important player in the audiovisual market producing content and investing in cultural industries from around the world.[2] The company started off as a DVD rental service in 1997 and began streaming content ten years later. By 2013, Netflix was creating content and employing a discourse of distinction to promote its originals and itself as a novel kind of TV producer. Because of this, critics and journalists started to position the streamer as the future of television. Yet, in this essay, we aim to deconstruct this notion as well as point the limitations to the company's distinction discourse. Our principal argument is that there is an unreasonable focus on the notion of "novelty" linked to video streaming services and the kind of products they offer, when, in reality, a large part of their financial investments and most successful products are legacies from linear television.

Different than linear-TV, structured around a programming schedule, Netflix makes content available in a non-linear manner. By freeing itself from TV's schedule, Netflix is able to engage "in a project of deterritorialization."[3] The streamer's library contains products from several audiovisual industries from around the globe. Although different in certain countries/regions, Netflix's library is its greatest weapon in attracting new subscribers, keeping them satisfied, and avoiding turnover.

Nonetheless, cultivating an attractive library has proven to be a tricky goal. Netflix's dependency on licensing agreements is fueling the so-called streaming wars, sparking disputes over the possession and production of desirable content, whether old or new around the world.

In Netflix's quest to forge an independent library, it received a great amount of media attention. Several online articles rushed to declare the end of television (once again) and to suggest that "Netflix is killing TV."[4] Media articles from around the world presented great enthusiasm with the "revolution" Netflix would bring to the medium.[5] However, recent data on Netflix's most-watched programs in the U.S. market reveal the popularity of TV shows from linear TV, such as the sitcoms *Friends* (NBC, 1994–2004) and *The Office* (NBC, 2005–2013) and the medical drama *Grey's Anatomy* (ABC, 2005–).[6] In this sense, the so-called "TV of the future" is still deeply connected with the "TV of the past."

Based on a review of the literature and of trade press coverage, in this essay, we shed light on Netflix's discourse of distinction and its fragilities. Here, we divided our analysis into three key variables: revenue model, formats, and consumption practices. Although Netflix reshaped the delivery of content to audiences and popularized binge-watching, we contend that the platform still reiterates practices associated with linear television. We aspire to contribute to the discussion on the future of television from an unconventional point of view. Despite the possibilities awakened by the feeling of unrestricted access, stylistic revolutions and ubiquity, as long as Netflix, and other streaming video services for that matter, depend on linear television's programming to compose their library, the future of television seems to lie in the medium's past.

Netflix's Discourse of Distinction

Since it began producing original content, Netflix has employed a discourse of distinction. The company tries to distinguish itself and its productions in a crowded television landscape. Producers and creators started to promote their Netflix shows calling them "cinematographic." This label encompasses anything from their narrative structure, high production value to their photography aesthetics, among other elements. In one instance, they even used expressions as "it's a 13-hour movie" to describe a complete season of *House of Cards* (2013–2018) or *Orange Is the New Black* (2013–2019).[7] What lies behind Netflix's discourse of distinction is a two-fold strategy that aims to: (1) distance its productions from linear TV; and (2) associate them with more legitimized art forms (e.g., film and the cinematic arts).

This is not the first time a producer of television content has tried to associate their productions with higher art forms. Actually, this process became the norm for a couple of cable networks, starting in the 1990s with HBO's branding campaign "it's not TV, it's HBO." This strategy engages with the concept of "quality television," which became popular in the 1980s and 1990s in the United States and was used to describe several distinct characteristics, such as creative freedom, aesthetic and narrative innovations, liberal and progressive programming, among several others.[8] Nevertheless, HBO's slogan takes this further by positioning HBO's content as so innovative and revolutionary that it was anything but TV. This controversial slogan is a discursive way of claiming a vicarious prestige, in which HBO borrows legitimatization from other more reputable art forms. Some of the network's creators promoted episodes of popular shows like *The Sopranos* (HBO, 1999–2006) as small movies,[9] while others framed episodes of *The Wire* (HBO, 2002–2008) as chapters in a novel.[10]

The association with cinema and literature would serve as a seal of distinction and position these productions as "not TV." In other words, these productions escaped the narrative and aesthetic norms traditionally attached to the television medium. This strategy is by no means unproblematic. When film directors want to distance themselves and their productions from Hollywood's blockbusters, they criticize the industry's practices as a way of elevating the status of their own works. Yet, these professionals do not go so far as to deny the medium; they are not making "not cinema." Cable television channels in the U.S., however, resorted to the "not TV" strategy as a way of attributing a distinctive value to their works. The viewers associated with this "not TV," notes Newman, "are generally more masculine, adult, and upscale by comparison with those associated with ordinary television, conceived as feminized mass culture addressed at a lowest common denominator."[11]

The conception that television is a "bad object"[12] and unworthy of the artistic status that film and literature have enjoyed is the result of an elitist view of quality and taste. To understand this process the notion of distinction proposed by Bourdieu is useful.[13] Cultural and intellectual elites, in a way, rationalize their distaste for television, a popular and massive medium, by demeaning its content. These elites use a positive distinction by claiming they prefer the consumption of books, plays, and films to television. However, Bourdon also notes a dimension of "negative distinction," in which individuals affirm they "do not have a TV at home" or "they don't even watch TV."[14]

It is interesting to note how this type of logic has gained a new aspect in the current television landscape. People who watch TV content quite regularly in streaming video services claim they don't watch television. Although it might sound sanctimonious, it is only an advancement of the "not TV" discourse promoted by HBO years ago. In other words, companies who often seek to distance themselves from television, through discursive strategies, fuel this confusion between technology and language.

The strategy of promoting yourself through distinction discourses today is no longer a privilege of HBO. Other cable channels and streaming services in the U.S. have used the same strategy to attract and foster subscriber fidelity. They promise sophisticated narratives, greater racial and gender representation, and more authorial freedom and autonomy.[15] Netflix, for example, guarantees "prestigious, full, participatory and personalized" content.[16] Moreover, the company's discourse of distinction is also tied to other social agents of validation, as critics, fan communities, and academic legitimation.

Television scholars have scrutinized the fragilities of HBO's distinction strategies.[17] Here, we propose that Netflix's distinction discourse is just as controversial. To unpack this, we need to focus on two separate levels: (1) original programming, and (2) the platform's content library. First, Netflix chooses to highlight the quality of its original commissions. *The Crown* (2016–) is certainly the drama that comes closest to the cinematographic aesthetic the company promotes. Yet, Netflix still produces shows that resemble U.S. television staples. Programs like the multi-camera sitcom *Fuller House* (Netflix, 2016–2020) or the reality cooking competition *Sugar Rush* (Netflix, 2018–) come to mind. Because Netflix is not bound to a twenty-four-hour programming schedule and its need to cater to several different audiences, not only in the United States but in over 190 countries, the company has diversified its original programming in such a way that it is difficult to guarantee the same level of quality and prestige to all its original productions. Otherwise, the company's library has a significant amount of licensed content from linear television. So, by choosing to combine their original productions with those from other linear TV channels, instead of breaking with TV's traditions, Netflix is strengthening them.

A Closer Look into Netflix's Strategies and Practices

To understand Netflix's distinction discourse and highlight its strengths and fragilities, we have focused on three key variables: revenue model, format and consumption practices.

Revenue Model

Here, we understand linear television refers to a model of television that is bound to the programming schedule.[18] It is also intricately organized around the goal of reaching the largest possible audience, who watches a specific program synchronously. Non-linear TV, on the other hand, has detached itself from TV's 24-hour schedule. Streaming video services organize their programs in a content library. This difference is relevant to highlight the changes and continuities between Netflix and linear TV. We can divide linear TV into ad-supported and subscription-supported. Non-linear TV platforms like Netflix, Amazon Prime, and Hulu share a subscription-supported revenue model.[19] Thus, streaming video services' primary interest is not related to catering to advertisers, but to attracting new subscribers and cultivating their loyalty. They also do not need subscribers to watch a specific content at the same time, or indeed at all. Their main goal is to keep users satisfied by frequently finding content that is worth their monthly payments.

It should be noted that the costs of subscriptions between linear TV channels and streaming video services can vary greatly, especially in peripheral markets. Let's consider Brazil for example. The country's Pay-TV has a very limited penetration reaching less than 10 percent of the population.[20] The main reason for this is that Brazil has very expansive cable bundles and a strong national broadcasting system that meets consumers' programming needs. Also, premium subscription-supported channels, such as HBO and Cinemax, are only included in the costliest packages. Meanwhile, in 2020, Netflix surpassed the number of Pay-TV subscribers in the country.[21] As of January 2021, Netflix reached an estimated 19 million subscribers in Brazil.[22] The preference for Netflix, then, can be associated with a better monetary value. Currently, Brazil is Netflix's second-largest market in the world, only behind the United States.

Netflix, unlike some of its U.S.-based competitors, does not have its own consolidated library, as does Warner's HBO Max or Universal's Peacock. Also, the service is not part of a larger business model, like Apple TV+ or Amazon Prime Video. In this sense, Netflix depends on subscribers' interest in accessing its content library. To attract subscribers and avoid turnover, Netflix needs to provide an attractive library. To do this, Netflix has depended on licensing agreements. According to Lotz, Netflix currently uses two main licensing models: acquisitions and commissions.[23] Acquisitions refer to content produced by other companies, which can be exclusive to Netflix or available in other windows. Commissions, on the other hand, are programs in which Netflix has some kind of financial or creative input, thus, creates. Given the nature of licensing agreements, these productions eventually leave the streamer's catalog and become unavailable to subscribers. Netflix's library of titles, in this sense, is subject to constant reconfiguration.

When transitioning from a video rental store to a streaming service,

Netflix invested heavily in acquisitions. Yet, with the end of these licensing agreements and a higher cost to maintain availability of popular products, the company has, in recent years, invested globally in commissions and co-commissions (when the production is available on linear TV in a certain country, but in the rest of the world it is exclusive to Netflix).[24] It is interesting to note that Netflix strategically makes it difficult for subscribers to distinguish between their acquisitions and commissions when cataloging their "Netflix Originals."[25] For example, Netflix lists the drama *Dynasty* (The CW, 2017) as a "Netflix Original" in libraries around the world, because the company has the global licensing rights; however, the linear TV channel The CW produces and airs the drama in the United States. Ultimately, this strategy fosters inaccurate understandings about Netflix's library, which works to solidify the company's positioning as a global producer/creator of content.[26]

Formats

Although Netflix has released original content for several years, it is still very difficult to pinpoint a specific programming strategy. Netflix commissioned and co-commissioned productions do not follow formats as rigid as those on linear TV. The main reason for this is that they are not bound to the schedule or to advertisement placements during an episode. In this sense, Netflix produces comedy and dramatic shows with a flexible number of episodes per season, like *Blood & Water* (Netflix, 2020–) and *Sweet Magnolias* (Netflix, 2020–), which had 6 and 10 episodes respectively. The duration of each episode also varies, depending on the production. Moreover, Netflix's original live-action commissions seem to be short-lived. Currently, the longest Netflix original is *Orange Is the New Black* with 7 seasons. On the other hand, several commissioned shows only lasted one season, such as *Girlboss* (2017), *I'm Not Okay with This* (2019), *Spinning Out* (2020), *The Irregulars* (2021), and *Jupiter's Legacy* (2021), among many others. In this sense, it is troubling to consider Netflix the future of television if its own original commissions have struggled to find lasting success.

Although the company has invested heavily in shows like *The Crown*, *House of Cards* and *Orange Is the New Black*, we wish to highlight two programming strategies that weaken Netflix's distinction discourse. First, the company has weaponized nostalgia[27] by reviving canceled shows in hopes of reawaking fandoms, like *Arrested Development* (Fox, 2003–2006/Netflix, 2013–2019) and *The Killing* (AMC, 2011–2013/Netflix, 2014). Netflix also appeals to the viewer's memory by updating old productions, such as *Fuller House* and *One Day at a Time* (Netflix, 2017–2019 / Pop TV, 2020).

The streamer has also replicated established formulas from linear TV in the United States, such as the black sitcoms *Family Reunion* (2019–) and *#BlackAF* (2020–). These shows can be considered a safer investment in a moment of great competition from other streaming video services.[28]

On the other hand, Netflix has invested heavily in a TV product that has always had its legitimacy questioned: reality shows. TV critics point to the emergence of reality shows in the library as a sign of a possible decline in the quality of programming offered by the company. Several journalistic articles framed the rise of reality shows as trash.[29] Yet, this popularization only astonishes those who believed in Netflix's discourse of distinction. This investment translates into a concern to make the company's library more attractive and for a good part of the reality show audience, they have been successful. Low investment programs, produced quickly, with financial returns that are often high and responsible for fostering conversations on social media, these products now occupy more space in streaming video services. Netflix's original reality shows grew from 2 in 2016 to over 60 in 2020.[30]

Even more revealing is the fact that Netflix is still dependent on its acquisitions, mainly productions from a TV model said to have died, i.e., broadcast TV shows. These titles fill the company's library and are some of the most popular programs available on the streamer. In a library with so many titles, viewers gravitate toward such productions as *The Office*, *Friends*, and *Grey's Anatomy*. According to data from Jumpshot, publicized by Vox in 2018, of the 20 most popular shows on Netflix's U.S. library, 17 came precisely from that model of television considered to be a "TV from the past."[31] It is interesting how even in the face of data like this, journalists, TV critics, and even some scholars still insist that television is dying.

Consumption Practices

Finally, it is in the consumption practices variable that we find the greatest distinctions in the Netflix model. For several decades, the main form of spectatorship of linear TV programs was appointment viewing, in which viewers took time from their daily schedules to see their favorite shows. The main argument Netflix uses to challenge linear TV norms is its non-dependence on a programming schedule. According to Reed Hastings, Netflix's CEO, appointment viewing is a form of "manageable dissatisfaction."[32] Hastings highlights that on Netflix viewers have more control to watch what they want when they want.

The distribution model favored by Netflix is part of a larger context in which time-shifting practices become more mainstream and there is a multiplicity of ways to access television content.[33] The one-drop model used by Netflix makes available all the episodes of a season at once. This distribution model boosts the practice of binge-watching, characterized as the habit of watching multiple episodes of a TV show in one sitting. The term started to appear in several journalistic articles in 2013 after Netflix released a full season of its original drama *House of Cards* in February.[34]

Despite Netflix's push to solidify binge-watching as a *new* consumption practice, before the advent of streaming services, the consumption of multiple episodes was viable through internet piracy, DVD-box sets, VHS tapes, or even television marathons.[35] However, Netflix did ease the practice by offering a large content library that is accessible through a subscription. Netflix constantly encourages binging by releasing new seasons from its original commissions on Fridays or on the eve of holidays. The company's "post play" function, which provides the viewer with a few seconds before it starts the next episode, and the main menu page of the interface, that exhibits the shows the viewer was watching, are other ways in which Netflix facilitates the binge-watching experience. Although other streaming services encourage binging, Jenner argues Netflix uses binge-watching as a unique branding strategy.[36]

Lastly, when video streaming services first popularized journalistic articles rush to not only state that they would (supposedly) kill TV, but also DVDs, which would become extinct.[37] These services would replace the DVD, just as the latter replaced VHS tapes. This flawed reasoning, in reality, reveals a paradigm shift, from a more permanent logic—in which the DVD represented the possession of a cultural asset—to a more ephemeral logic, focused on a subscription and temporary access to audiovisual products in a content library.[38] Yet, such ephemerality has led to titles vanishing from video streaming services. This process weakens Netflix's discourse of "freedom" and that the viewer is "in control." In reality, the company's library is constantly adding and removing content, placing the viewer at its mercy. We should note that, in 2019, when Netflix announced the departure of *Friends* and *The Office* from its library in the United States, DVD sales of both comedies soared in the country.[39]

The Future of Television Is…

What is the future of television? This question, which has concerned scholars for a couple of decades, routinely arises in the media, with journalists hastily putting an end to a medium that is still so prevalent today. Considering the latest technological innovations and new models of television distribution, Netflix soon established itself as emblematic of this "new" television. Although the company frequently employs a discourse of distinction and positions itself as a "new" type of producer, we contend that the notion of Netflix as the future of television is deceptive.

This is not the first time that critics and scholars have debated the future of television.

Television is a medium constantly in transformation. In spite of this, scholars, critics, and other business insiders are frequently anxious by the prospects that lie ahead. In a way, it is as if nothing would withstand the alluring arrival of something "new." In this sense, the debate concerning the end or the future of TV rests in some kind of faith in the redemption of the medium, which could occur after a novelty is introduced. This process is noticeable in the past with the debut and establishment of the videotape, color TV, remote controls, and cable TV. Today it manifests chiefly in discourses about streaming video services. We understand this search for redemption as the "eternal debate on television quality." It reveals that television is not completely legitimized and critics and scholars are still searching for ways to rehabilitate the medium and justify their interest in it and its productions.

Several journalistic texts committed to analyzing the emergence of Netflix seem to confuse the notion of television as a medium with the electronic set itself, commonly called TV. Even though this confusion seems insignificant, it can explain the contradiction why, critics and journalists argue that we are in the "Peak TV era," characterized by exorbitant numbers of production, circulation, and consumption of television productions, and, at the same time, also impudently claim that television is dying. If some individuals today disavow the TV set in the middle of the living room, others still spend countless hours watching television content on smartphones, tablets, laptops, etc. In this sense, when we say "TV" we ascribe to a collection of phenomena that comprise social, technological, cultural, aesthetic, and even legal issues. These appear in an audiovisual production with a particular grammar, financing systems, audience social practices, global flows, among numerous other matters.

Television's death is not a new topic among scholars, critics, and, particularly, journalists. The same longing for changes and transformations in the medium lies in the desire to determine its end.[40] Much of the discussion encompassing the end of television centers on the dispute between the medium and the Internet. According to Buonanno, the enchantment with "new media" and technological-based transformations experienced in the digital age makes television obsolescence a habitual theme in specialized media since the mid–1980s and a key concern in academia since the early 2000s.[41] The author contends (supported by the work of Graeme Turner) that these discussions revolved around two contrasting points of view: "broadcast pessimism" and "digital optimism."[42]

Yet, according to Dhoest and Simons, a great part of these works considered the future of television without reflecting carefully on the significant role of the audience.[43] In other words, discussions on the new television ages have continuously been related to a kind of technophilia, quickly captivated by a market discourse that the specialized media propagates. Dedicated scholars investigating what has changed in television, usually come to conclusions similar to Van Esler: "television as a medium is actually not terribly different, at least not enough to conclude that we have entered a new era."[44]

Currently, the aforementioned "competition with the Internet" is the largest source of anticipation concerning the imminent end of television. However, scholars from the field of Communication attest that both can coexist. Moreover, our own daily practices reinforce this notion. There is, then, a change in the discourse in which the thought of competition is overcome, but gives rise to the idea of incorporation. Television, then, would "disappear" not because people were going to substitute its content for other online practices, but as a result of it being available over the internet, on services such as Netflix. This reveals a disproportionate importance on the materiality of access and an utter disdain for language.

It is interesting to note that this process seems to only apply to the television medium. Reproducing this reasoning to the cinematographic arts would be to argue that movies could only exist as films when they air in the theater. Despite the significance of this form of exhibition for the cinematographic experience, it would be naive to consider that a movie watched on a TV set would automatically become television content. This notion, which considers the device as the basis of the relationship with the medium, reveals a lot about the driving force behind discussions on the potential interpenetrations between these contents' production and consumption forms. Here, we do not wish to maintain some kind of purism in the boundaries of what is, ultimately, televisuality, but it seems problematic that television is oftentimes diluted in the more widespread notion of "audiovisual media" while cinema, despite its many transformations, is comparatively exempted from this.

The rise and popularization of video streaming services, especially Netflix, has re-sparked media discourses about the death of television and the medium's future. Here we understand streaming video services reveal trends in the manner in which individuals desire to watch TV. In this sense, we comprehend that most inquiries on the end of TV should, in reality, question how long the linear television model will resist as the principal (or only) form of access to TV content. But even this discussion should be addressed with prudence, considering the strength of linear television in several countries, as in Brazil. Alternatively, the data on access to these services and a thorough examination of the company's programming and investment strategies might reveal what people want to watch. This weakens a significant part of the discussions already proposed, in the media and in academic circles, about the future of television.

If the remarkably saturated media environment has led video streaming services to bet on a more established TV language, which is familiar, on the other hand, these same services have had difficulty maintaining a content library consistent with a brand positioning aligned with a "not-television" discourse, notably with regard to the notion of quality television. Netflix's recent investments in reality shows and nostalgic content are just a sample of how the company dissociates itself from its own distinction discourses. In this process, Netflix ultimately reiterates models from a kind of television that (supposedly) has been dying for a while.

Notes

1. Lesley Goldberg, "Peak TV Update: Scripted Originals Dip 7% in 2020, FX Says," *The Hollywood Reporter*, January 29, 2021. https://www.hollywoodreporter.com/live-feed/peak-tv-update-scripted-originals-dip-7-in-2020-fx-says.

2. Ramon Lobato, *Netflix nations: The geography of digital distribution*. NYU Press, 2019.

3. Mareike Jenner, *Netflix and the Re-invention of Television*. Springer, 2018, 211.

4. Matt Ladue, "Will Netflix Kill TV?," *Pop Matters*, June 12, 2013. https://www.popmatters.com/171978-netflix-binge-viewing-and-the-end-of-television-2495753251.html.

5. Eduardo Salgado, "Como a revolução do streaming mudou as TVs e Hollywood," *Exame*, September 7, 2017. https://exame.com/revista-exame/como-a-revolucao-do-streaming-mudou-os-negocios-das-tvs/; Colin Cullis, "Streaming killed the TV star," *Capetalk*, October 19, 2016. http://www.capetalk.co.za/articles/193046/streaming-killed-the-tv-star-bizun.

6. Rani Molla, "Here are some of the most popular shows on Netflix—which may be leaving Netflix soon," *Vox*, December 21, 2018. https://www.vox.com/2018/12/21/18139817/netflix-most-popular-shows-friends-office-greys-anatomy-parks-recreation-streaming-tv

7. Chuck Tryon, "TV got better: Netflix's original programming strategies and the on-demand television transition." *Media Industries Journal* 2, no. 2 (2015), 107; Sarah Jane Griffiths, "Orange is the New Black: 'A 13-hour movie,'" *BBC News*, June 5, 2014. https://www.bbc.com/news/entertainment-arts-27721317.

8. Jane Feuer, Paul Kerr and Tise Vahimagi, *MTM: Quality Television*. British Film Institute, 1984;

Michael Z. Newman, "Quality TV as Liberal TV." *Western Humanities Review* 70, no. 3 (2016). http://www.westernhumanitiesreview.com/fall-2016-70-3/quality-tv-as-liberal-tv/

9. David Lavery and Robert Thompson, "David Chase, The Sopranos, and television creativity," in *This thing of ours*: investigating The Sopranos, ed. by David Lavery (New York: Columbia University Press, 2002), 23.

10. Ted Nannicelli, "It's all connected: televisual narrative complexity," In *The Wire*: urban decay and American television, ed. by Tiffany Potter, and C.W. Marshall (New York: Bloomsbury Publishing USA, 2009), 190.

11. Newman, "Quality TV as Liberal TV."

12. Michele Hilmes, "The bad object: Television in the American academy." *Cinema*

Journal 45, no. 1 (2005), 112; Jérôme Bourdon, "Is the End of Television Coming to an End?." *VIEW Journal of European Television History and Culture* 7, no. 13 (2018), 83-85.

13. Pierre Bourdieu, *Distinction: A social critique of the judgement of taste.* Cambridge: Harvard University Press, 1984.

14. Bourdon, "Is the End," 86.

15. Jenner, *Netflix and the Re-invention*," 171-178; Melanie Bourdaa, "Quality Television: construction and de-construction of seriality." In *Previously On*: Interdisciplinary studies on TV Series in the Third Golden Age of Television, ed. by Miguel Perez-Gomez (Sevilla, Spain: Frame, 2011), 34.

16. Tryon, "TV got better," 106.

17. Marc Leverette, Brian L. Ott, and Cara Louise Buckley, eds. *It's not TV: watching HBO in the post-television era* (New York: Routledge, 2009).

18. Amanda Lotz, *Portals: A treatise on internet-distributed television.* Michigan Publishing, 2017.

19. Amanda Lotz, "Q2: How does subscriber funding distinguish SVODs?," *Amanda D. Lotz*, last modified June 8, 2020. http://www.amandalotz.com/netflix-30-qa/2020/6/7/q2-how-does-subscriber-funding-distinguish-svods

20. According to the *Associação Brasileira de Televisão por Assinatura* (Brazilian Pay-TV/ Telecom Association), as of June 2021, Pay-TV services had 13.9 million subscribers in Brazil. http://www.abta.org.br/dados_do_setor.asp

21. Pablo Santana, "Netflix passa TV a cabo em número de assinantes no Brasil, segundo consultoria americana," *Infomoney*, August 28, 2020. https://www.infomoney.com.br/consumo/brasil-tem-mais-assinantes-da-netflix-de-que-tv-a-cabo-segundo-consultoria-americana/#:~:text=Os%20analistas%20da%20empresa%20afirmam,com%2060%20milh%C3%B5es%20de%20assinaturas

22. Carlos Palmeira, "Netflix: Cade revela por engano número de assinantes do streaming no Brasil,"

Tecmundo, October 11, 2021. https://www.tecmundo.com.br/minha-serie/226728-cade-revela-engano-numero-assinantes-netflix-brasil.htm

23. Amanda Lotz, "Q15: Why distinguish between commissions and acquisitions in analyzing SVODs?," *Amanda D. Lotz*, last modified July 23, 2020. http://www.amandalotz.com/netflix-30-qa/2020/7/23/q15-why-distinguish-between-commissions-and-acquisitions-in-analyzing-svods

24. Lotz, "Q15: Why distinguish."

25. Tomaz Penner and Joseph Straubhaar, "Netflix originals and exclusively licensed titles in Brazilian catalog: a mapping producing countries." *MATRIZes* 14 (1):135.

26. Melina Meimaridis, Daniela Mazur and Daniel Rios, "From São Paulo to Seoul: Netflix's strategies

in peripheral markets." *Comunicación Y Sociedad* (2021): 7–8.

27. Mayka Castellano and Melina Meimaridis, "'Weaponizing Nostalgia': Netflix, Revivals, and Brazilian Fans of Gilmore Girls." In *Netflix Nostalgia*: Streaming the Past on Demand, ed. Kathryn Pallister (Lanham: Lexington Books, 2019), 173–174.

28. Castellano and Meimaridis, "'Weaponizing Nostalgia': Netflix," 170.

29. Aubrey Hansen, "Netflix Stoops to New Lows With Reality Show 'Too Hot to Handle,'" *CNN*, April 15, 2020. https://www.ccn.com/netflix-stoops-to-new-lows-with-reality-show-too-hot-to-handle/; John Doyle, "No sex, no sin: Why Netflix's repulsive Too Hot to Handle is an icky hit," *The Globe and Mail*, April 21, 2020. https://www.theglobeandmail.com/arts/television/article-no-sex-no-sin-why-netflixs-repulsive-too-hot-to-handle-is-an-icky/

30. Clara Balbi, "Depois da era de ouro das séries, streaming abraça os programas trash," *Folha de São Paulo*, July 18, 2020. https://www1.folha.uol.com.br/ilustrada/2020/07/depois-da-era-de-ouro-das-series-streaming-abraca-os-programas-trash.shtml?origin=uol

31. Molla, "Here are some of...."

32. Nancy Haas, "And the Award for the Next HBO Goes to...," *GQ Magazine*, January 29, 2013. https://www.gq.com/story/netflix-founder-reed-hastings-house-of-cards-arrested-development

33. Mareike Jenner, "Binge-watching: Video-on-demand, quality TV and mainstreaming fandom." *International Journal of Cultural Studies* 20, no. 3 (2017): 317.

34. Jenner, *Netflix and the Re-invention,*" 109.

35. Charlotte Brunsdon, "Bingeing on box-sets: the national and the digital in television crime drama," in *Relocating Television*: Television in the Digital Context, ed. by Jostein Gripsrud (London: Routledge, 2010), 66.

36. Jenner, *Netflix and the Re-invention,*" 163–168.

37. John Patrick Pullen, "5 Reasons Streaming Is Making DVDs Extinct," *Time Magazine*, June 15, 2015. https://time.com/3921019/streaming-dvds/

38. J.P. Kelly, "'This Title Is No Longer Available': Preserving Television in the Streaming Age." *Television & New Media* (2020): online first.

39. Michael Schneider, "'Friends' DVD, Digital Sales Soar as It Takes a Break From Streaming," *Variety*, February 20, 2020. https://variety.com/2020/tv/news/friends-netflix-streaming-hbo-max-dvd-digital-sales-1203506810/

40. Toby Miller, "A televisão acabou, a televisão virou coisa do passado, a televisão já era." In *A TV em transição*: tendências de programação no Brasil e no mundo, ed. by João Freire Filho (Porto Alegre: Sulina, 2009), 9–10.

41. Milly Buonanno, "Thematic Issue on The End of Television (Not Yet): Editor's Introduction." *Media and Communication* 4, no. 3 (2016): 95

42. Buonanno, "Thematic Issue on The," 95.

43. Alexander Dhoest and Nele Simons, "Still 'watching' TV? The consumption of TV fiction by engaged audiences." *Media and communication* 4, no. 3 (2016): 177.

44. Mike Van Esler. "Not yet the post-TV era: Network and MVPD adaptation to emergent distribution technologies." *Media and Communication* 4, no. 3 (2016): 131.

Works Cited

Balbi, Clara. "Depois da era de ouro das séries, streaming abraça os programas trash," *Folha de São Paulo*, July 18, 2020. https://www1.folha.uol.com.br/ilustrada/2020/07/depois-da-era-de-ouro-das-series-streaming-abraca-os-programas-trash.shtml?origin=uol.

Bourdaa, Melanie. "Quality Television: Construction and De-Construction of Seriality." In *Previously On: Interdisciplinary Studies on TV Series in the Third Golden Age of Television*, edited by Miguel Perez-Gomez, 33–43. Sevilla, Spain: Frame, 2011.

Bourdieu, Pierre. *Distinction: A Social Critique of the Judgement of Taste*. Cambridge: Harvard University Press, 1984.

Bourdon, Jérôme. "Is the End of Television Coming to an End?" *VIEW Journal of European Television History and Culture* 7, no. 13 (2018): 80–95, http://doi.org/10.18146/2213-0969.2018.jethc144.

Brunsdon, Charlotte. "Bingeing on Box-Sets: The National and the Digital in Television Crime Drama." In *Relocating Television: Television in the Digital Context*, edited by Jostein Gripsrud, 61–75. London: Routledge, 2010.

Buonanno, Milly. "Thematic Issue on The End of Television (Not Yet): Editor's Introduction." *Media and Communication* 4, no. 3 (2016): 95–98, http://dx.doi.org/10.17645/mac.v4i3.661.

Castellano, Mayka, and Melina Meimaridis. "'Weaponizing Nostalgia': Netflix, Revivals, and Brazilian Fans of Gilmore Girls." In *Netflix Nostalgia: Streaming the Past on Demand*, edited Kathryn Pallister, 169–184. Lanham, MD: Lexington Books, 2019.

Cullis, Colin. "Streaming killed the TV star," *Capetalk*, October 19, 2016. http://www.capetalk.co.za/articles/193046/streaming-killed-the-tv-star-bizun.

Doyle, John. "No Sex, No Sin: Why Netflix's repulsive Too Hot to Handle is an icky hit," *The Globe and Mail*, April 21, 2020. https://www.theglobeandmail.com/arts/television/article-no-sex-no-sin-why-netflixs-repulsive-too-hot-to-handle-is-an-icky/.

Dhoest, Alexander, and Nele Simons. "Still 'watching' TV? The consumption of TV fiction by engaged audiences." *Media and communication* 4, no. 3 (2016): 176–184, http://dx.doi.org/10.17645/mac.v4i3.427.

Feuer, Jane, Allen Eyles, Paul Kerr, Tise Vahimagi, and David Meeker, eds. *MTM: "quality television."* British Film Institute, 1984.
Goldberg, Lesley. "Peak TV Update: Scripted Originals Dip 7% in 2020, FX Says," *The Hollywood Reporter*, January 29, 2021. https://www.hollywoodreporter.com/live-feed/peak-tv-update-scripted-originals-set-record-2019-1266256.
Griffiths, Sarah Jane. "Orange is the New Black: 'A 13-hour movie,'" *BBC News*, June 5, 2014. https://www.bbc.com/news/entertainment-arts-27721317.
Haas, Nancy. "And the Award for the Next HBO Goes to...," *GQ Magazine*, January 29, 2013. https://www.gq.com/story/netflix-founder-reed-hastings-house-of-cards-arrested-development.
Hansen, Aubrey. "Netflix Stoops to New Lows With Reality Show 'Too Hot to Handle,'" *CNN*, April 15, 2020. https://www.ccn.com/netflix-stoops-to-new-lows-with-reality-show-too-hot-to-handle/.
Hilmes, Michele. "The bad object: Television in the American academy." *Cinema Journal* 45, no. 1 (2005): 111–117, http://dx.doi.org/10.1353/cj.2006.0008.
Jenner, Mareike. "Binge-watching: Video-on-demand, quality TV and mainstreaming fandom." *International Journal of Cultural Studies* 20, no. 3 (2017): 304–320, https://doi.org/10.1177/1367877915606485.
Jenner, Mareike. *Netflix and the Re-invention of Television*. Springer, 2018.
Kelly, J.P. "'This Title Is No Longer Available': Preserving Television in the Streaming Age." *Television & New Media* (2020): online first. https://doi.org/10.1177/1527476420928480.
Ladue, Matt. "Will Netflix Kill TV?," *Pop Matters*, June 12, 2013. https://www.popmatters.com/171978-netflix-binge-viewing-and-the-end-of-television-2495753251.html.
Lavery, David, and Robert Thompson. "David Chase, The Sopranos, and television creativity." In *This Thing of Ours: Investigating* The Sopranos, edited by David Lavery, 18–25. New York: Columbia University Press, 2002.
Leverette, Marc, Brian L. Ott, and Cara Louise Buckley, eds. *It's Not TV: Watching HBO in the Post-Television Era*. New York: Routledge, 2009.
Lobato, Ramon. *Netflix Nations: The Geography of Digital Distribution*. NYU Press, 2019.
Lotz, Amanda D. *Portals: A Treatise on Internet-Distributed Television*. Michigan Publishing, University of Michigan Library, 2017.
Lotz, Amanda. "Q2: How does subscriber funding distinguish SVODs?" *Amanda D. Lotz*, last modified June 8, 2020. http://www.amandalotz.com/netflix-30-qa/2020/6/7/q2-how-does-subscriber-funding-distinguish-svods.
Lotz, Amanda. "Q15: Why distinguish between commissions and acquisitions in analyzing SVODs?," *Amanda D. Lotz*, last modified July 23, 2020. http://www.amandalotz.com/netflix-30-qa/2020/7/23/q15-why-distinguish-between-commissions-and-acquisitions-in-analyzing-svods.
Meimaridis, Melina, Daniela Mazur, and Daniel Rios. "From São Paulo to Seoul: Netflix's strategies in peripheral markets." *Comunicación Y Sociedad* (2021): 1–26. https://doi.org/10.32870/cys.v2021.8038.
Miller, Toby. "A televisão acabou, a televisão virou coisa do passado, a televisão já era." *A TV em transição: tendências de programação no Brasil e no mundo*, edited by João Freire Filho, 9–26. Porto Alegre: Sulina, 2009.
Molla, Rani. "Here are some of the most popular shows on Netflix—which may be leaving Netflix soon," *Vox*, December 21, 2018. https://www.vox.com/2018/12/21/18139817/netflix-most-popular-shows-friends-office-greys-anatomy-parks-recreation-streaming-tv.
Nannicelli, Ted. "It's all connected: televisual narrative complexity." In *The Wire: Urban Decay and American Television*, edited by Tiffany Potter, and C.W. Marshall, 190–202. New York: Bloomsbury Publishing USA, 2009.
Newman, Michael Z. "Quality TV as Liberal TV." *Western Humanities Review* 70, no. 3 (2016). http://www.westernhumanitiesreview.com/fall-2016-70-3/quality-tv-as-liberal-tv/.
Palmeira, Carlos. "Netflix: Cade revela por engano número de assinantes do streaming no Brasil," *Tecmundo*, October 11, 2021. https://www.tecmundo.com.br/minha-serie/226728-cade-revela-engano-numero-assinantes-netflix-brasil.htm.

Penner, Tomaz Affonso, and Joseph Straubhaar. "Netflix Originals and Exclusively Licensed Titles in Brazilian Catalog: A Mapping Producing Countries." *MATRIZes* 14 (1):125–49. 2020. https://doi.org/10.11606/issn.1982-8160.v14i1p125-149.

Pullen, John Patrick. "5 Reasons Streaming Is Making DVDs Extinct," *Time Magazine*, June 15, 2015. https://time.com/3921019/streaming-dvds/.

Salgado, Eduardo. "Como a revolução do streaming mudou as TVs e Hollywood," *Exame*, September 7, 2017. https://exame.com/revista-exame/como-a-revolucao-do-streaming-mudou-os-negocios-das-tvs/.

Santana, Pablo. "Netflix passa TV a cabo em número de assinantes no Brasil, segundo consultoria americana," *Infomoney*, August 28, 2020. https://www.infomoney.com.br/consumo/brasil-tem-mais-assinantes-da-netflix-de-que-tv-a-cabo-segundo-consultoria-americana/#:~:text=Os%20analistas%20da%20empresa%20afirmam,com%2060%20milh%C3%B5es%20de%20assinaturas.

Schneider, Michael. "'Friends' DVD, Digital Sales Soar as It Takes a Break From Streaming," *Variety*, February 20, 2020. https://variety.com/2020/tv/news/friends-netflix-streaming-hbo-max-dvd-digital-sales-1203506810/.

Tryon, Chuck. "TV got better: Netflix's original programming strategies and the on-demand television transition." *Media Industries Journal* 2, no. 2 (2015), https://doi.org/10.3998/mij.15031809.0002.206.

Van Esler, Mike. "Not yet the post–TV era: Network and MVPD adaptation to emergent distribution technologies." *Media and Communication* 4, no. 3 (2016): 131–141, http://dx.doi.org/10.17645/mac.v4i3.548.

Streaming Audience Data, Ratings and the Future of "Popular" Television

Michael L. Wayne

With more than 193 million subscribers in more than 190 countries, Netflix embodies many of the characteristics associated with subscription video on-demand platforms in television's streaming age. Nowhere is this more apparent than with regards to audience data. On one hand, platforms like Netflix collect and analyze data with detail and precision that was unimaginable twenty years ago. On the other hand, these subscriber-supported platforms have little economic incentive to publicize their audience data. This juxtaposition of advanced data capabilities with strict anti-transparency policies is frustrating for industry observers and media scholars alike. To explore these issues, this essay uses a variety of publicly available secondary data to construct a history of the industrial discourses surrounding Netflix's audience data.

The analysis starts with a brief discussion of the significance of audience data for U.S. commercial television, some background regarding Netflix's relationship to traditional television networks, and a description of the media industry studies methods employed in this research. The following sections detail Netflix's public discourse related to its own audience data and television audience data more generally. Between 2007 and 2018, the company enacted strict anti-transparency policies. As a result, executives were often asked to comment on audience data that would not be released. This public discourse about proprietary data provided Netflix opportunities to differentiate itself from its linear competitors, explicitly criticize traditional industry practice, and deflect criticism about programming decisions. In 2019, however, the platform began releasing viewership data for a very limited number of "Netflix original" titles.[1] The public discussions related to these selective data releases primarily highlight the popularity of the platform's original content which differs from earlier discourses that served a variety of organizational goals.

Although the release of any audience data is a significant departure, Netflix's longstanding refusal to comment on viewers' geographic location and its unwillingness to publicize data for most of its content library reflects the reality that anti-transparency policies are still very much the norm. Yet, in contrast to the company's preferred image of itself as a revolutionary force in television, the shift from using public discussions of audience data to position itself outside of and superior to traditional networks to using audience data as proof of popularity is unmistakably a shift towards traditional industry practice. Nonetheless, Netflix's ongoing resistance to transparency alongside the lack of comparative metrics for both traditional networks and other video streaming services has made it increasingly difficult to define popular television. Ultimately, then, whatever shared sense of collective audience-hood was discursively produced by widely accepted albeit thoroughly flawed ratings systems like Nielsen is being replaced by the industrial discourses associated with black-box audience data within which claims of popularity and cultural significance cannot be substantively challenged.

Audience Measurement and the Television Industry

It is nearly impossible to overstate the importance of ratings for the American commercial television industry. These ratings, produced by the supposedly independent Nielsen Company, function as currency in the economic transactions between advertisers and networks. Derived from viewing data collected from a "statistically representative" sample of households using a variety of methods including time diaries and monitoring devices known as "people meters," Nielsen ratings establish the cost of advertising spots during a given program or time of day on a given network. Rather than reflecting actual numbers of viewers, however, ratings "function as a social-discursive-economic convention, a streamlined currency that suits the needs and interests of various factions of the television industry."[2] In his seminal analysis of television executives during the network era, Gitlin notes that virtually all industry activity was oriented towards producing ratings success.[3] Even as the growth of cable and satellite television increasingly led to the pursuit of niche rather than general audiences, Nielsen ratings remained the central metric of success in a rapidly changing industry.

Premium cable is the only segment of the U.S. commercial television industry where the importance of ratings is less than total. Subscriber-supported networks like HBO and Showtime do not feature traditional commercial advertising. Instead, they generate revenue from viewers who pay an additional monthly fee (a premium) for access to these channels and from carriage fees paid by pay-television providers for the right to include these channels in their bundle. As a result, the definitions of success associated with these networks are largely divorced from the ratings system and advertising revenue. Instead, success is typically conceptualized in more abstract notions like critical acclaim, "buzz," and "quality." The network most closely associated with such alternative discourses of success is HBO which introduced its famous marketing slogan "It's Not TV" in 1996. Since then, the network has cultivated a brand identity as the home of quality television that drew on a wide range of its programming but was primarily centered on the shift towards producing adult, edgy, authored, and high-budget original drama series. While HBO's brand was initially constructed through the promotional efforts of the network itself, and then increasingly depended on signature shows to stand in for the network, it also increasingly relied on critical acclaim and industry awards to support its claim to be the home for creative talent. As scholars have noted, however, HBO's marketing strategy relies upon the long-standing marginalization of television and its audiences.[4] HBO is not only different from traditional television; it is superior to traditional television. Specifically, the network invokes the rhetoric of "quality TV" to assert the medium's progress and place it in the same cultural category as cinema or literature. This rhetoric has been very effective. Original series produced by premium cable networks have accrued more prestige that any other type of programming in the post-network era and helped redefine successful television in cultural and commercial terms.

Netflix largely followed HBO's model to establish its brand identity once it started producing original series in 2011. For example, the company uses the discourse of quality TV in relation to technological progress and emerging modes of audience engagement. In working to define its "programming against traditional television," Tryon argues that Netflix echoes HBO branding strategies by reconceptualizing "streaming as a more engaging form of television, one that exists on a technological and cultural cutting edge."[5] In particular, the company often emphasizes binge-viewing as a mode of audience behavior that improves upon traditional television's liveness and linear scheduling. Yet, however much Netflix relies on the discourses premium cable networks used to distance themselves from advertiser-supported networks, streaming technology places the service outside of the traditional television industry in ways that were simply not available to HBO or Showtime.

As a distributor of television content with no need for traditional television distribution systems, Netflix's decision to move into original programming brought them into direct competition with both subscriber- and advertiser-supported networks. Although founder and CEO Reed Hastings explained the company's original programming strategy in terms of economic efficiency,[6] other executives were more transparent about the company's competitive intentions. In a 2013 interview with *GQ* magazine, then-chief content officer now-co-CEO Ted Sarandos asserted that Netflix's primary goal was "to become HBO faster than HBO can become us."[7] This organizational strategy was confirmed later that year when the company released a document titled "Netflix Long Term View" which began with the statement, "Over the coming decades and across the world, Internet TV will replace linear TV."[8] Previous scholarship argues that Netflix's approach to industry practice is usefully understood through the prism of the company's competition with traditional networks. Regarding the policy of refusing requests to include other network's promotional branding when subscribers watch licensed content, for example, Wayne notes that the platform's user interface obscured other television brands to better position the service as the audience's primary point of identification.[9] Building on such scholarship, this essay examines Netflix's public discussions of audience data and ratings in the context of these competitive dynamics.

Methods

To understand the industrial discourses related to proprietary streaming audience data, this research examines a variety of publicly available secondary data from sources including trade press articles, press releases, trade and popular press interviews, videos of industry roundtables, promotional appearances, and more than ten years of Netflix's quarterly earnings call transcripts and letters to shareholders (2010–2020). Regarding trade publications, searches for material related to Netflix's discussion of audience data were conducted in prominent outlets such as *Variety*, *The Hollywood Reporter*, *Deadline*, and *The Wrap*. Although media industry trade publications and materials are a commonly used data source in media and communication research,[10] the use of these sources is hardly straightforward. As many scholars note, it is necessary to approach trade press material critically and to be cognizant of the inherent limitations associated with such data.[11] Nonetheless, in conjunction with other materials, the trade press offers substantive insight into industry dynamics and provides useful perspectives regarding the development of institutional processes.

To analyze the collected data, this essay employs the methodological approach variously described as media historiography, media industry studies, or trade press analysis.[12] This approach uses elements of the production culture perspective to examine common meanings and values expressed by media executives. As John Caldwell observes, material aimed primarily at investors and industry professionals functions as paratexts that "promote and validate the 'aura' and notion of an elite space inside the locked worlds" of organizations within the cultural industries.[13] As such, these paratexts construct highly controlled narratives that reveal industrial discourse, relationships within and between industries, and trends in the modern TV industry. Relatedly, materials directed towards the audience such as interviews outside of industrial contexts or televised show business reports are understood as "publicly disclosed deep texts and rituals."[14] As a kind of industrial theorizing, these materials are a public performance of "the ways that practitioners work, think, and talk about how they work and think" for viewers "positioned as lucky enough to have been given access to those 'inside' the production process."[15] In addition to the use of trade press analysis as a means to access general television industry discourse, this analysis also follows Burroughs' approach to understanding Netflix's particular articulation of streaming discourse.[16] In combining industry and discourse analysis, Burroughs uses notions of streaming to highlight moments of continuity and rupture characteristic of the ongoing negotiations between new and old media. In a similar fashion, this essay identifies significant themes within Netflix executives' public discussions of audience data and television ratings. The findings generated by this analysis are presented in two sections.

The first section addresses the time from Netflix's entry into the streaming market in 2007 until late 2018 when the only official information about the platform's audience was the number of domestic (U.S.) subscribers and the number of global subscribers (after 2010) released each fiscal quarter. During this period, executives simply declined to discuss the characteristics of the service's subscribers or their viewing behaviors. When asked about the viewership for *House of Cards* (2013–2018), Netflix's most successful early original series, Sarandos characteristically responded, "We've said publicly, and we'll continue to say publicly, that we are not releasing viewing numbers."[17] According to multiple trade press reports, secrecy was also internal practice as this information was withheld from high profile showrunners. Yet, it is precisely in the context of such strict anti-transparency policies that Netflix's public discourses about viewership and ratings take on increased significance. They provide a window into the platform's view of itself and its relations with the television industry.

The second section examines Netflix's public discussions of audience data between late-2018 and mid–2020. During this period, the company selectively published viewership numbers for a small number of original titles while executives promised more transparency. The incorporation of selective data releases into Netflix's broader anti-transparency policy has multiple implications. In one sense, efforts to demonstrate popularity with audience data is a traditional industry practice. In another sense, however, Netflix's use of non-standard viewership metrics reflects the distance between the world's most popular video streaming service and the U.S. commercial television industry. This essay concludes with a consideration of streaming audience data in relation to the emerging realities of "popular" television.

Anti-Transparency Data Policy and the Practice of Discussing Without Releasing

Prior to 2019, the company's discussions of audience data can be understood in relation to three overlapping organizational goals: to differentiate Netflix from the traditional television industry, to denigrate traditional television industry practices, and to deflect criticism. First, when discussing audience data, Netflix executives frequently distinguish the service from traditional networks with claims that some industry norm is "irrelevant" or "insignificant" in the context of streaming television. When addressing ratings, for example, executives consistently state that traditional metrics of success are incompatible with the company's subscriber-supported model. Discussing the platform's anti-transparency policies in 2014, Sarandos said, "We don't plan on releasing ratings since it's irrelevant to us, we don't sell advertising, we don't negotiate carriage fees, there's no reason for us to give a specific number of how shows are performing."[18] Sarandos also differentiates Netflix from networks with regards to the importance of traditionally valued audience segments. He explained, "Eighteen-to-forty-nine-year-old viewing is so insignificant to us. I can't even tell you how many eighteen-to-forty-nine members we have. We don't track them. It's an advertising-driven demographic that means nothing to us."[19] Netflix's data capabilities further differentiate the service from traditional television. Rather than relying on demographic data generated by audience samples, digital technology allows the company to collect behavioral data for all subscribers' activities on the platform. According to Sarandos, "With streaming, we have insight into every second of the viewing experience. I know what you have tried and what you have turned off. I know at what point you turned it off. It's very sophisticated."[20] This data allows Netflix executives to claim that the company "knows" the audience in ways traditional networks do not. Discussing the relationship between the platform's data capabilities and the company's programming decisions, Cindy Holland, former vice president of Original Series, claims that Netflix targets content to specific "taste communities" rather than demographic groups.[21] As a result, the service differs from traditional networks as Netflix executives like Holland "program to suit [the audience's] tastes" rather than their own as she implies other executives do.

It should be noted, however, that Netflix's discourse regarding the relationship between audience data and executive programming decisions has changed over time. For example, in 2012, executives framed the multi-season commitment to *House of Cards* as a data-driven decision. According to then-Chief Communications Officer Jonathan Friedland (who was fired in 2018 for his repeated use of racially insensitive language in the workplace), the heavy upfront investment in the Kevin Spacey led political drama was justified by the platform's audience data. He explained, "We know what people watch on Netflix and we're able with a high degree of confidence to understand how big a likely audience is for a given show based on people's viewing habits."[22] By 2015, however, executives were openly acknowledging the limits of data-driven programming. At the Sundance Film Festival that year, Sarandos explained to media scholar Tim Wu that Netflix's programming decisions were made based on both data and industry experience. The executive explained, "In practice, it's probably a seventy-thirty mix. Seventy is the data, and thirty is judgment. But the thirty needs to be on top, if that makes sense."[23] This shift away from data-driven decision making continued and, in 2019, Sarandos was quite explicit about the limited value of audience data. Regarding the choice to green light some shows and not others, he said, "The data doesn't help you on anything in that process. Picking content and working with the creative community is a very human function."[24] Although the company's framing of its programming decisions became more traditional in recent years, public discussions of audience data do not always differentiate the company from its network competitors in neutral terms.

Second, Netflix executives use discussions of viewership and ratings to explicitly denigrate longstanding television industry norms. This is especially clear in reference to the Nielsen ratings system. For example, in 2013, Sarandos told reporters, "Overnight ratings work against quality on television. That's why I don't want to adopt the one convention that I think is anti-quality."[25] In response to industry calls for greater transparency, Sarandos made the same point several years later, saying, "If we turn it into a weekly arms race by doing box scores of every live-plus-3 or live-plus-7, I think it's going to have the same result that it has for television, which has been remarkably negative in terms of the quality of shows."[26] Of course, anti-ratings discourse is hardly new. In 2005, for example, HBO's then-CEO Chris Albrecht observed, "Other networks aim to make things popular and then maybe work on making them good. We [at HBO] say, 'We gotta be good, and wouldn't it be nice if it were popular.'"[27] Yet, what separates Netflix's statements about Nielsen ratings from earlier industry criticism is the totality of the critique.

In contrast with Sarandos' concerns regarding the quality of television content, other executives claim the demographic categories that serve as the basis of the ratings system have little value. Describing the platform's "mountain of data," Todd Yellin, VP of product innovation notes, "That mountain is composed of two things. Garbage is 99 percent of that mountain. Gold is one percent.... Geography, age, and gender? We put that in the garbage heap. Where you live is not that important."[28] In addition to criticizing the industry's reliance on ratings data, Netflix has also criticized Nielsen directly. In 2017, the ratings giant began producing ratings for streaming content without Netflix's participation and shortly thereafter publicly announced some viewing estimates related to the second season of *Stranger Things* (2016–).[29] A spokesperson for the streaming platform responded, "Nielsen only measures a fraction of [Netflix] members' viewing. For example, they don't measure mobile viewing. Our series are global and member viewing patterns vary greatly (what device they watch on, where they're watching, what they are watching), making it very difficult to model, even if they had accurate samples."[30] Beyond the criticism of Nielsen's methodology, the broader criticism of audience sampling here is particularly notable. Of course, before the widespread adoption of digital technology, sampling was the only economically feasible means of generating audience data for the industry.

Third, Netflix also references audience data to deflect criticism. Here, the case of *Marco Polo* is particularly instructive. The first ten-episode season of this big-budget historical epic cost a reported ninety million dollars and was widely understood to reflect Netflix's global ambitions.[31] Billed as the streamer's response to the success of HBO's *Game of Thrones* (2011–2019), the show was savaged by American television critics who found it to be a "disappointment" and "dramatically inert."[32] A month after *Marco Polo*'s premier and just two weeks after the second season renewal was announced, CEO Reed Hastings told an interviewer the show was "a massive success" that had "been super popular with the audience."[33] The second season, with a budget of more than 100 million dollars, premiered in July 2016. Discussing *Marco Polo*'s performance later that year, Sarandos told an industry roundtable that the show was "hugely popular all throughout Asia and Europe."[34] Given Netflix's subscriber-based economic model, he explained, the series' lack of popularity with American audiences and its harsh reception by television critics was "really irrelevant because it's doing exactly what it was supposed to do." In these instances, the practice of discussing but not releasing audience data allows Netflix to deflect the criticism most networks face regarding an underperforming big-budget project. Instead of being forced to answer for low ratings and unmet expectations, anti-transparency policies ensure that executives can claim success or redefine the parameters of success without be challenged. Of course, claiming success and succeeding are two different things. In December 2016, Netflix canceled *Marco Polo* after just two seasons, taking a reported $200 million loss on the project.[35]

Selective Data Releases and the Promise of Greater Transparency

After more than a decade of ignoring industry demands and refusing to comment on press speculation, Netflix publicized specific audience data related to a specific title for the first time on December 28, 2018. The official Twitter account for Netflix Films (@NetflixFilm) claimed that more than forty-five million subscriber accounts viewed the Netflix original film *Bird Box* (2018) during the seven days following its premier.[36] After initially refusing to comment on the metrics associated with this data, the next day, a company spokesman explained that a "view" of *Bird Box* was defined as a subscriber account watching 70 percent of the total running time including credits but that this definition was specific to this title and "should not be taken as a metric for all Netflix content."[37] The reasons behind the company's decision to publish viewership numbers for this particular film and the decision to begin selective data releases more broadly was never disclosed. Nonetheless, it seems likely that the decision to first publish audience data to demonstrate the popularity an original film rather than a television series was related to the consistently poor reviews Netflix films had received from critics.

Less than a month later, the company publicized "original" series viewership data for the first time. In the quarterly shareholder letter, Netflix estimated that the recently launched series *You* (2018–) and *Sex Education* (2019–) were both on pace to be seen by more than forty million households during the first four weeks following their premiere.[38] According to press reports, viewership for series was defined as a subscriber account watching at least seventy percent of a single episode of a given show.[39] As surprising as the disclosure of viewing data was, the company's justification for doing so was perhaps more surprising. In an interview following the earnings report, Sarandos explained the company's decision to disclose viewing data in traditional industry terms. Claiming this audience data as "cultural metrics," he asserted that eighty million Netflix views "means exactly the same thing as eighty million plus people buying a movie ticket to seeing it or eighty million households watching a TV show."[40] For subscribers, he continued, this data tells them that they are "in the zeitgeist ... watching the programming that the rest of the world is loving at the same time." Given the platform's brand identity grounded in around individualized viewing experiences and more than a decade of insistence that streaming data bore no relation to television ratings, Sarandos' references to collective audience experience and traditional industry metrics of success represents a significant departure for Netflix.

Nonetheless, the television industry's response to Netflix's newfound willingness to publicize audience data was highly critical. At the Television Critics Association winter press tour, FX CEO John Landgraf told reporters, "Netflix is not telling you the full story."[41] In particular, he took exception to Netflix's methodology noting that the company did not use the industry standard of average audience measurement which would have provided an "an apples to apples comparison of viewership." Instead, Landgraf claimed, Netflix publicized grossly inflated viewership numbers for *You* and *Sex Education* with the goal of presenting the service's original content as significantly more popular than it is. He also accused Netflix of inflating perceptions of overall viewership overall by "reporting their singles like home runs." In the months and years that followed, Landgraf's claims regarding Netflix's use of selective data release to increase public perception of the service's popularity became common wisdom within the industry, the trade press, and even the popular press.

Several months later, Netflix executives began promising more transparency. In April 2019, Sarandos told investors that the company planned to begin releasing "more specific and granular data" with the goal of becoming "more fully transparent about what people are watching on Netflix around the world."[42] At the same time, the company announced plans to test a new "Top 10" feature that would allow subscribers to see which shows and movies were currently the most popular across the service. In July, as the platform announced that 40.7 million member accounts had watched at least part of *Stranger Things*' third season using the same methodology as earlier in the year.[43] In October, Netflix released lists of its most viewed movies and series for the previous twelve months.[44] By December, executives were still promising more transparency. At an industry event, Scott Stuber, the head of original films at Netflix, told reporters, "You'll see more numbers from us, more transparency, more articulation of what's working and not.... So, we're definitely headed in that direction as a company."[45]

As 2019 ended, however, the promised transparency had not materialized. Instead, Netflix released a single year-end top ten list including both shows and movies produced with a new metric for audience size. According to this new definition, viewership is "the number of accounts choosing to watch at least two minutes of a series, movie or special during its first 28 days on Netflix in 2019."[46] The company explained that this new metric is "a far more pure way to measure popularity rather than 70% metric we've used in the past (which discriminates against longer form content)." Purity aside, less than a month later, Netflix disclosed the practical benefits of the new two-minute view. As the company explained in its quarterly letter to shareholders, "The new metric is about 35% higher on average than the prior metric. For example, 45 [million] member households chose to watch *Our Planet* [(2019)] under the new metric vs. 33 [million] under the prior metric."[47] Not surprisingly, the industry's response was again highly critical. One unnamed network executive told *The Hollywood Reporter* that this move is "obviously to goose [Netflix's] numbers" while another wondered why a company like Netflix "who trades in 'viewership' isn't held to the same standard of independent verification as the rest of us."[48] This criticism had no discernable impact and, in February 2020, Netflix introduced a new daily top-ten feature on its user interface which allows subscribers to see that day's most popular content in their country. Yet, a ranked list of the most watched titles on a given day provides very little information without knowledge of the differences related to each title and the overall percentage of viewing represented. As such, it seems that Netflix publicizes approximately the same amount of substantive audience data through selective releases as it did when the company refused to publicly comment on viewing numbers.

Netflix's Audience Data and the Ongoing "End" of Popular Television

Using the framework of media industry studies, this essay examines industrial discourses related to Netflix's audience data under conditions shaped by the company's anti-transparency policy. Until late-2018, executives used discussions of proprietary audience data to position the platform outside of the traditional television industry, to critique traditional industry players, and to deflect criticism. During this period, the company presented the popularity of its original series as axiomatic. As Sarandos explained in 2014, "You know in the culture that *Orange Is the New Black* [(2013–2019)] and *House of Cards* are enormous hits."[49] By early 2019, selective releases of audience data for what are presumably Netflix's most popular series became standard practice. Although Hastings has described the willingness to publicize any data as part of the company's efforts to "grow up a little,"[50] Netflix's use of non-standard metrics remains a point of contention within the industry. Setting aside questions of whether selective data releases represent a move towards meaningful transparency (they don't), this research has two significant implications for scholars concerned with video streaming services.

In the broadest sense, the industrial discourse related to Netflix's audience data confirms what media scholars have long claimed about transitions between old and new media. New media forms do not replace old ones; the interplay of old and new is an ongoing negotiation between established and emerging practices. What Netflix says and doesn't say about its audience data and ratings more generally must be understood within the context of the television industry. Even as the company seeks to position itself as an outsider, its executives work to promote the company as a streaming television platform and television content producer. Of course, Netflix is not the only firm managing the tensions between old and new media. As conglomerate-backed video streaming services like Amazon's Prime Video, Disney+, and HBO Max attempt to catch up with Netflix both in terms of subscribers and cultural influence, it seems likely that discussions of audience data will become more varied without necessarily becoming more substantive. Given the different content libraries and target audiences of these services, each might well come to conceptualize success and discuss popularity in distinctive ways. What seems less likely, however, is that market dynamics will develop in such a way to incentivize data transparency for subscriber-based platforms.

In a more narrow sense, this essay highlights the ways in which Netflix's public discussions of its audience data severely limit possibilities for collective understandings of popular television in the age of streaming. The company's anti-transparency policies ensure that connections between popularity and viewer behavior are articulated on its own terms. Netflix content is popular because Netflix says so. Yet, there is little reason to approach the increasingly unknowable realities of popular television as a radical break from the past. The U.S. commercial television industry has never been interested in accurate and transparent audience data for itself or the public. To whatever degree the Nielsen ratings system effectively provided a shared currency for the television industry, it provided the public with an inaccurate image of American audiences as the company ignored many well-known inadequacies ranging from methodological problems associated with time diaries to the practice of under-sampling viewers of color. Along these lines, future television industry scholarship can mostly usefully address the streaming age by discarding "post–TV" thinking and, instead, seek to understand contemporary practices and discourses as extensions of the medium's past.

Notes

1. Netflix uses the label "original" more liberally than traditional television networks. Much of what Netflix promotes as original is more accurately described as exclusive in a particular market.

2. Jennifer Hessler, "Peoplemeter Technologies and the Biometric Turn in Audience Measurement," *Television & New Media*, 2019, 3.

3. *Inside Prime Time* (New York: Pantheon Books, 1983).

4. Janet McCabe and Kim Akass, "Sex, Swearing and Respectability: Courting Controversy, HBO's Original Programming and Producing Quality TV," in *Quality TV: Contemporary American Television and Beyond*, ed. Janet McCabe and Kim Akass (London, UK: I.B. Tauris, 2007), 62–76.

5. "TV Got Better: Netflix's Original Programming Strategies and the On-Demand Television Transition," *Media Industries Journal* 2, no. 2 (2015): 106.

6. Reed Hastings and David Wells, "Investor Letter Q1 2012," April 23, 2012, http://files.shareholder.com/downloads/NFLX/170689058x0x562104/9EBB887B-6B9B-4C86-AEFF-107C1FB85CA5/Investor%20Letter%20Q1%202012.pdf.

7. Nancy Hass, "Reed Hastings on Arrested Development, House of Cards, and the Future of Netflix," *GQ* (blog), January 29, 2013, http://www.gq.com/story/netflix-founder-reed-hastings-house-of-cards-arrested-development.

8. Netflix, "Netflix Long Term View," April 24, 2013, http://files.shareholder.com/downloads/NFLX/2441659654x0x656145/e4410bd8-e5d4-4d31-ad79-84c36c49f77c/IROverviewHomePageLetter_4.24.13_pdf.pdf.

9. "Netflix, Amazon, and Branded Television Content in Subscription Video On-Demand Portals," *Media, Culture & Society* 40, no. 5 (2018): 735, https://doi.org/10.1177/0163443717736118.

10. Allie Kosterich and Philip M. Napoli, "Reconfiguring the Audience Commodity: The Institutionalization of Social TV Analytics as Market Information Regime," *Television & New Media* 17, no. 3 (2016): 254–271.

11. Alisa Perren, "The Trick of the Trades: Media Industry Studies and the American Comic Book Industry," in *Production Studies, The Sequel!*, ed. Miranda Banks, Bridget Conor, and Vicki Mayer (Routledge, 2015), 247–257; Amanda D. Lotz, "The Post-Network Era: 2000s–Present," in *A Companion to the History of American Broadcasting*, ed. Aniko Bodroghkozy (Wiley Blackwell, 2018), 153–67.

12. Lotz, "The Post-Network Era"; Perren, "The Trick of the Trades"; Thomas F. Corrigan, "Making Implicit Methods Explicit: Trade Press Analysis in the Political Economy of Communication," *International Journal of Communication* 12 (2018): 2751–72.

13. "Critical Industrial Practice: Branding, Repurposing, and the Migratory Patterns of Industrial Texts," *Television & New Media* 7, no. 2 (2006): 130, https://doi.org/10.1177/1527476403255811.

14. John Caldwell, *Production Culture: Industrial Reflexivity and Critical Practice in Film and Television* (Duke University Press, 2008), 347.

15. Caldwell, 348.

16. "House of Netflix: Streaming Media and Digital Lore," *Popular Communication* 17, no. 1 (January 2, 2019): 1–17, https://doi.org/10.1080/15405702.2017.1343948.

17. Netflix, "Q2 2013 Netflix, Inc. Earnings Conference Call Transcript" (July 22, 2013), https://s22.q4cdn.com/959853165/files/doc_financials/quarterly_reports/2013/q2/NFLX-Transcript-2013-07-22T22_00.pdf.

18. Katyln Quintanilla, "The Programmer's Summit, HRTS Luncheon Recap," *Hollywood Radio & Television Society* (blog), February 14, 2014, https://hrts.org/the-programmers-summit-hrts-luncheon-recap/.

19. Yvonne Villarreal, "It's Still 'Netflix and No Ratings'—Ted Sarandos Rejects a Numbers 'Arms Race,'" *Los Angeles Times*, January 17, 2016, https://www.latimes.com/entertainment/la-et-ct-sarandos-tca-netflix-20160117-story.html.

20. Ted Sarandos, Carsey-Wolf Center at UC Santa Barbara, June 2012, https://www.carseywolf.ucsb.edu/wp-content/uploads/2018/02/Interview_Ted-Sarandos.pdf.

21. Jason Lynch, "Netflix Thrives By Programming to 'Taste Communities,' Not Demographics," *AdWeek* (blog), July 29, 2018, https://www.adweek.com/tv-video/netflix-thrives-by-programming-to-taste-communities-not-demographics/.

22. Roberto Baldwin, "Netflix Gambles on Big Data to Become the HBO of Streaming," *Wired*, November 29, 2012, https://www.wired.com/2012/11/netflix-data-gamble/.

23. Tim Wu, "Netflix's Secret Special Algorithm Is a Human," *The New Yorker*, January 27, 2015, https://www.newyorker.com/business/currency/hollywoods-big-data-big-deal.

24. Dade Hayes, "Netflix's Ted Sarandos Weighs In On Streaming Wars, Agency Production, Big Tech Breakups, M&A Outlook—Update," *Deadline* (blog), June 22, 2019, https://deadline.com/2019/06/netflix-ted-sarandos-weighs-in-on-streaming-wars-agency-production-big-tech-breakups-ma-outlook-1202636595/.

25. Dawn Chmielewski, "Ted Sarandos Upends Hollywood with Netflix Revolution," *Los Angeles Times*, August 25, 2013, https://www.latimes.com/entertainment/envelope/cotown/la-et-netflix-ted-sarandos-20130825-dto-htmlstory.html.

26. Villarreal, "It's Still 'Netflix and No Ratings'—Ted Sarandos Rejects a Numbers 'Arms Race.'"

27. Kurt Andersen, "How HBO Could Get Back Its Mojo," *New York Magazine*, August 8, 2005, https://nymag.com/nymetro/news/columns/imperialcity/12199/.

28. Brian Barrett, "Netflix's Grand, Daring, Maybe Crazy Plan to Conquer the World," *Wired*, March 27, 2016, https://www.wired.com/2016/03/netflixs-grand-maybe-crazy-plan-conquer-world/.

29. Tony Maglio, "'Stranger Things': 15.8 Million Watched Season 2 Premiere in 1st Weekend," *The Wrap* (blog), November 2, 2017, https://www.thewrap.com/stranger-things-2-tv-ratings-netflix-nielsen/.

30. Lara O'Reilly, "CMO Today: CNN to Launch Digital Subscriptions; Nielsen's 'Stranger Things 2' Ratings; Advertising Escapes Tax Reform," *Wall Street Journal*, November 3, 2017, sec. Business, https://www.wsj.com/articles/cmo-today-cnn-to-launch-digital-subscriptions-nielsens-stranger-things-2-ratings-advertising-escapes-tax-reform-1509710449.

31. Emily Steel, "How to Build an Empire, the Netflix Way," *The New York Times*, November 29, 2014, sec. Business, https://www.nytimes.com/2014/11/30/business/media/how-to-build-an-empire-the-netflix-way-.html.

32. Neil Genzlinger, "O.K., the Women Can Kill, but They Have to Be Nude," *The New York Times*, December 11, 2014, sec. Arts, https://www.nytimes.com/2014/12/12/arts/television/marco-polo-fur-and-armor-drama-from-netflix.html; Emily VanDerWerff, "We Watched All of Netflix's Marco Polo. You ... Don't Have To.," *Vox* (blog), December 15, 2014, https://www.vox.com/2014/12/15/7392517/marco-polo-review-netflix.

33. Timothy Stenovec, "Netflix CEO Says 'Marco Polo" Is A Hit, And We'll Never Know Otherwise,'" *The Huffington Post* (blog), January 23, 2015, https://www.huffpost.com/entry/netflix-reed-hastings-marco-polo_n_6525776.

34. The Hollywood Reporter, *TV Executives Roundtable with Ted Sarandos, Bonnie Hammer and More*, 2016, https://www.hollywoodreporter.com/video/watch-thr-s-full-tv-918281.

35. Lesley Goldberg, "'Marco Polo' Canceled at Netflix After Two Seasons | Hollywood Reporter," *The Hollywood Reporter* (blog), December 12, 2016, https://www.hollywoodreporter.com/live-feed/marco-polo-canceled-at-netflix-two-seasons-955561.

36. NetflixFilm, Twitter post, December 28, 2018, 8:30 p.m. https://twitter.com/NetflixFilm/status/1078735051406204928.

37. Todd Spangler, "'Bird Box' Viewed by 45 Million Netflix Members in First Week, Company Says," *Variety* (blog), December 28, 2018, https://variety.com/2018/digital/news/bird-box-netflix-45-million-views-first-week-1203096379/.

38. Netflix, "Q4 2018 Letter to Shareholders" (Letter, January 17, 2019), https://s22.q4cdn.com/959853165/files/doc_financials/quarterly_reports/2018/q4/01/FINAL-Q4-18-Shareholder-Letter.pdf.

39. Rick Porter, "Netflix Reveals Viewership Numbers for 'You,' 'Sex Education' and More," *The Hollywood Reporter* (blog), January 17, 2019, https://www.hollywoodreporter.com/live-feed/netflixs-you-track-40-million-viewers-1177025.

40. Netflix Investor Relations, "Netflix Q4 2018 Earnings Interview," YouTube Video, 34:33, January 17, 2019, https://www.youtube.com/watch?v=mYsKCfWV0fs.

41. Lisa de Moraes, "FX Chief John Landgraf Smacks Down Netflix Big Ratings 'Myth'—TCA," *Deadline* (blog), February 4, 2019, https://deadline.com/2019/02/john-landgraf-smacks-down-netflix-ratings-myth-tca-1202549106/.

42. Julia Alexander, "Netflix Execs Say They'll Finally Start Releasing Viewership Data Soon," *The Verge* (blog), April 17, 2019, https://www.theverge.com/2019/4/17/18412309/netflix-transparency-data-viewers-ratings-subscribers-bird-box-numbers.

43. Rick Porter, "'Stranger Things 3' Racks Up Record Viewership, According to Netflix," *The Hollywood Reporter* (blog), July 8, 2019, https://www.hollywoodreporter.com/live-feed/stranger-things-racks-up-record-viewership-netflix-1223028.

44. John Koblin, "Netflix's Top 10 Original Movies and TV Shows, According to Netflix," *The New York Times*, October 17, 2019, sec. Business, https://www.nytimes.com/2019/10/17/business/media/netflix-top-ten-movies-tv-shows.html.

45. Adam B. Vary, "Netflix Film Chief Scott Stuber Says Streamer Planning to Release More Audience Numbers," *Variety* (blog), December 5, 2019, https://variety.com/2019/film/news/netflix-viewership-numbers-1203426670/.

46. Matt Patches, "Netflix Says These Are Its Most Popular Movies and Shows of 2019," *Polygon* (blog), December 30, 2019, https://www.polygon.com/2019/12/30/21042995/netflix-top-10-movies-shows-2019-viewers.

47. Netflix, "Q4 2019 Letter to Shareholders" (Letter, January 21, 2020), https://s22.q4cdn.com/959853165/files/doc_financials/2019/q4/FINAL-Q4-19-Shareholder-Letter.pdf.

48. Rick Porter, "Netflix's New Ratings Math Sacrifices Clarity for Flashy Numbers," *The Hollywood Reporter* (blog), January 23, 2020, https://www.hollywoodreporter.com/live-feed/netflixs-new-ratings-math-sacrifices-clarity-flashy-numbers-1272214.

49. Dominic Patten, "HRTS: Netflix Keeping Its Metrics To Itself, Ted Sarandos Says," *Deadline* (blog), February 6, 2014, https://deadline.com/2014/02/netflix-metrics-staying-private-ted-sarandos-says-hrts-678316/.

50. Max Goldbart, "Netflix Aiming to Be More Open about Data, Says Reed Hastings," *Screen Daily* (blog), September 20, 2019, https://www.screendaily.com/news/netflix-aiming-to-be-more-open-about-data-says-reed-hastings/5143077.article.

Works Cited

Alexander, Julia. "Netflix Execs Say They'll Finally Start Releasing Viewership Data Soon." *The Verge* (blog), April 17, 2019. https://www.theverge.com/2019/4/17/18412309/netflix-transparency-data-viewers-ratings-subscribers-bird-box-numbers.

Andersen, Kurt. "How HBO Could Get Back Its Mojo." *New York Magazine*, August 8, 2005. https://nymag.com/nymetro/news/columns/imperialcity/12199/.

Baldwin, Roberto. "Netflix Gambles on Big Data to Become the HBO of Streaming." *Wired*, November 29, 2012. https://www.wired.com/2012/11/netflix-data-gamble/.

Barrett, Brian. "Netflix's Grand, Daring, Maybe Crazy Plan to Conquer the World." *Wired*, March 27, 2016. https://www.wired.com/2016/03/netflixs-grand-maybe-crazy-plan-conquer-world/.

Burroughs, Benjamin. "House of Netflix: Streaming Media and Digital Lore." *Popular Communication* 17, no. 1 (January 2, 2019): 1–17. https://doi.org/10.1080/15405702.2017.1343948.

Caldwell, John. "Critical Industrial Practice: Branding, Repurposing, and the Migratory Patterns of Industrial Texts." *Television & New Media* 7, no. 2 (2006): 99–134. https://doi.org/10.1177/1527476403255811.

______. *Production Culture: Industrial Reflexivity and Critical Practice in Film and Television*. Duke University Press, 2008.

Chmielewski, Dawn. "Ted Sarandos Upends Hollywood with Netflix Revolution." *Los Angeles Times*, August 25, 2013. https://www.latimes.com/entertainment/envelope/cotown/la-et-netflix-ted-sarandos-20130825-dto-htmlstory.html.

Corrigan, Thomas F. "Making Implicit Methods Explicit: Trade Press Analysis in the Political Economy of Communication." *International Journal of Communication* 12 (2018): 2751–72.

Genzlinger, Neil. "O.K., the Women Can Kill, but They Have to Be Nude." *The New York Times*, December 11, 2014, sec. Arts. https://www.nytimes.com/2014/12/12/arts/television/marco-polo-fur-and-armor-drama-from-netflix.html.

Gitlin, Todd. *Inside Prime Time*. New York: Pantheon Books, 1983.

Goldbart, Max. "Netflix Aiming to Be More Open about Data, Says Reed Hastings." *Screen Daily* (blog), September 20, 2019. https://www.screendaily.com/news/netflix-aiming-to-be-more-open-about-data-says-reed-hastings/5143077.article.

Goldberg, Lesley. "'Marco Polo' Canceled at Netflix After Two Seasons | Hollywood Reporter." *The Hollywood Reporter* (blog), December 12, 2016. https://www.hollywoodreporter.com/live-feed/marco-polo-canceled-at-netflix-two-seasons-955561.

Hass, Nancy. "Reed Hastings on Arrested Development, House of Cards, and the Future of Netflix." *GQ* (blog), January 29, 2013. http://www.gq.com/story/netflix-founder-reed-hastings-house-of-cards-arrested-development.

Hastings, Reed, and David Wells. "Investor Letter Q1 2012," April 23, 2012. http://files.shareholder.com/downloads/NFLX/170689058x0x562104/9EBB887B-6B9B-4C86-AEFF-107C1FB85CA5/Investor%20Letter%20Q1%202012.pdf.

Hayes, Dade. "Netflix's Ted Sarandos Weighs In On Streaming Wars, Agency Production, Big Tech Breakups, M&A Outlook—Update." *Deadline* (blog), June 22, 2019. https://deadline.com/2019/06/netflix-ted-sarandos-weighs-in-on-streaming-wars-agency-production-big-tech-breakups-ma-outlook-1202636595/.

Hessler, Jennifer. "Peoplemeter Technologies and the Biometric Turn in Audience Measurement." *Television & New Media*, 2019, 1527476419879415.

The Hollywood Reporter. *TV Executives Roundtable with Ted Sarandos, Bonnie Hammer and More*, 2016. https://www.hollywoodreporter.com/video/watch-thr-s-full-tv-918281.

Koblin, John. "Netflix's Top 10 Original Movies and TV Shows, According to Netflix." *The New York Times*, October 17, 2019, sec. Business. https://www.nytimes.com/2019/10/17/business/media/netflix-top-ten-movies-tv-shows.html.

Kosterich, Allie, and Philip M. Napoli. "Reconfiguring the Audience Commodity: The Institutionalization of Social TV Analytics as Market Information Regime." *Television & New Media* 17, no. 3 (2016): 254–71.

Lotz, Amanda D. "The Post-Network Era: 2000s–Present." In *A Companion to the History of American Broadcasting*, edited by Aniko Bodroghkozy, 153–67. Wiley Blackwell, 2018.

Lynch, Jason. "Netflix Thrives By Programming to 'Taste Communities,' Not Demographics." *AdWeek* (blog), July 29, 2018. https://www.adweek.com/tv-video/netflix-thrives-by-programming-to-taste-communities-not-demographics/.

Maglio, Tony. "'Stranger Things': 15.8 Million Watched Season 2 Premiere in 1st Weekend." *The Wrap* (blog), November 2, 2017. https://www.thewrap.com/stranger-things-2-tv-ratings-netflix-nielsen/.

McCabe, Janet, and Kim Akass. "Sex, Swearing and Respectability: Courting Controversy, HBO's Original Programming and Producing Quality TV." In *Quality TV: Contemporary American Television and Beyond*, edited by Janet McCabe and Kim Akass, 62–76. London, UK: I.B. Tauris, 2007.

Moraes, Lisa de. "FX Chief John Landgraf Smacks Down Netflix Big Ratings 'Myth'—TCA." *Deadline* (blog), February 4, 2019. https://deadline.com/2019/02/john-landgraf-smacks-down-netflix-ratings-myth-tca-1202549106/.

Netflix. "Netflix Long Term View," April 24, 2013. http://files.shareholder.com/downloads/NFLX/2441659654x0x656145/e4410bd8-e5d4-4d31-ad79-84c36c49f77c/IROverviewHomePageLetter_4.24.13_pdf.pdf.
______. "Q2 2013 Netflix, Inc. Earnings Conference Call Transcript," July 22, 2013. https://s22.q4cdn.com/959853165/files/doc_financials/quarterly_reports/2013/q2/NFLX-Transcript-2013-07-22T22_00.pdf.
______. "Q4 2018 Letter to Shareholders." Letter, January 17, 2019. https://s22.q4cdn.com/959853165/files/doc_financials/quarterly_reports/2018/q4/01/FINAL-Q4-18-Shareholder-Letter.pdf.
______. "Q4 2019 Letter to Shareholders." Letter, January 21, 2020. https://s22.q4cdn.com/959853165/files/doc_financials/2019/q4/FINAL-Q4-19-Shareholder-Letter.pdf.
O'Reilly, Lara. "CMO Today: CNN to Launch Digital Subscriptions; Nielsen's 'Stranger Things 2' Ratings; Advertising Escapes Tax Reform." *Wall Street Journal*, November 3, 2017, sec. Business. https://www.wsj.com/articles/cmo-today-cnn-to-launch-digital-subscriptions-nielsens-stranger-things-2-ratings-advertising-escapes-tax-reform-1509710449.
Patches, Matt. "Netflix Says These Are Its Most Popular Movies and Shows of 2019." *Polygon* (blog), December 30, 2019. https://www.polygon.com/2019/12/30/21042995/netflix-top-10-movies-shows-2019-viewers.
Patten, Dominic. "HRTS: Netflix Keeping Its Metrics to Itself, Ted Sarandos Says." *Deadline* (blog), February 6, 2014. https://deadline.com/2014/02/netflix-metrics-staying-private-ted-sarandos-says-hrts-678316/.
Perren, Alisa. "The Trick of the Trades: Media Industry Studies and the American Comic Book Industry." In *Production Studies, The Sequel!*, edited by Miranda Banks, Bridget Conor, and Vicki Mayer, 247–57. Routledge, 2015.
Porter, Rick. "Netflix Reveals Viewership Numbers for 'You,' 'Sex Education' and More." *The Hollywood Reporter* (blog), January 17, 2019. https://www.hollywoodreporter.com/live-feed/netflixs-you-track-40-million-viewers-1177025.
______. "Netflix's New Ratings Math Sacrifices Clarity for Flashy Numbers." *The Hollywood Reporter* (blog), January 23, 2020. https://www.hollywoodreporter.com/live-feed/netflixs-new-ratings-math-sacrifices-clarity-flashy-numbers-1272214.
______. "'Stranger Things 3' Racks Up Record Viewership, According to Netflix." *The Hollywood Reporter* (blog), July 8, 2019. https://www.hollywoodreporter.com/live-feed/stranger-things-racks-up-record-viewership-netflix-1223028.
Quintanilla, Katyln. "The Programmer's Summit, HRTS Luncheon Recap." *Hollywood Radio & Television Society* (blog), February 14, 2014. https://hrts.org/the-programmers-summit-hrts-luncheon-recap/.
Sarandos, Ted. Carsey-Wolf Center at UC Santa Barbara, June 2012. https://www.carseywolf.ucsb.edu/wp-content/uploads/2018/02/Interview_Ted-Sarandos.pdf.
Spangler, Todd. "'Bird Box' Viewed by 45 Million Netflix Members in First Week, Company Says." *Variety* (blog), December 28, 2018. https://variety.com/2018/digital/news/bird-box-netflix-45-million-views-first-week-1203096379/.
Steel, Emily. "How to Build an Empire, the Netflix Way." *The New York Times*, November 29, 2014, sec. Business. https://www.nytimes.com/2014/11/30/business/media/how-to-build-an-empire-the-netflix-way-.html.
Stenovec, Timothy. "Netflix CEO Says 'Marco Polo' Is A Hit, And We'll Never Know Otherwise." *The Huffington Post* (blog), January 23, 2015. https://www.huffpost.com/entry/netflix-reed-hastings-marco-polo_n_6525776.
Tryon, Chuck. "TV Got Better: Netflix's Original Programming Strategies and the On-Demand Television Transition." *Media Industries Journal* 2, no. 2 (2015): 104–16.
VanDerWerff, Emily. "We Watched All of Netflix's *Marco Polo*. You ... Don't Have To." *Vox* (blog), December 15, 2014. https://www.vox.com/2014/12/15/7392517/marco-polo-review-netflix.
Vary, Adam B. "Netflix Film Chief Scott Stuber Says Streamer Planning to Release More Audience Numbers." *Variety* (blog), December 5, 2019. https://variety.com/2019/film/news/netflix-viewership-numbers-1203426670/.

Villarreal, Yvonne. "It's Still 'Netflix and No Ratings'—Ted Sarandos Rejects a Numbers 'Arms Race.'" *Los Angeles Times*, January 17, 2016. https://www.latimes.com/entertainment/la-et-ct-sarandos-tca-netflix-20160117-story.html.
Wayne, Michael L. "Netflix, Amazon, and Branded Television Content in Subscription Video On-Demand Portals." *Media, Culture & Society* 40, no. 5 (2018): 725–41. https://doi.org/10.1177/0163443717736118.
Wu, Tim. "Netflix's Secret Special Algorithm Is a Human." *The New Yorker*, January 27, 2015. https://www.newyorker.com/business/currency/hollywoods-big-data-big-deal.

A New Age of Diversity and Visibility

AHNGELI SHIVAM

Introduction

Contemporary creative productions such as film and television have become an easily accessible staple in today's, particularly Western, societies and comprise significant parts of mainstream entertainment. As they have become a constant influence on people's daily lives, their importance is tied to social responsibility. Among other things, film and television shape ideologies and inform the public about topics they know little about, including, but not limited to, minorities and other cultures.[1] Hence, as a potentially sole gateway for many people to a realm of the unknown, at their best, these media can shed light on marginalized populations, prejudices, and exclusionary practices.

The aforementioned responsibility is especially applicable to cultural productions by and about transpacific producers, as they are under more scrutiny for "authentic" representation and struggle to be seen in the first place. I understand the highly complex "transpacific" as both a geographical region—encompassing Asia, the United States, the Western coastal regions of the Americas, and Oceania—and as a fluid conglomeration of cultural influences as established by Erin Suzuki in "Transpacific." Suzuki argues that "within the context of contemporary Asian American studies, the concept of the transpacific has come to express the ways that different Asian, Pacific Island, and American cultures and communities mutually shape one another as they circulate throughout the region."[2] I assert that contemporary creative productions by individuals from the transpacific and about transpacific experiences function as important tools of social justice, resistance, and reshaping the normed spaces of production and society. This challenge concurs with the technological and social context of streaming services that offer an unprecedented opportunity for heterogeneous on-screen representation by increasing diversity behind the camera. For this purpose, I examine three distinct but linked media entities that uniquely interrogate dominant paradigms of power, creativity, and collaboration which influence each other and the larger media landscape (mediascape): the executive level, the writers' room, and the "matrix stage." These entities illustrate a certain function and importance for the ethical representation for and by transpacific cultural producers and also highlight the limitations they face with the current, albeit changing, state of affairs. Subsequently, I illustrate how these key stages are directly influenced and shaped by streaming services and a transpacific cultural producer such as Mindy Kaling. As I take a closer look at some of her medial works, particularly on streaming platforms, specifically the first episode of Netflix's coming-of-age series *Never Have I Ever* (2020–) (hereafter referred to as *NHIE*), I illustrate how Kaling has been able to use streaming services and their dynamics to influence these key areas to create a more diverse and political form of representation. This representation does not originate from respectability politics, public relations, or politically correct visibility, but challenges the terms dictated by these supposed paradigms.

Hollywood: Past and Future

In "Asian America on Demand: Asian Americans, Media Networks, and a Matrix Stage," L.S. Kim expounds that the audiovisual entertainment industry works on false pretenses as diversity has historically and still is prevalently addressed superficially for reasons of public relations and political correctness. She contends that there frequently is no deeper historical and conceptual consideration to on-screen diversity, even though the media has the power to actually deliver substance on diversity and other cultures. It can further correct false information and images of systemic racism, foster equality, and potentially inspire further justice, as Asian American media activism and movements, such as the Media Action Network for Asian Americans and Asian Pacific American Media Coalition have shown. Instead, this power is often lost in a capitalistic process. Kim continues:

> There are three false premises on which Hollywood operates, and that viewers tend to believe:
> 1. Talking about race and the media is interpreted as "complaints" about racism, and diversity is about political correctness (rather than creativity)....
> 2. Change automatically comes with time, and progress in racial representation is teleological....

> 3. Viewers identify with characters who are "like" them … [which] defies the reality of innumerable non–White people who have identified with main (that is, White) characters … [and] underestimat[es] the ability of White people to identify with characters of color and to have compassion for their stories or experiences.[3]

Corroborated by statistical evidence such as the University of California, Los Angeles' yearly Hollywood Diversity Report, there is a continuous, albeit improving, lack of diversity on-screen. Nonetheless, especially in the last three decades and with the surge in television and streaming service productions, there has been an increased debate around the under- and misrepresentation of minorities in mainstream media. Historically, Hollywood has focused on white characters in films and series and often disregarded any sort of diversity in their main cast, be it disability, gender, race, or often class, and rather used diverse characters as on-screen tokens. Consider popular shows such as *Seinfeld* (1989–1998), *Friends* (1994–2004), or *How I Met Your Mother* (2005–2014). Major strides have been made and for example *The Cosby Show* (1984–1992) was a pioneering television show when it first aired and over time individuals such as African American creator, writer, and producer Shonda Rhimes have changed, and continue to change, the representation of diversity within the mediascape with shows such as *Grey's Anatomy* (2005–). However, the overall slow shift to added diversity is illustrated by shows such as Margaret Cho's *All American Girl* (1994–1995) which was canceled after just one season and the fact that it took 20 years for a new Asian American television series—American Broadcasting Company's sitcom *Fresh Off the Boat* (2015–2020)—to be created and aired.

This overarching exclusionary pattern is coherent with the lack of diversity behind the camera—in writers' rooms and other positions of power, especially, producers and network executives. These individuals are in positions that have the potential to provoke social change as they greenlight the cultural productions to be created and shown. If these positions are solely inhabited by a homogeneous group, e.g., white able men, who believe in the outdated Hollywood premises outlined by Kim and are afraid of changing formats for they might turn out to be unsuccessful, representation in the mediascape will not change. One has to recognize, media and representation are not only about profit or creating relatable on-screen characters that reflect a country such as the United States' demographics, but for a population to be able to self-express and to have a voice in so-called mainstream media. As Ling-hsuan Larry Tung discusses in "Images of Asians and Asian-Americans: The Under-representation and Misrepresentation of Asians and Asian-Americans on American Television," Asians and Asian Americans account for a significant part of the

United States' demographics—including multiracial Asian Americans, 7.2 percent of the population as of the 2020 census[4]—yet, they have frequently been under- or misrepresented and stereotyped in American television. To counteract this historic imbalance in positional power and lack of diversity on-screen, production companies have to detach from the idea that representation will naturally evolve, that recognition and identification for their widest possible audience is limited to whiteness, and understand that diversity is actually a prominent business imperative.

Although steps have been and are being taken, specifically since the late 1990s and early 2000s, there is still much progress to be desired. These findings are corroborated by Kim in "Representation of Race." Among other things, Kim analyzes "improved" racial representations in diversifying media but reiterates how the power over how roles and shows are created and finally greenlit still resides with the industry's often white male executives, producers, and showrunners. However, these shortcomings are increasingly addressed by streaming services and their productions.

Second-generation Indian American Kaling is an ideal example for the disruption of the norm and a bridge between the powerful executive level and the creative writers' room positions. Kaling has not only written two memoirs, but has also extensively worked as an actress, writer, director, producer, and creator. As Kaling elaborates in her second memoir *Why Not Me?* (2015), after working on projects such as *The Office* (2005–2013), she desired to be more involved behind the scenes and wanted to be in a position of actual say: "[N]o matter how much you contribute, the only person who has the final say is the showrunner … [and] I wanted to be the judge, jury, and executive producer.… [S]o, at the end of season 7, when my original contract with Universal expired, they hired me to stay on as a writer and actress with *The Office*, and included a development deal for a pilot."[5]

Kaling used this opportunity to create and star as OB-GYN Dr. Mindy Lahiri in Fox and then Hulu's sitcom *The Mindy Project* (2012–2017) [hereafter referred to as *TMP*], a contemporary onscreen representation of an Indian American woman as she balances her medical profession and romantic life. *TMP* challenges pre-existing cultural, gendered, and medial frames and enables the discussion of the portrayal of South Asians, gendered stereotypes, normed Western beauty standards, and cultural identity in popular culture. Kaling, a pioneering transpacific woman, is an integral part for the advancement of social justice in contemporary media as she does not only frequently occupy behind-the-scenes creative positions but also one of power as a producer and director. As such, she hires and casts diverse individuals for on- and off-screen work and ensures minorities have increased "authentic" representation. This is something

Kaling considers her responsibility: "'My role is not just artist. It's also activist because of the way I look. On so many shows and films, race was a gesture, and in mine it's the premise.'"[6] Yuen elaborates: "Rather than become defeated by the onslaught of inconsequential or stereotyped roles, actors of color such as.... Kaling reframe their jobs as opportunities to subvert, redeem and challenge stereotypes."[7] Other than *TMP* and *NHIE*, Kaling also co-created *Champions* (2018) and Hulu's miniseries *Four Weddings and a Funeral* (2019) based on the 1994 film of the same title but with a more diverse cast and a modern setting. She also wrote and starred in *Late Night* (2019), which was produced and distributed by Amazon Studios and became part of Amazon's streaming service Prime Video.

Kaling's comedy-drama *Late Night* can be seen as a crucial step to furthering the understanding of an Asian American experience on- and off-screen as it not only introduces the audience to what function and influence a writers' room has, but it also critically and humorously addresses the importance of diversity within it. The writers' room inhabits a central creative position in the process of cultural productions, as the writers usually create the core content of medial productions, which is subsequently vetted and potentially turned into a script. As Nancy Wang Yuen explains in *Reel Inequality*, "[f]ixing characters of color is a common goal for actors of color who work on projects written by whites. It often involves adding dimension to a caricature,"[8] transferring the responsibility to the person of color rather than everyone involved in the production. Thus, these writers hold social responsibility for how minorities are represented in contemporary media.

Late Night's storyline follows Molly Patel, played by Kaling herself, as the only untrained, female, and non-white writer—a so-called diversity hire—on an acclaimed but increasingly failing talk show hosted by Katherine Newbury, played by Emma Thompson. Patel unexpectedly and unconventionally proves herself within and beyond the workplace and ultimately saves the show from being canceled while gaining her colleagues' respect. The film, inspired by Kaling's experience and difficulties being a diversity hire for *The Office*,[9] highlights the lack of female late night show hosts in real life, the under- and misrepresentation of minorities, systemic racism and gender discrimination, mental health and public vulnerability, ageism in Hollywood, conservative networks, and the overall lack of diversity behind and in front of the camera. Most importantly, however, *Late Night* emphasizes that diversity and inclusivity need to be *actively* pursued, as, e.g., the writers' room ultimately has the ability to create "authentic" diverse on-screen characters.

Following the executive level and the writers' room, the final and most inclusive medial entity is the so-called matrix stage, a term coined by film and media scholar Kim. It is a key element in the process of utilizing the reach and effect media can have and advancing accurate representation. Kim describes it as "a space where different forms of producing and consuming media overlap and blend, opening up new possibilities for collaboration and meaning making. It is this practice of participating in a matrix stage that can lead to cultural change through Asian American media."[10] It is an intersectional space, primarily enabled by the internet and streaming services, in which the audience—critics and private consumers—and cultural producers—artists, directors, networks and streaming services—can interact and collaborate and make media more inclusive, diverse, realistic, and demographic-oriented; it is where the margin and the mainstream meet. Like Tung, Kim encourages multiple communities to take part in the inclusivity discourse and recognize their own influential power as consumers and creators. "Asian American artists and viewers-producers are taking up transmedia mechanisms to establish themselves as performers, fans, critics, and above all, as citizens. They are interacting in a matrix where race is made and unmade, credited and dismisses, discussed and negotiated."[11] Racially diverse series such *Brooklyn Nine-Nine* (2013–2021) and *Lucifer* (2016–2021) exemplify how the matrix stage works in practice. After being cancelled, they were either picked up by a different broadcasting station or a streaming service, as their fan bases demanded a continuation of the show and online campaigns went viral.

However, the concept of a matrix stage in media exceeds individual case studies but marks a substantial change in the mediascape itself, as it presents a new approach to the production of diversified, including transpacific, media, where we as a collaborative community participate in the shaping of what is widely considered mainstream productions and offer insights into under- or misrepresented societies. Thus, we are able to move away from Anglo- and Americentric and patriarchal modes of production and toward a representational system not based on social hierarchy and easy racial tropes but one of accuracy and inclusivity.

Yuen discusses how transpacific actors as well as cultural producers influence the way race is being portrayed and have an obligation to dismantle the stereotypes they encounter within and beyond Hollywood. However, she acknowledges the difficulties people of color encounter during those attempts, but contends that resistance/media activism also redefines what it means to *be* an actor, cultural producer, and even American today. Yuen also suggests alternatives to traditional Hollywood as potential forms of activism and resistance:

> Panethnic theaters and independent films have served as sites of empowerment for artists of color to reclaim and reimagine themselves and their community through performance and art. Actors of color continue to participate

> in these movements because racial inequality and stereotypes still exist in Hollywood.... [W]ith the gap between independent and mainstream films narrowing, and the willingness of streaming services such as Netflix and Amazon to buy independent films, this is an increasingly viable medium for actors and artists of color who want to tell their own stories outside mainstream Hollywood.[12]

Indeed, this shift toward marginalized communities, transpacific productions, and accurate representation is now frequently enabled by the popularity of streaming services which continue to largely replace the traditional forms of creating and watching films and television in many (Western) countries:

> [A]n explosion in original streaming video-on-demand content—for example, the number of scripted digital shows increased by 512 percent since the 2012–13 season—continued to drive what many hail as a 'renaissance' in quality television programming. Television content in 2016–17, distributed across more than 100 platforms, was a far cry from earlier periods when programming was dominated by ... just handful of broadcast networks.[13]

These platforms offer more inclusive formats, free from the limitations and censorships of public television and the need to please a broad viewership. They include cultural productions by people from the transpacific and about their experiences, which is often indicative of more diverse people in charge and in their writers' room, as exemplified by many of Kaling's medial works. Furthermore, these platforms emphasize that with such an on-demand service, they do not have to seek and represent what they assume is their audience's common denominator, but are free to create and offer more diverse content, such as *NHIE*. After *TMP*, *Champions*, and *Four Weddings and a Funeral*, *NHIE* is the fourth series (co-) created by Kaling. Including Dr. Lahiri in *TMP*, Maya, played by Nathalie Emmanuel, in *Four Weddings and a Funeral*, and Michael Prashant Patel, played by Josie Totah, in *Champions*, it is Kaling's fourth show to star a lead person of color and her third show to feature an empowered woman of color protagonist. *Champions* featured a young Indian American homosexual main character, once again naturalizing diversity on screen, while *NHIE*'s plot was inspired by Kaling's own life growing up in an Indian American household as a second-generation immigrant.

Challenging Norms: Never Have I Ever—*Season 1, Episode 1*

NHIE is a Netflix Original Series, Universal Television Production, and Kaling International Inc. coming-of-age sitcom co-created by Kaling and Lang Fisher, who have also worked together on *TMP*. As Kaling explained in an NPR interview, "[she] was initially hesitant to revisit her teen years for the project" because it would "'be too painful and embarrassing to relive those experiences.'"[14] However, being so involved and utilizing the options streaming services provide, Kaling was able to hire "a staff of young Indian women" for *NHIE*'s writers' room, which made her feel less alone and changed her outlook.[15] Thus, this diversity in creative roles as well as positions of power enabled them to create a series which has been "virtually absent from American screens until now."[16] *NHIE* also processes loss and pays tribute, Kaling having lost her mother and Fisher her father. The sitcom was viewed by 40 million households within four weeks of its release.[17]

Devi Vishwakumar, played by Maitreyi Ramakrishnan, is a 15-year-old Sherman Oaks high school sophomore who deals with puberty and adolescence, balancing a biracial identity, school, filiality, and parental expectations while carving her own path as an only child. As Netflix sums up *NHIE*'s plot: "After a traumatic year, an Indian-American teen just wants to spruce up her social status—but friends, family and feelings won't make it easy on her."[18] Kaling and Lang aimed at bringing a new kind of nerd to the screen, not a bookworm or wallflower "who struggle[s] to stand up for themselves … [but a] belligerent, confident nerd … [who] want[s] big things for themselves."[19]

NHIE's "Pilot" represents and empowers marginal communities, as it naturalizes on-screen diversity beyond race and respectability politics and utilizes humor and the streaming service sitcom format sprinkled with popular culture references as a tool for social justice, collaboration, and visibility. It is as diverse in its cast as it is in its topics covered in its pilot episode, which can be accredited to its female writers, Kaling and Fisher.

The episode opens with Devi, *NHIE*'s Indian American protagonist, at her family's Hindu shrine at their home, praying to various gods in her daily worship, also called Puja, to help her in regard to the new school year, appearance, love life, and reputation in an unusual mix of religion and adolescence. She is a high school student who lives in the San Fernando Valley, California, with her mother Dr. Nalini Vishwakumar, played by Poorna Jagannathan, a single mother and full-time dermatologist, who enters Devi's room and warns her not to drop her blessed Geometry book while explaining its significance: "Devi, that textbook has been blessed. If it touches the ground, I have to take it back to the priest."[20] Devi's parents, Nalini and father Mohan, played by Sendhil Ramamurthy, moved to the United States in September 2001, which was a particularly difficult time for immigrants due to the aftermath of the September 11 attacks.[21] The episode's flashback elaborates on the differences among the Vishwakumar parent and first filial generation: "[Devi's parents] stayed true to their Indian roots.... Devi was all-American"[22]—whether it is in eating habits, language—both accent and slang vocabulary—or mannerisms. However, the flashback also sums up the trials and tribulations the Vishwakumar family endured in the past year: Mohan dies of a heart attack and shortly after Devi inexplicably becomes paraplegic for three months until she miraculously recovers.[23] This "physical manifestation of a teenager's grief" was inspired by Fisher's brother, who experienced this after their parents got divorced,[24] further highlighting how personal biographies and inclusive mindsets in creative positions directly affect on-screen representation.

Another character introduced at the beginning of the "Pilot" is Devi's cousin Kamala, played by Richa Moorjani, who moved in after Mohan's passing and helped around the house and Devi with her condition. Devi struggles to warm up to her seemingly perfect and beautiful cousin who is in the United States to finish her Biology PhD at the California Institute of Technology, and who, according to Devi, is "just so Indian."[25] Her mother however reminds Devi of the importance of family, the constant responsibility and filial duty they have toward it, and that she could learn from her cousin's ambition. Being in the United States on a temporary basis, Kamala personifies the most prominent bridge to Indian culture, family, and filiality in *NHIE*'s pilot episode. Among the Vishwakumars, Kamala most recently entered the United States, diversifying immigration patterns within the family itself. Kamala is not only expected to return to India after her studies, she is also expected to partake in an arranged marriage, which she sarcastically comments on: "A husband from India? Someone I've never met before. Perfect stranger. How exciting."[26] The imposed model minority identity on Kamala transcends her race but strongly pertains to cultural gender roles; thus, she is not only expected to be a model child in terms of her academic achievement, she is also expected to be a wife as soon as she closes that chapter of her life. Overall, her situation gives the audience an insight on still ongoing traditions in India and the position of women in its patriarchal culture.

Having survived the difficult past year, Devi is now wondering how she can "shed her old identity as the paralyzed Indian girl, whose dad dropped dead at a school function."[27] Although Devi seems to be outspoken and confident on the surface, she struggles with adolescence and is considered a nerd at school; thus, on the first day of the new school year, she has decided that she and her best friends need to rebrand themselves; "[w]e are glamorous women of color, who deserve a sexy high school life."[28] Devi's best friends, Chinese American Eleanor Wong, played by Ramona Young, and multiracial Fabiola Torres, played by Lee Rodriguez, represent solidarity among women of color rather than female rivalry and although they or rather Devi wants them all to be "cool" and accepted into the mainstream, they appear happy as accomplished, potentially stereotyped model minority, teenagers who already consider eating in the teachers' lounge cool. Although Eleanor and Fabiola maturely refuse Devi's idea to completely change their personality—a self-proclaimed actress and president of the drama club and captain of the high school robotics team, respectively—they reluctantly agree to her solution to elevate their popularity through boyfriends instead. Their "squad['s]"[29] diverse interests illustrate young girls not only excelling in school but also in theater and engineering, yet, unfortunately, the boyfriend plan appears to tie their worth or rather their popularity to men. However, all the boys Devi has chosen for her friends are minorities as well: a Russian exchange student, a popular GSM classmate that has not come out yet, and a Mexican American. This choice departs from the idea that only white heterosexual Anglophone men are desirable.

Ben Gross, played by Jaren Lewison, Devi's school nemesis, comes from a Jewish family, is an only child, boasts about his father and their wealth, and is an academic equal to Devi. Ben created and spread the "gently racist nickname, the UN"[30] to describe Devi, Eleanor, and Fabiola because they are "an ethnically diverse group of academically-focused … dorks."[31] According to Ben, calling them the UN however is not about race, but "because [they] are unfuckable nerds."[32] Ben further claims that Devi's disability was fake and generally preys on her insecurities due to him feeling academically threatened; "he and Devi had been vying for the number one spot in the class every year since the first grade."[33]

Devi has an unproductive, yet refreshing temper, as it is something you rarely see in on-screen young women of color—"Devi has, what you might consider, a short fuse, and sometimes, she's a straight up psycho"[34]—especially in her competition with Ben, which interestingly reiterates the model minority stereotype in its ambition but not in its execution. In contrast, Ben is *NHIE*'s pilot episode's prime example for male white fragility. This includes Ben's defensiveness about his father's looks and his own physical appearance.

In order to prove her attractiveness to Ben and get a boyfriend, the following day, Devi shows up in a sexy outfit, which can be read as both empowering and a reclamation of selfhood and body, but also as self-objectification driven by patriarchal motives. However, Devi's flaws do not only make her more of a rounded character, *NHIE* uses them to distance its protagonist from the idea that a minority has to fit a certain image or play according to the rules of respectability politics.

Devi expected for her two best friends to dress sexy as well. However, unbeknownst to Devi, Eleanor already has a boyfriend which breaks several conventions, not because Eleanor is Chinese American and her boyfriend Oliver Martinez, played by Martin Martinez, is Latino, but because she is an actress and he is from the tech crew, which would send an unimaginable shock wave through the drama club according to Eleanor,[35] naturalizing their ethnically diverse relationship on-screen and making their story equally important, not limiting them to the roles of on-screen tokens.

Devi's reaction to Eleanor supposedly betraying her by having a secret boyfriend only further highlights her human flaws and defects, which challenges superficial presentation over the *re*presentation of rounded characters of color and therefore contributes to social justice. By not picturing Devi as a model minority, Kaling uses Netflix to distance the character of Devi from a hegemonic misrepresenting system in which only empowered people of color are allowed to exist. Instead, by challenging imposed terms of visibility and representation itself, *NHIE* portrays a "real" person. As the narrator explains: "When you're a normal person with genuinely balanced reactions to things, it may be hard to understand why we hotheads fly off the handle."[36] Devi storms home, screams, throws her blessed Geometry book out of the window, breaks the window in the process, and then lies about it to her family, claiming it was a bird.[37] Devi tries to process the day she has had: "Does [Eleanor] think Devi's too unhinged to handle it? Or that Devi would be jealous of her? Do both of her friends think she's just a pitiful, lonely, wheelchair girl without a freaking dad?"[38]

Based on her loss, her disability, and her changed living situation, Devi started seeing Dr. Jamie Ryan, played by Niecy Nash, an African American child psychologist. Rather than discuss her late father, her subsequent paralysis and grief, and work on her grief journal in her latest sessions, Devi primarily talks to her therapist about her crush on Japanese American Paxton Hall-Yoshida, played by Darren Barnet, an upperclassman at their high school, her school nemesis Ben, and her two best friends. The matrix stage likely influenced *NHIE*'s lead male casting choices and the aforementioned proposed boyfriends, as Kaling and *TMP*'s first seasons were heavily criticized for its protagonist Lahiri only dating white men. Even though Devi may not take her therapy sessions too seriously in *NHIE*'s pilot, its depiction naturalizes therapy for teenagers and destigmatizes mental health issues. Generally, Devi struggles with her feelings and the need for an acceptable or "normal" appearance. She does not even care who her boyfriend would be, as long as she has one and he makes her look good: "'It doesn't matter how it makes me feel. It matters how it makes me look.... I just want to be a normal girl, who isn't called mean names, and could actually have a boyfriend. I don't even care who he is, as long as he wanted to be with me.'"[39]

Paxton, an aloof jock and flat character in the pilot episode, is *NHIE*'s romantic lead, which is unusual in two significant ways. Firstly, having an

Asian American romantic lead is rare, as the idea that having white main characters is the only way to make a plot or character relatable is still rampant in the United States' mediascape. Series such as *Crazy Ex-Girlfriend* (2015–2019) have been forerunners in highlighting Asian men as desirable partners and romantic leads in recent romantic comedic series. Secondly, pairing the Indian American female lead with an East Asian American, specifically Japanese, who has to retake a class, is significant when considering the origins and the rise of the model minority myth. Furthermore, based on the cultural differences, including outdated traditions of exclusively having relationships with individuals from one's country and religion, older generations of both cultures would most likely forbid such a pairing. Thus, this casting and plot choice breaks several cultural norms. Additionally, in order to accurately reflect Barnet's ethnicity, -Yoshida was added to his character's last name after colleagues heard Barnet speaking Japanese to *NHIE*'s assistant director Yuko Ogata.[40]

Throughout the pilot episode, which gives the audience insights into different cultures and most importantly the major diverse characters of the series, the core of *NHIE*, coming-of-age and grief, does not come too short either. Devi's first two pictured days are intercepted by a dream of her late father Mohan, whom she communicates with. This visual and emotional "experience [is] drawn directly from Kaling and co-creator Lang Fisher's lives" and their experience with parental loss.[41] After Devi confides her struggles and hurt to her father, he reminds her that John McEnroe, Mohan's favorite tennis player, would never let anyone push him around and neither should Devi. McEnroe, who is *NHIE*'s peculiar yet amusing narrator, is not only a connection to Devi's father, an emotional depth Devi is not ready to fully explore yet, he also helps to contextualize Devi's rage. Overall, courage truly seems to be the message of *NHIE*'s diverse pilot episode, whether it is standing up to your bully at school, standing up for yourself and being clear about what kind of marriage or relationship you want in the future, or standing up to your friend who wants to change your personality in order to be cool. *NHIE* also provides viewers with various insights on Hinduism, Indian culture, and Indian American identity, yet simply naturalizes its presence in a series rather than make it its task to educate its audience. To end my analysis of *NHIE*'s section on destigmatization and naturalized on-screen diversity, equality, social justice, and the importance of representation behind and in front of the camera in Devi's loving father's words: "You fight back with your spirit, little one. You stand up for yourself."[42] Thus, even though Devi proposes sex to Paxton at the end of the first episode instead of working through her grief, experienced disability, and desire to be accepted into mainstream society, it leaves the viewer sympathetic for a grieving flawed teenager struggling with what life is throwing at her and it leaves them hopeful for further growth. Therefore, *NHIE* does not encourage some form of orthodoxy of progressivism but embraces social justice as a challenge of the representation itself by depicting a flawed female protagonist of color.

Conclusion

By interrogating and transforming crucial functions of cultural productions, including, but not limited to, the ones outlined in this essay, and through collaborative efforts in multiple forms of media activism, transpacific cultural producers resist cultural erasure through medial social justice. For many transpacific cultural producers such as Kaling, their work in media surpasses entertainment, but encapsulates activism. Furthermore, often through streaming services, they envision new formats of visibility, assert cultural citizenship, reshape mainstream productions and create new spaces for previously displaced and/or silent minorities far beyond the one-dimensionalized token side-kicks of political correctness. As activist, writer, filmmaker, and scholar Renee Tajima-Peña sums up the past and continuous work the diverse transpacific community undertakes and calls for in "Toward a Third Wave: Why Media Matters in Asian American Studies":

> This is a manifesto, a call for advancing a third wave of collaboration among artists, scholars, and community[,] a deeper engagement in the production of knowledge, the creation of culture, and, ultimately, the advancement of social justice. It is a call to marshal all of our resources, whether intellectual, creative, or the power of social action. Interactive, online technologies unleash new possibilities[.][43]

Representing more and different types of diversity through streaming services and the correlating matrix stage continues to contribute to a social justice effort that includes, but is not limited to, orthodox progressive kinds of representation of empowered minority figures. Instead, it is a more complex and nuanced representation of individuals which reify cultural identities in the public sphere. Instead of curtailing transpacific voices in minority categories, their productions can be means for the transformation of not only American society, but the role of entertainment as a form of education and social justice.

Notes

1. Ling-hsuan Larry Tung, "Images of Asians and Asian-Americans: The Underrepresentation and Misrepresentation of Asians and Asian-Americans on American Television," *Intercultural Communication Studies* 15, no. 1 (2006): 87.

2. Erin Suzuki, "Transpacific," in *The Routledge Companion to Asian American and Pacific Islander Literature*, ed. Rachel C. Lee (New York: Routledge, 2014), 352.

3. L.S. Kim, "Asian America On Demand: Asian Americans, Media Networks, and a Matrix Stage," in *The Routledge Companion to Asian American Media*, ed. Lori Kido Lopez and Vincent Pham (New York: Routledge, 2017), 170.

4. "RACE: 2020: DEC Redistricting Data (PL 94–171)," United States Census Bureau, accessed December 14, 2021, https://data.census.gov/cedsci/table?q=%202020&g=0100000US&tid=DECENNIALPL2020.P1.

5. Mindy Kaling, *Why Not Me?* (New York: Three Rivers Press, 2016), 44–45.

6. Nancy Wang Yuen, *Reel Inequality: Hollywood Actors and Racism* (New Brunswick: Rutgers UP, 2016), 107.

7. Nancy Wang Yuen, *Reel Inequality: Hollywood Actors and Racism* (New Brunswick: Rutgers UP, 2016), 107.

8. Nancy Wang Yuen, *Reel Inequality: Hollywood Actors and Racism* (New Brunswick: Rutgers UP, 2016), 115.

9. Terry Gross, "Mindy Kaling Brings A New Nerd To TV, And Finds She 'Was Not Alone' As A Teen," *National Public Radio*, April 27,, 2020, https://www.npr.org/2020/04/27/845440741/mindy-kaling-brings-a-new-nerd-to-tv-and-finds-she-was-not-alone-as-a-teen.

10. L.S. Kim, "Asian America On Demand: Asian Americans, Media Networks, and a Matrix Stage," in *The Routledge Companion to Asian American Media*, ed. Lori Kido Lopez and Vincent Pham (New York: Routledge, 2017), 171.

11. L.S. Kim, "Asian America On Demand: Asian Americans, Media Networks, and a Matrix Stage," in *The Routledge Companion to Asian American Media*, ed. Lori Kido Lopez and Vincent Pham (New York: Routledge, 2017), 179.

12. Nancy Wang Yuen, *Reel Inequality: Hollywood Actors and Racism* (New Brunswick: Rutgers UP, 2016), 134.

13. Darnell Hunt, Ana-Christina Ramón, and Michael Tran. *Hollywood Diversity Report 2019* (Los Angeles: University of California Los Angeles, College of Social Sciences, 2019), 8.

14. Terry Gross, "Mindy Kaling Brings A New Nerd To TV, And Finds She 'Was Not Alone' As A Teen," *National Public Radio*, April 27,, 2020, https://www.npr.org/2020/04/27/845440741/mindy-kaling-brings-a-new-nerd-to-tv-and-finds-she-was-not-alone-as-a-teen.

15. Terry Gross, "Mindy Kaling Brings A New Nerd To TV, And Finds She 'Was Not Alone' As A Teen," *National Public Radio*, April 27,, 2020, https://www.npr.org/2020/04/27/845440741/mindy-kaling-brings-a-new-nerd-to-tv-and-finds-she-was-not-alone-as-a-teen.

16. Priya Arora, "Mindy Kaling's Netflix Show Tells a New Kind of Story: One Like Hers," *The New York Times*, April 27, 2020, https://www.nytimes.com/2020/04/27/arts/television/mindy-kaling-never-have-I-ever-netflix.html.

17. Dominic Patten, "Netflix Reveals Strong Viewership Numbers For Mindy Kaling's 'Never Have I Ever' & Spike Lee's 'Da 5 Bloods' In Earnings Report," *Deadline*, July 16, 2020, https://deadline.com/2020/07/netflix-viewership-results-mindy-kaling-never-have-i-ever-steve-carell-space-force-spike-lee-da-5-bloods-earnings-report-q2-1202987697/.

18. "Never Have I Ever," *Netflix*, accessed July 14, 2020, https://www.netflix.com/title/80179190.

19. Terry Gross, "Mindy Kaling Brings A New Nerd To TV, And Finds She 'Was Not Alone' As A Teen," *National Public Radio*, April 27,, 2020, https://www.npr.org/2020/04/27/845440741/mindy-kaling-brings-a-new-nerd-to-tv-and-finds-she-was-not-alone-as-a-teen.

20. Mindy Kaling and Lang Fisher, "Pilot," in *Never Have I Ever*, dir. Tristram Shapeero (*Netflix*: April 27, 2020), 00:04:49–00:04:54.

21. Ahmad, Muneer I. "A Rage Shared by Law: Post-September 11 Racial Violence as Crimes of Passion." *California Law Review* 92, no. 5 (2004): 1259–1330. https://doi.org/10.2307/3481418.

22. Mindy Kaling and Lang Fisher, "Pilot," in *Never Have I Ever*, dir. Tristram Shapeero (*Netflix*: April 27, 2020), 00:01:56–00:02:03.

23. Mindy Kaling and Lang Fisher, "Pilot," in *Never Have I Ever*, dir. Tristram Shapeero (*Netflix*: April 27, 2020), 00:02:11–00:04:16.

24. Terry Gross, "Mindy Kaling Brings A New Nerd To TV, And Finds She 'Was Not Alone' As A Teen," *National Public Radio*, April 27,, 2020, https://www.npr.org/2020/04/27/845440741/mindy-kaling-brings-a-new-nerd-to-tv-and-finds-she-was-not-alone-as-a-teen.

25. Mindy Kaling and Lang Fisher, "Pilot," in *Never Have I Ever*, dir. Tristram Shapeero (*Netflix*: April 27, 2020), 00:05:51–00:05:53.

26. Mindy Kaling and Lang Fisher, "Pilot," in *Never Have I Ever*, dir. Tristram Shapeero (*Netflix*: April 27, 2020), 00:14:45 00:14:50.

27. Mindy Kaling and Lang Fisher, "Pilot," in *Never Have I Ever*, dir. Tristram Shapeero (*Netflix*: April 27, 2020), 00:04:19–00:04:25.

28. Mindy Kaling and Lang Fisher, "Pilot," in *Never Have I Ever*, dir. Tristram Shapeero (*Netflix*: April 27, 2020), 00:07:23–00:07:27.

29. Mindy Kaling and Lang Fisher, "Pilot," in *Never Have I Ever*, dir. Tristram Shapeero (*Netflix*: April 27, 2020), 00:06:22.

30. Mindy Kaling and Lang Fisher, "Pilot," in *Never Have I Ever*, dir. Tristram Shapeero (*Netflix*: April 27, 2020), 00:09:14–00:09:16.

31. Mindy Kaling and Lang Fisher, "Pilot," in *Never Have I Ever*, dir. Tristram Shapeero (*Netflix*: April 27, 2020), 00:09:05–00:09:12.

32. Mindy Kaling and Lang Fisher, "Pilot," in *Never Have I Ever*, dir. Tristram Shapeero (*Netflix*: April 27, 2020), 00:12:22–00:12:24.

33. Mindy Kaling and Lang Fisher, "Pilot," in *Never Have I Ever*, dir. Tristram Shapeero (*Netflix*: April 27, 2020), 00:09:37–00:09:42.

34. Mindy Kaling and Lang Fisher, "Pilot," in *Never Have I Ever*, dir. Tristram Shapeero (*Netflix*: April 27, 2020), 00:11:31–00:11:37.

35. Mindy Kaling and Lang Fisher, "Pilot," in *Never Have I Ever*, dir. Tristram Shapeero (*Netflix*: April 27, 2020), 00:20:23–00:20:27.

36. Mindy Kaling and Lang Fisher, "Pilot," in *Never Have I Ever*, dir. Tristram Shapeero (*Netflix*: April 27, 2020), 00:21:08–00:21:15.

37. Mindy Kaling and Lang Fisher, "Pilot," in *Never Have I Ever*, dir. Tristram Shapeero (*Netflix*: April 27, 2020), 00:21:38–00:21:50.

38. Mindy Kaling and Lang Fisher, "Pilot," in *Never Have I Ever*, dir. Tristram Shapeero (*Netflix*: April 27, 2020), 00:21:24–00:21:38.

39. Mindy Kaling and Lang Fisher, "Pilot," in *Never Have I Ever*, dir. Tristram Shapeero (*Netflix*: April 27, 2020), 00:23:06–00:23:25.

40. Olivia Singh, "'Never Have I Ever' star Darren Barnet on his favorite scene from season 1, 'humanizing' Paxton Hall-Yoshida, and forging his own path," *Insider*, May 19, 2020, https://www.insider.com/never-have-i-ever-darren-barnet-paxton-interview-2020-5.

41. Terry Gross, "Mindy Kaling Brings A New Nerd To TV, And Finds She 'Was Not Alone' As A Teen," *National Public Radio*, April 27,, 2020, https://www.npr.org/2020/04/27/845440741/mindy-kaling-brings-a-new-nerd-to-tv-and-finds-she-was-not-alone-as-a-teen.

42. Mindy Kaling and Lang Fisher, "Pilot," in *Never Have I Ever*, dir. Tristram Shapeero (*Netflix*: April 27, 2020), 00:16:30–00:16:35.

43. Renee Tajima-Peña, "Toward a Third Wave: Why Media Matters in Asian American Studies," *Journal of Asian American Studies* 17, no. 1 (February 2014): 94–95.

Works Cited

Ahmad, Muneer I. "A Rage Shared by Law: Post-September 11 Racial Violence as Crimes of Passion." *California Law Review* 92, no. 5 (2004): 1259–1330. https://doi.org/10.2307/3481418.

Arora, Priya. "Mindy Kaling's Netflix Show Tells a New Kind of Story: One Like Hers." *The*

New York Times, April 27, 2020. https://www.nytimes.com/2020/04/27/arts/television/mindy-kaling-never-have-I-ever-netflix.html.

Ganatra, Nisha, dir. *Late Night*. United States: Amazon Studios, 2019.

Gross, Terry. "Mindy Kaling Brings A New Nerd To TV, And Finds She 'Was Not Alone' As A Teen." *National Public Radio*, April 27, 2020. https://www.npr.org/2020/04/27/845440741/mindy-kaling-brings-a-new-nerd-to-tv-and-finds-she-was-not-alone-as-a-teen.

Hunt, Darnell, Ana-Christina Ramón, and Michael Tran. *Hollywood Diversity Report 2019*. Los Angeles: University of California Los Angeles, College of Social Sciences, 2019.

Kaling, Mindy and Lang Fisher, writers. *Never Have I Ever*. Season 1, Episode 1, "Pilot." Directed by Tristram Shapeero, featuring Maitreyi Ramakrishnan, Poorna Jagannathan, and Richa Moorjani. *Netflix*, April 27 2020.

Kaling, Mindy. *Why Not Me?* New York: Three Rivers Press, 2016.

Kim, L.S. "Asian America On Demand: Asian Americans, Media Networks, and a Matrix Stage." In *The Routledge Companion to Asian American Media*, edited by Lori Kido Lopez and Vincent Pham, 170–180. New York: Routledge, 2017.

______. "Representation of Race." In *Battlegrounds: The Media: Volumes 1 and 2*, edited by Robin Andersen and Jonathan Gray, 452–459. Westport: Greenwood Press, 2008.

"Never Have I Ever." *Netflix*. Accessed July 14, 2020. https://www.netflix.com/title/80179190.

Patten, Dominic. "Netflix Reveals Strong Viewership Numbers For Mindy Kaling's 'Never Have I Ever' & Spike Lee's 'Da 5 Bloods' In Earnings Report." *Deadline*, July 16, 2020. https://deadline.com/2020/07/netflix-viewership-results-mindy-kaling-never-have-i-ever-steve-carell-space-force-spike-lee-da-5-bloods-earnings-report-q2-1202987697/.

Singh, Olivia. "'Never Have I Ever' star Darren Barnet on his favorite scene from season 1, 'humanizing' Paxton Hall-Yoshida, and forging his own path." *Insider*, May 19, 2020. https://www.insider.com/never-have-i-ever-darren-barnet-paxton-interview-2020-5.

Suzuki, Erin. "Transpacific." In *The Routledge Companion to Asian American and Pacific Islander Literature*, edited by Rachel C. Lee, 352–364. New York: Routledge, 2014.

Tajima-Peña, Renee. "Toward a Third Wave: Why Media Matters in Asian American Studies." *Journal of Asian American Studies* 17, no. 1 (February 2014): 94–99. Project MUSE.

Tung, Ling-hsuan Larry. "Images of Asians and Asian-Americans: The Under-representation and Misrepresentation of Asians and Asian-Americans on American Television." *Intercultural Communication Studies* 15, no. 1 (2006): 87–93.

"2019: ACS 1-Year Estimates Data Profiles." United States Census Bureau. Accessed September 29, 2020. https://data.census.gov/cedsci/table?q=united%20states&g=0100000US&tid=ACSDP1Y2019.DP05&hidePreview=false.

Yuen, Nancy Wang. *Reel Inequality: Hollywood Actors and Racism*. New Brunswick: Rutgers University Press, 2016.

Contemplating the "Original" in an Age of Branded Content, Branded Networks, Branded Genres and Branded Adaptations

KATERINA MARAZI

Introduction

Today's vast visual culture includes a plethora of entertainment productions. Viewing options have become enriched and personalized via video streaming services such as Netflix, Amazon, and Hulu. Who has not seen a Netflix original? And yet, the term original does raise questions. According to the Oxford English Dictionary, the term "original" means: (n) "the earliest form of something, from which copies may be made"; "a book or recording that has not been previously made available in a different form"; (adj) "present or existing from the beginning; first or earliest"; "created personally by a particular artist, writer, musician, etc.; not a copy"; "not dependent on other people's ideas; inventive or novel." At a first glance, these meanings correspond to meaning(s) the field of Adaptation has assigned to the primary texts upon which adaptations are based. At a second glance, the use of "original" in the video streaming services, such as Netflix, does not appear to fall in line with that of adaptation but rather with how the term is utilized in a branded context.

Certain concepts invite reconsideration, particularly when industrial and cultural practices impact how these concepts are treated and understood. The context of immediate concern noted by Michael L. Wayne[1] is that of a struggle between the established and the emerging. This paper views Disney as a long-standing established brand, one that can compete against other brands, like Warner Bros., in a race of who will release their branded adaptations first.[2] Netflix is among the emerging contestants. While the two cases of Disney and Netflix offer an array of fruitful areas for investigation, this paper is primarily concerned with their treatment of the concept "original."

The question set forth here is: What is an "original" in a branded context as opposed to an adaptation context? While the answer may appear self-evident and simple, it prompts an array of numerous interrelated questions that can be examined from various perspectives as the effects of such clashes do trickle towards multiple directions, such as branded storytelling, branded marketing, industrial intertextuality, branded experiences and even reconfiguring or branding terms such as "original." Drawing on scholars such as Linda Hutcheon, John Fiske, John Bryant and Derek Johnson, the Netflix branding practice of "original" will be examined in connection with the Disney brand adaptation practices related to *The Jungle Book* (2016) whilst considering the Marvel/Netflix superhero productions to examine the treatment of the term "original" and determine if an "original" is just that or what the brand says it is.

While the term "original" can be associated with adaptations and video streaming services, the term does not appear in the respective *Oxford English Dictionary* meanings of "adaptation" or "brand." It does, however, appear in the way Netflix markets its original content and it can be found in academic publications pertaining to adaptations. The following section provides context to the term "original" by initially juxtaposing the respective dictionary meanings of "adaptation" and "brand" to academic publications in the fields of adaptation and branding respectively. Following that, the paper cross-references how the term is understood in each context, given recent practices, in order to determine either a point of convergence or divergence.

One Term, Different Contexts

According to the *Oxford English Dictionary*, "adaptation" means: (n) "the action or process of adapting or being adapted"; "a film, television drama, or stage play that has been adapted from a written work"; "the process of change by which an organism or species becomes better suited to its environment." The dictionary definition contains a meaning pertinent to adaptation—though rather limiting given the plethora of adaptation types. It acknowledges, similarly to academic publications, that adaptation is both a product and a process. To offer points of comparison from an academic standpoint, this paper adopts Linda Hutcheon's definition. Hutcheon describes adaptation as follows: "a *formal entity or product*, an adaptation is an announced and extensive transposition of a particular work or works," one example being a film adaptation of Shakespeare's plays.[3] Adaptations should also be considered as "a *process of creation,* the act of adaptation always involves both (re-)interpretation and then (re-) creation."[4] Baz Luhrmann's *Romeo and Juliet* (1996) is a reinterpreted/ recreated film adaptation of the respective Shakespeare play. Finally, Hutcheon informs that "from the perspective of its *process of reception,* adaptation is a form of intertextuality; we experience adaptations (*as adaptations*) as palimpsests through our memory of other works that resonate through repetition with variation."[5] In other words, the more adaptations of Romeo and Juliet we experience, the more intertextual references and associations we can make. Hutcheon's definition enriches the dictionary definition by adding the dimension of reception and not limiting the types of adaptations that may occur. Nevertheless, the term "original" is not evident in either. The term, however, is utilized in older academic publications related to adaptation particularly when the focal debate was that of the adaptation's fidelity towards the original.

Imelda Whelehan offers an overview of contemporary dilemmas the field of adaptation was facing at that time, chief amongst them the fidelity of the adaptation towards the original work. Often referred to as "original source," "original," or "original work," the term refers to the text an author or studio has acquired copyrights to in order to proceed with an adaptation. This falls in line with the respective dictionary definition of "original," namely that which existed first, which belongs legally to someone else and, by extension, can be considered a novel idea. The value of the "original" in this context relied heavily on the aspect of fidelity. According to Whelehan, Geoffrey Wagner (1975) was the first to identify three types of adaptation that correspond to degrees of fidelity.[6] John Bryant, on the one hand, does include the term "original" in his account of fluid texts but, on the other hand, he notes that the fluid-text approach can assist in the reconsideration of certain concepts, such as the "original," as well as dilemmas and aims at equating all works.[7]

Meanwhile, the respective dictionary meanings for "brand" are: (n) "a type of product manufactured by a particular company under a particular name"; "a brand name"; "a particular identity or image regarded as an asset"; "an identifying mark burned on livestock or criminals or slaves with a branding iron"; (v) "assign a brand name"; "promote by means of advertising and distinctive design." Etymologically speaking, the word "brand" is defined as "marking with a branding iron," for instance when burning the skin of animals, especially cattle, to indicate ownership or property. In this light, production companies brand the texts they produce. The American Marketing Association defines the word brand as "a name, a term, a strategy, a symbol or any other characteristic that creates associations with the product, the service or the company and distinguishes it from others."[8] Similarly, Matthew Healey indicates that brands are understood as "a promise of satisfaction," while the process of branding is the "continuous struggle between producers and customers to define that promise and meaning."[9] Zervaki also highlights that brand and branding are: a promise; the way products distinguish from other similar products; what consumers believe about a company; the feeling created via the interaction with a product, service or company; the tangible representation of a company's values; a set of expectations that have been met and satisfied; the trust between a company and consumers; the intangible value of a company; a set of unique benefits; the reasons for purchasing something; the story of the brand; the symbol of the brand; how messages and their meanings are communicated with or without words; a consumer's experience; and the impression left to consumers after their latest interaction with the brand.[10]

Branding is not to be confused with marketing, though the two remain tightly interrelated. According to Zervaki, branding refers to the strategy a company adopts while marketing refers to the actual tactics the company will follow to realize the adopted strategy.[11] The Netflix Original is primarily part of the Netflix brand incorporated as a major marketing tool to attract audiences. Thus, branding precedes marketing; it is a dynamic non-linear process, an umbrella term that encompasses marketing, design, and trademarks. Zervaki stresses that branding is something that triggers a feeling in the minds of consumers, sets consumer expectations and is the impression people have of a company, its services, and its products. The "original" Netflix content raises or creates expectations for consumers when compared to other content available via the Netflix platform or in comparison to other platforms. It enables the distinction between companies, products, and services. After all, it is not only Netflix that has adopted the brand identity characteristic or promise of "original" content; Amazon Prime also utilizes it. Most importantly, branding is predominantly connected with the creation and negotiation of identity in the sense of who we are, who we want to be and how we want consumers to perceive us.[12] In other words, Netflix—and evidently Amazon Prime—offers access to content created by other productions studios but they also offer their own "original" content.

The following section brings forth the established context of franchise adaptations and the emerging context of video streaming services. The "original" remains the focal point of convergence but, as the section aims to demonstrate, the term has now acquired a brand identity value dimension rather than simply being considered the first of its kind or novel in its status.

Established and Emerging Contexts: Original and Point of Convergence

The field of adaptation has moved past initial debates bestowed upon it from other disciplines, as Robert Stam (2005) notes.[13] Scholars like Hutcheon, Stam, and Thomas Leitch in "Twelve Fallacies in Contemporary Adaptation Theory" (2003)[14] move beyond the confinement of fidelity. Publications such as *Adaptation Studies: New Challenges, New Directions* (2013) and *The Routledge Companion to Transmedia Studies* (2018) acknowledge the value of adaptations, unveil intentions behind adapting texts, adopt a description/definition of adaptation more akin to that offered by Hutcheon and consider the interrelationship of adaptations with emerging storytelling and industry practices such as that of transmedia storytelling. This is logical when scholars like Will Brooker[15] note that certain adaptations, such as comic books, may not even have an original text, or when scholars like Bryant[16] argue that an adaptation is the sum of its works and since both "original" and adaptation are considered texts, their value ought to be equated. The multitude of Batman texts illustrates the above and to experience all the texts, or as many as possible, is to fully experience the Batman character. André Bazin emphasizes an overlooked feature: "One must first know to what end the adaptation is designed: for the cinema or for its audience? One must also realize that most adapters care far more about the latter than about the former."[17] There is an economic incentive influencing and prompting this practice. What is more, as Disney's *The Jungle Book* (2016) demonstrates, this practice is also guided by a need to further strengthen the organization's brand identity. Consequently, the point of convergence between branding and adaptations primarily appears at the level of franchise adaptations.

Clare Parody considers the industrial context of adaptations, an area relatively overlooked at that point. The industrial entertainment practices of Hollywood involve the production of franchise storytelling via adaptations resulting in "the creation of narratives, characters, and settings that can be used both to generate and give identity to vast quantities of interlinked media products and merchandise, resulting in a prolonged, multitextual, multimedia fictional experience."[18] Franchise adaptations are always part of a market strategy and a main feature occurring from such adaptations is that of intertextuality which can lead to a sense of instability.[19] Both Parody and Paul Grainge note brand identity as "the most important interacting protocol" for both the development and management of a fictional brand.[20] Grainge further informs that what is adapted can be viewed as a brand identity "the intellectual property, advertising language, and presentational devices that cohere, authorize, and market the range of media products that together comprise the franchise experience."[21] Janet Wasko[22] and Michaela Robbins and Fritz G. Polite[23] provide informative overviews of Disney's historical, social, global and brand impact. As a major, established brand player, Disney's intent to firmly brand its intellectual properties is no secret.

Text Turf-War: The Case of Disney's The Jungle Book

Amongst many dominating issues found in the context of franchise adaptations is that of corporate ownership. Nicholas Benson investigates "Disney's hold over public domain texts," such as Rudyard Kipling's *The Jungle Book*, and examines the textual and paratextual strategies employed in its recent live-action film to maintain control over *The Jungle Book* text.[24] He focuses on Disney's 1967 animated cartoon version, *The Jungle Book* (2016), and Kipling's text in comparison with Warner Bros.' attempt to challenge it with their *Mowgli: Legend of the Jungle* (2018) which, as Benson notes, resulted in a textual turf-war. Benson observes that the main strategy to guide both the management of text and paratexts was that of industrial intertextuality. The choices Disney made regarding the live-action film "were not made as ways of improving upon or overshadowing the animated version, but rather the new movie functioned to reinforce and expand upon the legacy of that animated film."[25] Constantine Verevis argues that "just as adaptations of literary properties often lead viewers back to source novels for a first reading, remakes encourage viewers to seek out original film properties."[26] Even though *The Jungle Book* (2016) is an adaptation of Kipling's text, it is also a live-action remake of Disney's *The Jungle Book* (1967) animated cartoon. Benson argues that the "original" in the case of the live-action version is the animated cartoon, a strategy that reinforces "latent cultural nostalgia" but also prompts a "Disney interpretation of the story."[27] And this is not the first instance where Disney has utilized industrial intertextuality as the *Pirates of the Caribbean* case could demonstrate.

Disney's strategy promotes specific interpretations and readings of the text and appoints authenticity to their version. Benson explains that "[b]y incorporating narrative elements from the book into this latest Disney brand version, Disney not only limited the portions of the source material Warner Brothers could use to distinguish their version but weakened their claims that their darker more adult version was somehow more authentic."[28] The textual turf-war becomes more intriguing because Disney managed to release their version in 2016, thus forcing Warner Brothers to push "the release date of their film back several years until eventually selling the distribution rights to Netflix in 2018."[29] Established brands, such as Disney, are in a position to appoint their branded texts as an "original" potentially overshadowing the actual source material, namely Kipling's text, as well as hinder other companies from appointing the term to their own branded texts. And yet, both Disney and Warner Brothers produced versions of the same source material. Similarly, Netflix utilizes the term "original" to distinguish between the content it distributes and that which it actually produces. Nevertheless, Netflix content is similar to what other production companies create. What can shed further light on the use of "original" is to consider how Netflix views its brand in its brand marketing tactics.

Original Content or Original Experience?

Video streaming services unavoidably act within a brand context. Ramon Lobato and Amanda D. Lotz note that "Netflix's catalog, cultural status, brand recognition, and market power also vary enormously from country to country" and while arguably Netflix is more global than "any previous screen producer and distributor" they question "what is at stake in imagining Netflix as global?"[30] Juan Llamas-Rodriguez examines the global (or international) Netflix brand and how it consists of national (or local) Netflix subbrands.[31] Yu-Kei Tse highlights that "the future of online television, in Netflix's vision, seems to be both borderless and postnational. In practice, however, Netflix continues to abide by national and regional regulations, as other transnational television systems do."[32] In other words, Netflix offers what other video streaming services offer which could minimize the branding strategy of Netflix "original" to simply mean that which is produced by Netflix. Meanwhile, Michael L. Wayne makes the case for the portal-as-content and portal-as-brand strategy observed in video streaming services drawing attention to "how the identities of global streaming services blend established and emerging branding strategies in national markets."[33] What is more intriguing is how Netflix actually views itself as a brand which can shed light on the notion of "original."

The television industry aims to establish strong channel brand identities like that of HBO. Wayne informs that "the most popular subscription video on-demand (SVOD) services have not used original content targeting specific audience demographics to construct distinctive brand identities."[34] Instead, Wayne argues that streaming services actually present themselves as "portals" that pose as "generalized viewing platforms for subscribers" where the brand identities of these services "are largely defined by the experiences that the portal offers viewers: a personalized television viewing experience made possible through internet distribution."[35] In 2016 of the almost 1200 shows available on Netflix, only 98 (8%) were Netflix Originals.[36] The small percentage does not appear sufficient to justify the wide array of content on Netflix as "original"; nevertheless, the services it offers can potentially balance out this notion of "original." For instance, Allègre L. Hadida et al. employ two institutional frameworks, the commitment logic and the convenience logic, that reflect the established and emerging entertainment companies respectively in order to examine to what extent these relationships are complementary or result in competition.[37] Meanwhile, Chuck Tryon surmises that "instead of treating streaming and on-demand formats as revolutionizing television, we should instead see them as convenient narratives that serve to promote more desired modes of media consumption."[38] When asked about the company's brand identity, chief content officer Ted Sarandos notes that "There's no such thing as a 'Netflix show.' That as a mind-set gets people narrowed. Our brand is personalization."[39] Similarly, vice president for original content Cindy Holland informs that "Our brand is as broad as the tastes of our members."[40] As a result, the term "original" is not associated exclusively with content but with a particular personalized viewing experience.

Taking the company brand into consideration is also highlighted by Catherine Johnson who focuses on the case study of HBO and two of its flagship programs and views branding as "*the* defining industrial practice" in the TVIII context, also referred to as "the digital era of US television."[41] Branding enables the effective competition of television networks in an otherwise crowded marketplace "by creating strong, distinctive and loyal relationships with viewers" because the networks as well as the television programs can act as brands.[42] These programs can be "profitably exploited across a range of different media platforms" thus increasing the gains of the owner of the associated trademark.[43] Therefore, to have such a broad definition of the Netflix brand certainly requires further research into video streaming services in the future as these brands are still emerging in a sense. The Marvel/Netflix collaboration can depict the struggles notable between an established and an emerging brand, particularly when considering advantages that established brands have such as licensing their content. Tim Westcott (1999) argues that "licensing is a game for the big players and it is likely to remain so as long as the likes of Disney, Warner Bros. and Nickelodeon continue to exercise their vertically integrated muscle around the world."[44] This power struggle is also evident when Netflix ceased collaborating with Marvel in 2019 in light of the Disney+ launch as well as the Hulu shares owned by Fox, Disney, Comcast and Time/Warner.[45] Marvel's parent company, Disney, was now offering their "original" viewing experience, a type of viewing Netflix claims characterizes their brand. which could insinuate that the viewing experience Netflix offers is not entirely "original" or unique. No longer needing a portal to distribute its content, Disney apparently did not want to have its content associated with other brands. The long-standing negotiations between Disney/Marvel with Sony for the film rights to the Spider-Man intellectual property are also an indication of this.

In the Face of Genre, Is It Original? The Case of Marvel/Netflix and Superheroes

From an adaptation standpoint, it is becoming clear that the term "original" has not been widely considered in light of industrial practices. While adaptation studies acknowledge intertextual and intermedial relationships, they do not appear to focus on vertical intertextuality or industrial practices that can inform how certain terms are now viewed or understood. Drawing on John Fiske's intertexuality and its connection to genre, the Marvel/Netflix collaboration for the five superhero series they developed demonstrates how far adaptations the value of "original" diverges from that of source material towards that of brand organization.

A term that echoes industrial intertextuality is brandcasting, utilized by scholars like Jennifer Gillan, Grainge and Johnson, and Jana Radošinská. Radošinská informs that "[t]elevision production is nowadays very diverse—this fact also means that television branding is becoming far more complex as there are more parts of the production chain to 'brand.'"[46] Brandcasting as a term "has been developed in order to thoroughly reflect on processes of television branding which often result in hybrid communication forms merging media content and promotional material" and she argues the "television drama serials produced by *Marvel* and exclusively distributed by *Netflix* can be seen as hybrids of content and promotion which significantly expand *Marvel's* global popularity and *Netflix's* increasing influence in the sphere of digital media production and distribution."[47] Even though the superhero genre itself is considered hybrid,[48] the idea of brandcasting highlights how "original" pertains more to organizations and services than to the products.

Brand identity, as David Aaker informs, consists of two components, the core, and the extended identity, where the latter is comprised of four perspectives (product, organization, personality, and symbol). "The core identity—the central, timeless essence of the brand—is most likely to remain constant as the brand travels to new markets and products."[49] I appoint Coogan's "The Definition of the Superhero" as being the core of superhero brands:

> [a] heroic character with a selfless, pro-social mission; with superpowers—extraordinary abilities, highly developed physical, mental, or mystical skills, or advanced technology; who has a superhero identity embodied in a codename and iconic costume, which typically express his biography or character, powers, or origin (transformation from ordinary person to superhero); and is generally distinct, i.e. can be distinguished from characters of related genres (fantasy, science fiction, detective, etc.) by a preponderance of generic conventions. Often superheroes have dual identities, the ordinary one of which is usually a closely guarded secret.[50]

Based on this definition, to see one superhero is to have seen them all. The "original" aspect, as that which is different, is notable at the extended identity level because the core cannot solely function as the brand's identity but requires textures that fill out the picture, attribute concrete meanings and dimensions and allow for differences at the extended identity level.[51] For example, all superheroes share the same core identity but each superhero differs concretely in how the abstract core identity is manifested with regard to their superpowers and abilities, the good versus evil conflict they engage in (their modus operandi and raison-d'etre) and the matter of secret or dual identity. In the case of the Marvel/Netflix superheroes series we see four distinct superheroes, Daredevil, Jessica Jones, Luke Cage, and Iron Fist, respectively (teaming up in a fifth series, *The Defenders* 2017), and we can distinguish amongst all four given the superhero branding at the extended identity level as well as at the brand organization level (Marvel/Netflix and not DC/Warner Bros). Other added textures appear in extended identities such as comic books and graphic novels, films, television or animated series, video and computer games, animated figures, merchandise and theme park rides. The core identity of a brand, however, is influenced and enriched by the very identity of its organization.

The brand organization is responsible for managing the extended identities and preserving a relationship with consumers. As Aaker points out it is "more enduring and more resistant to competitive claims than are product attributes" because it is easier to duplicate a product than it is an organization.[52] Moreover, organizational attributes such as being innovative or "original" are hard to evaluate; therefore, they pose as features that are debatable.[53] The Marvel brand is not the only one producing superhero products. Rival company DC also deals with the same product types. Both produce blockbuster films, comic books and TV series. Their brand names, attributes, their intellectual properties and their brand management distinguish them. In addition, the aims, intentions, and stature of the organization also affect the output of products, as well as their characteristics as Disney's *The Jungle Book* (2016) demonstrates. Brand organizations, in other words, offer recognition for products instead of demoting a product to a generic level.

Generic can be viewed in two ways: one, it implies a generic product as opposed to a brand product of the same category (e.g., generic superhero category versus specific Batman brand); two, it can be understood as the genre of the product or service. There is fluidity in the brand identity of superheroes if we view the definition of superhero as being the core of the brand. The same applies to video streaming services. Derek Johnson asserts that the "franchise system thus lends itself not so much to generic types of products or services, but to those that can be developed as recognizable, unique coherent brands with qualities that motivate consumers to seek [them] out."[54] They are distinguished by their brand name and since they all offer the same services, producing "original" content is an additional way to further distinguish them. The second view of generic pertains to the similarity in a product, its genre so to speak. DC's Batman and Marvel's Ironman are both superheroes, but the brand identity of DC or Marvel acts as the differentiating marker. Genre, while not equated to franchises, can be viewed as the abstract starting point that provides both recognition via similar, continuous forms and rules, while the extended identity of the brand is what distinguishes each product type. Intertextuality does not simply exist horizontally, or across texts, it also exists vertically.

According to Fiske, the genre "serves the dual needs of a commodity: on the one hand standardization and familiarity, and on the other, product differentiation. But the work of genre is more than economic, it is cultural as well. [...] Genre spells out to the audience the range of pleasures it might expect and thus regulates and activates memory of similar texts and the expectations of this one."[55] Genre caters to the area in between the abstract and concrete. This connects it to intertextuality which Fiske argues exists "in the space *between* texts."[56] One can view genre, text and organization from a brand identity perspective as they are all intertexually interrelated. Fiske points out that genres, in addition to being a cultural practice that grant structure and conventions, "are intertextual or even pre-textual, for they form the network of industrial, ideological, and institutional conventions that are common to both producer and audiences out of which arise both the producer's program and the audiences' readings."[57] Though we engage with texts at a horizontal intertextual level, the brand dimension does become more prominent when we engage with vertical intertextuality. For Fiske, "[v]ertical intertextuality consists of a primary text's relations with other texts which refer to it specifically. These secondary texts, such as criticism or publicity, work to promote the circulation of selected meanings of the primary text."[58] What is more, they reveal the organization behind the text and can even account for audience reception and responses. What is interesting when considering the meaning of "original" in light of intertextuality and genre is that, on the one hand, in the case of adaptations, both source material and adaptation are accountable to concrete manifestations of their genre core. This can render the idea of an "original" in adaptation studies a moot point or at the very least simply accommodate the meaning of "original" as being that which appeared first. When it comes to branding, however, genre or generic does not enable the brand to distinguish itself from others, to become "original" in the sense of being unique or recognizable, hence the additional need for branding.

An organization's personality raises the bar for identification, brand loyalty and value when it comes to how consumers engage with them. Aaker clarifies that brand personality can "serve as the foundation for meaningful differentiation, especially in contexts where brands are similar with respect to product attributes."[59] Consumer anthropologist Grant McCracken considers the brand's personality to be part of its cultural meaning capable of corresponding with consumer needs for self-expression, as well as constructing and maintaining their social profile.[60] For example, loyal consumers of Marvel superheroes will continue to follow Marvel productions but may not exhibit the same loyalty towards Netflix "original" superhero content. What the Disney and Netflix example demonstrates is that the matter of "original," whether that pertains to the product or the service, is tightly connected to the organization. CEO of Brand Entertainment Studios Steve Marrs sums this up quite effectively when he notes: "If you can create an environment that is entertaining to your desired consumers and allows them to be entertained in the context of the brand, then you have an ideal form of communication with your consumer that is relevant, original, and impactful."[61] In other words, the "originality" of either product or service is primarily connected to branded authorship, corporate or otherwise, and how that brand identity feature is treated, promoted and overall received.

Conclusion

Industrial practices prompted the reconsideration of the term "original" in this paper. In that light, I return to Bryant's view on adaptation. Bryant considers cultural revision as being the proper arena of adaptation and claims that "if adaptation is to achieve its proper textual legitimacy, we need a broader conception of geneticism in which the notion of *work* embraces all versions of a text, including sources and adaptations, and the *creative process* is extended to include all forms of revision, both authorial and cultural."[62] The combination of the fluid text approach and brand identity can certainly aid in this venture as both take those who adapt and those who receive adaptations into consideration by acting as the point of convergence between horizontal and vertical intertextuality. Attempting to reconsider the term "original" with this converging point in mind, what is observed is that in a context of industrial intertextuality the meaning of "original" is influenced or determined by copyright laws and corporate authorship. Ultimately, how those practices develop will determine the treatment and understanding of terms such as "original."

Notes

1. Michael Wayne, "Netflix, Amazon, and Branded Television Content in Subscription Video On Demand Portals," *Media, Culture & Society* 40, no. 5 (2017): 725–741, https://doi.org/10.1177/0163443717736118
2. Nicholas Benson, "All Hail Disney: Establishing Corporate Authorship Through Industrial Intertextuality," *Quarterly Review of Film and Video* 37, no. 1 (2020): 25–47, https://doi.org/10.1080/10509208.2019.1593032
3. Linda Hutcheon, *A Theory of Adaptation* (New York: Routledge, 2006), 7.
4. Hutcheon, *A Theory of Adaptation*, 8.
5. Hutcheon, *A Theory of Adaptation*, 8.
6. Imelda Whelehan, "Adaptations: The Contemporary Dilemmas," in *From Text to Screen, Screen to Text*, ed. Deborah Cartmell and Imelda Whelehan, 3-20. (London and New York: Routledge, 1999), 8.
7. John Bryant, "Textual Identity and Adaptive Revision: Editing Adaptation as a Fluid Text," in *Adaptation Studies: New Challenges, New Directions*, ed. Jørgen Bruhn, Anne Gjelsvik and Eirik Frisvold Hanssen (London and New York: Bloomsbury Publishing Plc., 2013), 47-68.
8. Dimitra Zervaki, "Ti Einai Alitheia To Branding & To Brand," Epixeiro. 11 February 2015, https://www.epixeiro.gr/article/2218:
9. Matthew Healey, *What is Branding*? (N.p.: Rockport Publishers, 2010), 6.
10. Zervaki, n.pg.
11. Zervaki, n.pg.
12. Zervaki, n.pg.
13. Robert Stam and Alessandra Raengo, ed. *Literature and Film: A Guide to the Theory and Practice of Film Adaptation* (Massachusetts: Blackwell Publishing, 2005).
14. Thomas M. Leitch, "Twelve Fallacies in Contemporary Adaptation Theory," *Criticism* 45, no. 2 (Spring 2003): 149–171, https://www.jstor.org/stable/23126342
15. Will Brooker, *Hunting the Dark Knight: Twenty-First Century Batman* (London and New York: I.B. Tauris, 2012).
16. Bryant, "Textual Identity and Adaptive Revision," 47-68.
17. André Bazin, "Adaptation, or the Cinema as Digest," in *Film Adaptation*, ed. James Naremore, 19-27. (New Jersey: Rutgers University Press, 2000), 21.
18. Clare Parody, "Franchising/Adaptation," *Adaptation* 4, no. 2 (September 2011): 210-218, https://doi.org/10.1093/adaptation/apr008 : 211.
19. Parody, "Franchising/Adaptation," 212.
20. Parody, "Franchising/Adaptation," 212.
21. Parody, "Franchising/Adaptation," 214-215.
22. Janet Wasko, *Understanding Disney: The Manufacture of Fantasy* (Cambridge: Polity Press, 2003).

23. Michaela Robbins and Fritz G. Polite, "The Most Powerful Mouse in the World: The Globalization of the Disney Brand," *Global Journal of Management and Business* 14, no. 1-F (2014): 11-20, https://journalofbusiness.org/index.php/GJMBR/article/view/1441
24. Nicholas Benson, "All Hail Disney: Establishing Corporate Authorship Through Industrial Intertextuality," *Quarterly Review of Film and Video* 37, no. 1 (2020): 25-47, https://doi.org/10.1080/10509208.2019.1593032 : 25.
25. Benson, "All Hail Disney," 33-34.
26. Benson, "All Hail Disney," 34.
27. Benson, "All Hail Disney," 34-35.
28. Benson, "All Hail Disney," 37.
29. Benson, "All Hail Disney," 25.
30. Ramon Lobato and Amanda D. Lotz, "Imagining Global Video: The Challenge of Netflix," *Journal of Cinema and Media Studies* 59, no. 3 (Spring 2020): 132-136, 10.1353/cj.2020.0034: 132.
31. J. Llamas-Rodriguez, "Luis Miguel: La serie, Class-Based Collective Memory, and Streaming Television in Mexico," *Journal of Cinema and Media Studies*. 59, no. 3 (Spring 2020): 137-143, https://doi.org/10.1353/cj.2020.0035
32. Yu-Kei Tse, "Black Ships? Locating Netflix in Taiwan and Japan," *Journal of Cinema and Media Studies*. 59, no. 3 (Spring 2020). 143-148, https://doi.org/10.1353/cj.2020.0036 : 143.
33. Michael Wayne, "Netflix, Amazon, and Branded Television Content in Subscription Video On-Demand Portals," *Media, Culture & Society* 40, no. 5 (2017): 725-741, https://doi.org/10.1177/0163443717736118 : 151
34. Wayne, "Netflix, Amazon and Branded Television," 149.
35. Wayne, "Netflix, Amazon and Branded Television," 149-150.
36. Wayne, "Netflix, Amazon and Branded Television," 130.
37. Allègre L. Hadida, Joseph Lampel, W. David Walls and Amit Joshi, "Hollywood Studio Filmmaking in the Age of Netflix: a Tale of Two Institutional Logics," *Journal of Cultural Economics*, n. n. (January 2020): n.pg, https://doi.org/10.1007/s10824-020-09379-z
38. Chuck Tryon, "TV Got Better: Netflix's Original Programming Strategies and Binge Viewing," *Media Industries* 2, no. 2 (2015): 104-116, https://doi.org/10.3998/mij.15031809.0002.206 : 105
39. Wayne, "Netflix, Amazon and Branded Television," 150.
40. Wayne, "Netflix, Amazon and Branded Television," 150.
41. Catherine Johnson, "Tele-Branding in TVIII: The Network as Brand and the Programme as Brand," *New Review of Film and Television Studies* 5, no. 1 (2007): 5-24, https://doi.org/10.1080/17400300601140126 : 6
42. Catherine Johnson, "Tele-Branding in TVIII," 7.
43. Catherine Johnson, "Tele-Branding in TVIII," 8.
44. Catherine Johnson, "Tele-Branding in TVIII," 8.
45. Kevin Sanson and Gregory Steirer, "Hulu, Streaming, and the Contemporary Television Ecosystem," *Media, Culture & Society* 41, no. 8 (2019): 1210-1227, https://doi.org/10.1177/0163443718823144 : 1213
46. Jana Radošinská, "New Trends in Production and Distribution of Episodic Television Drama: Brand Marvel-Netflix in the Post-Television Era," *Communication Today* 8, no. 1 (2017): 4-29, https://www.ceeol.com/search/article-detail?id=525203 : 9
47. Radošinská, "New Trends in Production and Distribution," 5.
48. Saige Walton, "Baroque Mutants in the 21st Century?: Rethinking Genre Through the Superhero," In *The Contemporary Comic Book Superhero*, ed. Angela Ndalianis (New York and London: Routledge, 2009), 86-106.
49. David A. Aaker, *Building Strong Brands* (London: Free Press Business, 1996), 68.
50. Peter Coogan, "The Definition of Superhero," in *Super/Heroes: From Hercules to Superman*, ed. Wendy Haslem, Angela Ndalianis and Chris Mackie, 21-36. (Washington: New Academia Publishing, 2007), 21.
51. Aaker, *Building Strong Brands*, 69.
52. Aaker, *Building Strong Brands*, 83.

53. Aaker, *Building Strong Brands*, 83.
54. Derek Johnson, "Franchising Media Worlds: Content Networks and the Collaborative Production of Culture" (PhD diss., University of Wisconsin—Madison, 2009), 47
55. John Fiske, "Intertextuality," in *Popular Culture: Production and Consumption*, ed. C. Lee Harrington and Denise D. Bielby, 219-233. (Massachusetts: Blackwell Publishers, 2001), 223-224.
56. Fiske, "Intertextuality," 219.
57. Fiske, "Intertextuality," 220-221.
58. Fiske, "Intertextuality," 227.
59. Aaker, *Building Strong Brands*, 150-151.
60. Aaker, *Building Strong Brands*, 153.
61. Paul Grainge, *Brand Hollywood: Selling Entertainment in a Global Media Age*. (London and New York: Routledge, 2008), 37.
62. Bryant, "Textual Identity and Adaptive Revision," 48.

Works Cited

Aaker, David A. *Building Strong Brands*. London: Free Press Business, 1996.
Bazin, André. "Adaptation, or the Cinema as Digest." In *Film Adaptation*, edited by James Naremore, 19–27. New Jersey: Rutgers University Press, 2000.
Benson, Nicholas. "All Hail Disney: Establishing Corporate Authorship Through Industrial Intertextuality." *Quarterly Review of Film and Video* 37, no. 1 (2020): 25–47. https://doi.org/10.1080/10509208.2019.1593032.
Brooker, Will. *Hunting the Dark Knight: Twenty-First Century Batman*. London and New York: I.B. Tauris, 2012.
Bryant, John. "Textual Identity and Adaptive Revision: Editing Adaptation as a Fluid Text." In *Adaptation Studies: New Challenges, New Directions*, edited by Jørgen Bruhn, Anne Gjelsvik and Eirik Frisvold Hanssen, 47–68. London and New York: Bloosmbury Publishing Plc., 2013.
Coogan, Peter. "The Definition of Superhero." In *Super/Heroes: From Hercules to Superman*, edited by Wendy Haslem, Angela Ndalianis and Chris Mackie, 21–36. Washington: New Academia Publishing, 2007.
Fiske, John. "Intertextuality." In *Popular Culture: Production and Consumption*, edited by C. Lee Harrington and Denise D. Bielby, 219–233. Massachusetts: Blackwell Publishers, 2001.
Grainge, Paul. *Brand Hollywood: Selling Entertainment in a Global Media Age*. London and New York: Routledge, 2008.
Hadida, Allègre L., Joseph Lampel, W. David Walls and Amit Joshi. "Hollywood Studio Filmmaking in the Age of Netflix: a Tale of Two Institutional Logics." *Journal of Cultural Economics*, n. n. (January 2020): n. pg., https://doi.org/10.1007/s10824-020-09379-z.
Healey, Matthew. *What is Branding?* N.p.: Rockport Publishers, 2010.
Hutcheon, Linda. *A Theory of Adaptation*. New York: Routledge, 2006.
Johnson, Catherine. "Tele-Branding in TVIII: The Network as Brand and the Programme as Brand." *New Review of Film and Television Studies* 5, no. 1 (2007): 5–24. https://doi.org/10.1080/17400300601140126.
Johnson, Derek. "Franchising Media Worlds: Content Networks and the Collaborative Production of Culture." PhD diss., University of Wisconsin—Madison, 2009.
Leitch, Thomas M. "Twelve Fallacies in Contemporary Adaptation Theory." *Criticism* 45, no. 2 (Spring 2003): 149–171. https://www.jstor.org/stable/23126342.
Llamas-Rodriguez, Juan. "*Luis Miguel: La serie*, Class-Based Collective Memory, and Streaming Television in Mexico." *Journal of Cinema and Media Studies*. 59, no. 3 (Spring 2020): 137–143. https://doi.org/10.1353/cj.2020.0035.
Lobato, Ramon and Amanda D. Lotz. "Imagining Global Video: The Challenge of Netflix." *Journal of Cinema and Media Studies* 59, no. 3 (Spring 2020): 132–136. 10.1353/cj.2020.0034.

Parody, Clare. "Franchising/Adaptation." *Adaptation* 4, no. 2 (September 2011): 210–218. https://doi.org/10.1093/adaptation/apr008.
Radošinská, Jana. "New Trends in Production and Distribution of Episodic Television Drama: Brand Marvel-Netflix in the Post-Television Era." *Communication Today* 8, no. 1 (2017): 4–29. https://www.ceeol.com/search/article-detail?id=525203.
Robbins, Michaela, and Fritz G. Polite. "The Most Powerful Mouse in the World: The Globalization of the Disney Brand." *Global Journal of Management and Business* 14, no. 1-F (2014): 11–20. https://journalofbusiness.org/index.php/GJMBR/article/view/1441.
Sanson, Kevin, and Gregory Steirer. "Hulu, Streaming, and the Contemporary Television Ecosystem." *Media, Culture & Society* 41, no. 8 (2019): 1210–1227. https://doi.org/10.1177/0163443718823144.
Stam, Robert, and Alessandra Raengo, ed. *Literature and Film: A Guide to the Theory and Practice of Film Adaptation*. Massachusetts: Blackwell Publishing, 2005.
Tryon, Chuck. "TV Got Better: Netflix's Original Programming Strategies and Binge Viewing." *Media Industries* 2, no. 2 (2015): 104–116, https://doi.org/10.3998/mij.15031809.0002.206.
Tse, Yu-Kei. "Black Ships? Locating Netflix in Taiwan and Japan." *Journal of Cinema and Media Studies*. 59, no. 3 (Spring 2020). 143–148. https://doi.org/10.1353/cj.2020.0036.
Walton, Saige. "Baroque Mutants in the 21st Century?: Rethinking Genre Through the Superhero." In *The Contemporary Comic Book Superhero,* edited by Angela Ndalianis, 86–106. New York and London: Routledge, 2009.
Wasko, Janet. *Understanding Disney: The Manufacture of Fantasy.* Cambridge: Polity Press, 2003.
Wayne, Michael. "Netflix, Amazon, and Branded Television Content in Subscription Video On-Demand Portals." *Media, Culture & Society* 40, no. 5 (2017): 725–741. https://doi.org/10.1177/0163443717736118.
Whelehan, Imelda. "Adaptations: The Contemporary Dilemmas." In *From Text to Screen, Screen to Text,* edited by Deborah Cartmell and Imelda Whelehan, 3–20. London and New York: Routledge, 1999.
Zervaki, Dimitra. "Ti Einai Alitheia To Branding & To Brand"; *Epixeiro.* 11 February 2015. https://www.epixeiro.gr/article/2218.

Part 2

Beyond Netflix

Globalization and Second-Tier SVODs

Encore+

Orphaned Canadian Content in the Age of Digital Abundance

Daniel Keyes

On November 7, 2017, the Canadian Media Fund,[1] a federal agency and not-for-profit that collects carriage fees from licensed television broadcasters and distributes the fees to producers to create Canadian media content, launched with one-time annual funding Encore+,[2] a YouTube channel. Encore+ hosts older and often lost Canadian television programs and films that the CMF and Telefilm, its parallel film production national government agency, originally funded. In 2020, Encore+ boasts over 100,000 subscribers and "features over 2,000 acclaimed Canadian feature films, documentaries and television serial programs in English, French and by Indigenous creators"[3] and finally secured stable funding. An Encore+ press release from 2020 boasts it is "monetizing, preserving and relicensing their [rightsholder's] legacy titles to new streaming platforms. New generations of Canadians, and audiences worldwide are rediscovering and connecting with important Canadian stories, comedies and childhood favorites."[4] In November 2021, four years after the initial launch of Encore+, it has 165,000 subscribers and includes a tag "new content added weekly" to assure viewers that although it releases old content that new "old" Canadian content [Cancon] is continually being added rather than a stagnant repository of orphaned Cancon.[5] This essay relates the unique business model and partnership between Google/YouTube and a government agency dedicated to supporting the production of Canadian media content. It contextualizes the creation of Encore+ within the scholarly study of audiovisual media that includes archival perspectives on audiovisual preservation. Finally, this essay evaluates Encore+ aim to preserve and provide access for Canadian streaming video heritage by examining the affordances offered by this partnership between Google and the CMF.[6]

Encore+ offers a unique approach to making available a selection of a nation's commercial audiovisual back catalogue.[7] This essay synthesizes interviews conducted with media professionals[8] involved in either the creation of Encore+ or media preservation with analysis of the affordances of Encore+ streaming video on Google's YouTube platform. This analysis is contextualized with the tension in contemporary archival theories that tilts between the goals of access versus records preservation. The analysis considers the risks and benefits of operating a national level audiovisual participatory archives on the social medium platform YouTube. YouTube does not have a nationalist agenda but is eager to present content and build audiences for content that in the case of Encore+ has lost its commercial value in an age of digital abundance[9] when much analog and digital material is prone to loss.

Canadian Television Studies: The Vanishing Texts

In the mid-1990s, my doctoral dissertation studied CTV's[10] daytime talk show *The Shirley Show* (1989–1995). As with most commercial broadcast talk shows in North America, this show shot episodes in the fall and spring that would air a few weeks after tapings with episodes re-running during the summer hiatus season. *The Shirley Show*, like much commercial television content that has ceased production, vanished from access with the idea that old content does not sell advertisement. Yet, today on YouTube, if I search for the program with the Boolean string "Shirley Show ctv,"[11] I return a smattering of episodes and short segments from the show uploaded by individuals using monikers like "AmazingFilmNS"[12] who earn ad revenue for their curatorial copyright breaking labors. YouTube presents an incomplete and fragmentary archive for *The Shirley Show* that is indicative of the wider digital loss of audiovisual texts in this age of digital abundance. YouTube offers what Chun refers to as "enduring ephemerals" that circulated untethered from their origins loosely secured by hash tags and user comments as a digital fragment severed from its production origins in a type of perpetual present.[13] Such "Tower of Babel" type digital loss presents a challenge for scholars seeking to study the social and cultural significance of old linear broadcast television that having faded from the screen remains locked in storage units bound by copyright laws from digital re-distribution or illegally and idiosyncratically curated by fans on YouTube. Taylor notes Canada's public broadcaster, the Canadian Broadcast Corporation (CBC), has fared no better than its corporate rivals at presenting old Cancon paid by taxpayers. She notes that the long running CBC dramedy *The Beachcombers*

(1972–1990) has "361 videotaped episodes, most of them already digitized—can't be seen at watch.cbc.ca but pops up all over YouTube."[14] Encore+ has *The New Beachcombers*[15] (2002) film, but not the episodes, which again points to the fragmentary nature of Canadian commercial TV archives. The transition from linear terrestrial television to streaming digital television presents a number of challenges for the television scholars and would be curators.

Other Canadian television studies scholars echo this sentiment. Over the last 30 years. Canadian television scholars and archivists lament both the lack of access to Canadian audio-visual content and that audio-visual content once broadcast degrades in a patchwork of corporate storage facilities hidden from public view by copyright laws.[16] In 2010 Byer and Vanderburg recount Mary Jane Miller's prescient suggestion in 1990 for an audio-visual archive that would "exist in digital as well as material space, allowing all sorts of people, from all sorts of places, to be connected to it.... Along with Mary Jane [Miller], we are still dreaming of archive heaven."[17] I sympathize with the idea of a digital audiovisual archive heaven where I could locate the linear schedule for a region from a day in 1975 and explore the televisual flow of that period. Despite the potential for a digital streaming renaissance much of Canadian audiovisual[18] content languished on master tapes and reels of film due to copyright laws protecting content and content losing it commercial value following release. The knowledge that audiovisual content is ephemeral is one that has a history that predates the invention of streaming video and the arrival of Encore+ as a solution.

Audiovisual Archives and the Digital Turn in Canada

Canada's National Archives recognizes it could not capture all audiovisual texts in a June 1995 report titled *Fading Away: Strategic Options to Ensure the Protection of and Access to Audio-visual Memory.*[19] This report led to the creation of the A/V Trust as "a consortium of stakeholders" and a "non-profit corporation" to allow the protection and compatible access to "Canadian audio-visual heritage" via "a decentralized approach to the preservation of these cultural resources."[20] Unfortunately, the A/V Trusts' federal funding was denied in 2008 by the Conservative Harper government keen on reducing taxes by cutting cultural initiatives,[21] meaning this type of national approach to working with industry to sustain an audiovisual archive disappeared.

For some archivists, the idea of the archive as a carceral repository preserving original content with limited access to fragile documents gave way to the idea of digital, post custodial, open archives. Archivist Laura Millar announced in 2011 that Library and Archives Canada's "monopoly as stewards of the national documentary heritage is over."[22] In a move in sync with the failed A/V Trust initiative, she proposed that "archivists would no longer wait to acquire archives physically in order to ensure that they were protected and available. Instead, archivists could maintain records control by providing advice and support to records creators and by overseeing the management of agency records and archives."[23] Reflecting the rise in social media, more daring archival approaches are offered that move away from the fetish of preserving originals to consider how archives might be active, public-facing spaces championing access: Prelinger theorizes that digital archives must "seek validation by creating abundance rather than maintaining scarcity."[24] Huvila imagines archives where users work to fill in the gaps in records as a "participatory archives."[25] Digital "rogue archives" as articulated by De Kosnik constitute fan-based digital archives curated by fans and non-professional that excludes YouTube since it "deletes user-uploaded content because of copyright-related complaints,"[26] but includes "Internet Archive, Project Gutenberg, ibiblio, the Rhizome ArtBase, and many smaller, lesser-known archives founded by specific subcultures, minority groups, and artists' collectives."[27] Encore+ with its social media aspect operates a fan friendly "participatory archive"[28] and not the rogue archive as described by De Kosnik as Encore+ strives to work within its cultural nationalist framework to promote Cancon and within the copyright framework provided by Google/YouTube that sees Canadian artists rewarded for their effort. Yet the deal afforded by YouTube is that if a particular film or tv serial thrives on Encore+, it could disappear to be relicensed by Subscription Video on Demand [SVOD] services like Netflix. What is a financial success for the artist and for the CMF/Encore+ sparking renewed commercial interest in Cancon, injects a degree of precarity into Encore+ as an open archive. A copy of a film or tv program might appear on Encore+ salvaged from a media locker or the attics of a director and just as quickly disappear from Encore+ to appear behind a paywall elsewhere.

I am keenly aware that digitalization brings with it accelerated ephemerality. Digital platforms that today offer instant access to texts can vanish for a variety of reasons: 1. Copyright law that restricts access behind rights paywalls, 2. Software and/or hardware failure and/or obsolescence resulting in Error 404 "This site no longer exists" or Error 410 "This resource has been removed," and 3. Copyright holders who lose track of digital or analog texts as one media company swallows another media company unaware of the inventory of old media as is the case with many of Encore+'s rescue missions.

Canadian Media in the 2010s

The audiovisual mediascape in Canada in the last decade has shifted as viewers continue to move from subscribing to CRTC[29] licensed commercial cable providers like Shaw, Rogers, Bell, and Telus that offer linear commercial broadcast television to SVOD services. Canadian telecommunication giants Shaw's launched its ill-fated streaming service Shomi (2014–2016) while Bell's subscription service Crave continues to offer much premium HBO type American content to compete with American SVOD giants like AppleTV, Amazon's Prime, and Netflix. Beyond SVOD, the Canadian mediascape sees the move to Video on Demand [VOD] that prominently features American content with ad revenue going to Google and Facebook.[30] Google via YouTube's ad revenue model introduces the notion that non-subscription "free" video can harness a revenue model not unlike commercial broadcast television while gathering data on users.

The CMF supports the Canadian production of television, film, and new media. The CMF operates as public-private partnership drawing on money from the department of Canadian Heritage and licenses providers of television (Satellite, cable, etc.). Cable providers like Bell point to the double standard that while Canadian cable companies contribute to the CMF, American SVOD companies do not, nor do these American-based SVOD companies pay taxes in Canada.[31] The continuation of funding for the CMF from cable provider licensors is doubtful as licensors chide against the double standard that their main American competitors are devouring their market share, are not taxed, and do not support the CMF.[32] Ballingall and Boutilier quote Simon Ross the press secretary for Pablo Rodriguez, the Liberal federal Heritage minister in 2018, who insists "all [media] players must contribute. There is no free ride. But, we will not take an approach that will increase costs for Canadians. Our culture needs a global solution to address the challenges they face.... We want strong Canadian companies and platforms that show great Canadian content."[33] In 2014–15, Catalina Briceño working for the CMF's industry and market trends department surveyed Cancon on YouTube. She located 97 Canadian titles on YouTube with 25 percent claimed by legitimate rightsholders while 75 percent were claimed by illegitimate rightsholders or simply unclaimed.[34] Encore+ with its partnership between the CMF and Google/YouTube seems a timely answer to this aspiration that sees cultural nationalism playing nice with transnational algorithmic platforms to reward content creators.

Encore+: A Business Model[35]

As established Encore+ is a YouTube channel, funded by the CMF and partners like Telefilm that showcases Canadian taxpayer funded audiovisual content. Due to copyright law and the tendency of broadcasters and film studios to lock and forget media content in vaults after its initial commercial broadcast or release, much of Canada's commercial audiovisual heritage remains hidden.[36] Much of the hidden affective labor of Encore+ involves painstaking detective work, contacting directors and writers who are unaware that the rights on a property they have created have reverted to them and do not know where the master is located. Follow up includes contacting media companies that acquired a vault of content in a takeover and have little sense of the inventory. Much of this work relies on nurturing personal connection to scour the country for lost content rather than relying on a comprehensive and current film database. After elaborate legal work on copyright agreements for rightsholders, Encore+ digitizes analog media content and uploads it to YouTube.

The digital transfer firm Deluxe, based in Toronto, handles the transfer from analog to digital with the analog master tapes or reels and a digital copy returned to the rightsholder, who are free to remove their content from Encore+'s service or earn revenue from ads that run with the content on Encore+. The preservation of the masters is beyond the remit of Encore+. What Encore+ offers is preservation via digital duplication and dissemination, which agree with archivist Prelinger's dictum that generating copies might be the best way to preserve media for future generations.

For archival purists concerned with maintaining the original tape or film in perpetuity like Kealy Wilkinson with the Canadian Broadcast Museum Foundation, this approach is a half measure. Kealy Wilkinson pilloried the publicly funded CBC's 2018 plan to destroy its analog tape collection of programs as it converted the content to a state of the digital arts preservation system.[37] In an e-mail, Wilkinson expressed ambivalence with Encore+'s effort, but felt the project was a useful experiment but missed the mark of preserving vanishing Canadian media content.[38]

When the rights to audiovisual content typically revert to the initial creators after 25 to 30 years, Encore+ staff locate the analog content and clear copyright permissions with various unions (directing, acting, writing, music). To avoid directly competing with new television and films, Encore+ does not display material produced after 2013. The one exception to this practice is Encore's ImagineNative playlist that features 20 documentary and shorts made by Indigenous artists with some of this material being new.[39] However, the consequence of having content produced predominantly belonging to the late 1980s and early 1990s and not the

1950s or 1960s on Encore+ or contemporary content is that Encore+'s collections may appear chronologically lopsided. A newcomer to Canadian film and television discovering Cancon via Encore+ might wonder about the narrowness of the selection despite its abundance for a particular era. Abarca-Cantin indicates the dearth of commercial French-language content on YouTube means that this particular content enjoys global success with viewers.

Rightsholders' Experiences

Encore+ does not pay royalties according to union scale, but pays rightsholders based on the percentage of the ad revenue collected by YouTube. Rightsholders earn the majority of the ad revenue with Encore+ and YouTube taking tiny percentages. With some uploaded content, the ad revenue can be slight, but in other cases it can be substantial and may even spark interest in re-booting an old property or as already mentioned seeing the digital copy removed from Encore+ and re-licensed to another SVOD service like CBC's streaming service Gem[40] that will follow the regular royalty scheme agreed with various media unions. Some producers of old content object to Encore+'s model, preferring the guaranteed upfront royalty model of regular broadcast. Abarca-Cantin opines that the view from inside the CMF is that Encore+ returns "content that Canadians have already paid for."[41] Working with YouTube, the revenue that would normally flow to pirated copies of the content on YouTube is diverted via Encore+ to the legal rightsholders. Encore+ is careful to avoid copyright issues as YouTube runs a three strikes policy for all of its users that bars repeat offenders.[42] Ad revenue is slight for feature-length films as Encore+ wants to ensure viewers do not wander off in the click economy of YouTube; Encore+ feels the cinematic experience is ruined by too many commercial interruptions. As described by Catalina Briceño, ad revenue is not the main source of revenue for Encore+. Encore+ leverages YouTube's Content Identification[43] application to take revenue from "partners or to close down the pirate-user use of the content." She noted that originally "the archival aspect … was not baked into the project…. The whole preservation part revealed itself as we began the work of locating titles, securing masters … we discovered as we did this work that stuff was lost … it became clear why we were doing it. A big part of it was preservation. Realizing the bad state much of this material was in, made us aware of the preservation aspect."[44] The challenges of preservation are multiple in dealing with a multitude of digital and analog media.

Encore+ prepares semi-annual rightsholders reports detailing the hours a particular show is watched and gross revenue based on ads. My informants with Encore+ all expressed that negotiating licensing agreements with the various guilds in English Canada and Quebec was a time consuming and often vexed process. The success of Encore+ since 2017 that sees revenue diverted from pirates to rightsholder has helped to reassure rightsholders the project is worthy.

Authenticity and Provenance

For Encore+ rights management is time consuming with much support offered by the CMF's legal team looking for inventive ways to bring content to the channel. For example, the 1993 feature film *The Lotus Eater*[45] had one scene that was very expensive to use because of the soundtrack's use of copyright, so the soundtrack for that one scene, in agreement with the producer and director, was removed for the version posted on Encore+. As described by Abarca-Cantin, this removal was a difficult choice. In this light, Encore+ is less involved in the archival priority to preserve the pristine original and more interested in the possibilities of renewal via access. This approach aligns with media preservations Hölling who admits that electronic arts tend to demonstrate the principle that change is unavoidable and attempts to conserve electronic art in some Edenic original state are a fool's errand.[46] In the digital era, change is inevitable and thus preservation is a form of constant renewal that accepts alterations. In the case of the sonically redacted *The Lotus Eaters,* this renewal becomes the only legal way to provide access.

Encore+ does not note this change in its gloss on *The Lotus Eaters,* which I sense would rankle a film historian or archivist keen to know of this alteration and the provenance of the copy. Additionally, I suspect this sort of sonic redaction is exactly what would concern people like Kealy Wilkinson with the Canadian Broadcast Museum Foundation, who fear as aforementioned the CBC's mass destruction of the original masters in the rush to digitize content will inevitably generate irretrievable losses.[47] Abarca-Cantin's view is that audiences are still able to engage with this lost film with this slight modification that in no way ruins the experience of the film. Access trumps preservation provided the rightsholders are all in agreement that this redaction is the only way to publish the film on YouTube. She notes that in the case of Metha's *Hollywood Bollywood* (2002), Mongrel Media, the rightsholder, on learning that there was a claim against the film's soundtrack determined to remove it from Encore+ rather than attempt to resolve this claim. The stability of Encore+'s holding ultimately depends on market forces well beyond its control.

Abarca-Cantin notes that Encore+ limits the use of hash tags for each piece to a maximum of four, which does limit the ability for users to stumble across a film. To facilitate searches, Encore+ uploads key terms relating to actors and directors. Encore+ also uses YouTube's playlists[48] to organize its collection, which might work for users seeking an old Canadian film, but does little to give users a sense of the shape and overall structure of Encore+s holdings that tilt towards the niche of education and heritage content.[49]

User Experience

The average viewing time on YouTube hovers around 2 to 3 minutes. Encore+ with its long form content (e.g., CBC miniseries *Prairie Giant: The Tommy Douglas Story* [2006] with a three-hour run time[50]) has an average viewing time of 16 minutes. Encore+'s content promotes stickiness. YouTube's social media affordances offer a different type of engagement than offered by linear TV or SVOD as users are able to comment on programs. Encore+ uses BBTV[51] that specializes in the management of YouTube to manage user experience via YouTube and other social media. BBTV ensures the social media voice for the channel remains in Abarca-Cantin's words "active, authentic and knowledgeable." Encore+ thrives not just as a place to watch old Cancon but also as a place for viewers to engage with that content between themselves. For example, the TV movie *Deadly Friends a.k.a. The Death and Life of Nancy Eaton* (2003) has over 700 comments from users discussing mental health, violence, and the criminal system.[52] These comments demonstrate the vital role social media provides in ensuring the afterlife of long dormant media content that loosely follows the model of "participatory archives."[53] Additionally, Encore+ offers appointment type viewing experiences with relaunched content. In the spring of 2019 to coincide with Encore+'s re-release of the feature *Dancing in the Dark* (1986),[54] the original main actor for the film Martha Henry provided a live discussion about the film's production history and her own career as a feminist actor.[55] User interest drives acquisitions for Encore+. Sixty percent of Encore+ users are from outside of Canada, demonstrating that aging and often forgotten Cancon can with YouTube gain a new audience leveraging the affordance of YouTube and BBTV's management of the social media aspect of Encore+ to develop interest.

On its initial launch, journalists uniformly praised Encore+ as the long-awaited realization of the lost treasures of Cancon.[56] Over the last five years, Encore+'s steady growth in subscribers and ad revenue continues despite a lack of exposure by print television reviewers, who routinely tout the latest programs on SVOD services Crave, Netflix, Apple TV, etc. Encore+'s re-launch of the first Canadian feature film directed by a woman, Sally Springs' *Madeleine Is* (1969),[57] the playlist partnering with Vtape, an artist video collective, and the ImagineNative Film + Media Arts Festival that offers brilliant Indigenous films[58] deserve attention that print media has not given as these offerings fall outside the parameters of current slick commercial content streaming on SVOD. Encore+ performs important work not undertaken by other governmental entities like Library and Archives Canada, the CBC or the corporate sector to provide a digital afterlife for lost Cancon.

Conclusion

It took five years of planning to realize Encore+ in 2017. I asked one of the architects of Encore+, Deborah Drisdell, who had worked on the NFB's digital initiatives from 2006 to 2015, why the CMF in 2017 did not use the National Film Board's pay-per-use rental video streaming platform. Her response was that it would not have been robust enough for Encore+ and that YouTube's digital rights management made it the logical choice over other models. In hindsight with concerns about Google/YouTube's data mining, lack of user privacy, third party ads being used to influence voters, and partnering with an American company that does not pay taxes in Canada and whose ad revenue model has helped to gut newspapers in Canada,[59] it may appear as a marriage of unequal partners. Still I do not know if Encore+ with the NFB would have had the global success that Encore+ has generated (over 165,000 subscribers, old programs gaining new interests from SVOD buyers for redevelopment, resurrecting long lost films that did not make it beyond the Canadian festival circuit). So while one might cynically see Encore+ as a bargain bin of cast off Cancon where its 165,000 subscribers are easily dwarfed by YouTube videogame blogger and alt right star PewDiePie's 110 million subscribers,[60] I sense there is a value in having this admittedly lumpy but active archive providing this content.[61] Encore+ justifies the CMF's and Telefilm's mandates by demonstrating that Cancon can find an appreciative global audience. The pesky archival concerns of maintaining provenance and lack of context remain with Encore+ platformed on YouTube's curiously flattened sprawling populist audiovisual archive. The tradeoff is that the social media aspect of YouTube allows users to generate a new archive of comments appreciating these old former hidden texts.

Encore+ presents a living archive in terms of meaning making and engagement. So while I recognize Encore+'s weaknesses in regards to archival priorities like authenticity, preservation, and provenance, it provides an archive of responses for the texts it present. This public facing, living archive might prove valuable in understanding how old content circulates and continues to generate meaning as a precarious living post custodial archive on a corporate platform that could one day offer the message Error 410: this content has been removed. Encore+ provides an alternative to the walled gardens of SVOD that I hope will prove a stable place for Cancon audiovisual heritage to reside and grow.

Briceño, who currently holds a professorship at UQAM, suggests nations need to maintain their own audiovisual databases so that national copyright bureaus can ensure artists are remunerated and material is tracked.[62] For example in Taiwan, the Ministry of Culture offers a database that does not offer streaming access but shows where a specific film has been screened and licensing agreements and potential for licensing that ensure content can be located.[63] Additionally, Briceño suggests that national entities like Telefilm and the Canadian Media Fund need to think through their funding agreements with producers to provide a sunset window that might assume after a film's initial run or a television program's initial licensing that content finds a stable digital home.[64] India's National Film Development Corporation with a mandate similar to the CMF operates a platform called *Cinemas of India* that offers a rich multilingual streaming catalogue of Indian film with some films freely streaming while other are for purchase worldwide. I suspect given the global dominance of Google/YouTube, that Encore+ has higher viewer numbers than Cinemas of India, but I also assume Cinemas of India provides a more stable platform for accessing unloved older media content.

Notes

1. [hereafter referred to as the CMF].

2. Encore+. https://www.youtube.com/channel/UCH9jfFz0VzO-sqfh_TLVT7A/featured. This launch was meant to coincide with Canada 150 celebrations that celebrated the confederation of Canada in 1867, but funding for this project from the Canada 150 Fund that sponsored public events in 2017 was not awarded to Encore+.

3. "Encore+ YouTube Channel Reaches 100,000 Subscribers and 25 Million views Milestone" CMF, last modified August 18, 2020, https://www.cmf-fmc.ca/en-ca/news-events/news/august-2020/encore-youtube-channel-reaches-100-000-subscribers.

4. "Encore+" CMF.

5. This figure is taken directly from Encore+'s home page on November 11, 2021: https://www.youtube.com/c/EncorePlusMedia/featured. A summer 2021 press release from the CMF boasts "approximately 70 percent the platform's viewership is from international audiences." André Ferreira. "Encore+ YouTube Channel Research 150,000 subscribers and 40 M Views Milestone." CMF, last modified July 2, 2021. https://cmf-fmc.ca/news/encore-youtube-channel-reaches-150000-subscribers-and-40m-views-milestones/.

6. There were other contributors to Encore+'s launch and management. Reid notes "The

channel is spearheaded by the CMF, with support from Google Canada, Bell Media, BBTV and Deluxe Toronto." The Vancouver-based, and now European owned BBTV supports the social media aspect of the channel while the Toronto post production house Deluxe manages digital transfers. Bell Media is one of Canada's largest media companies with portfolios in telephone, internet, television cable and networks.

Regan, Reid. "CMF Unveils Its Cancon YouTube Channel." *Playback* November 8, 2017. http://playbackonline.ca/2017/11/08/cmf-unveils-its-cancon-youtube-channel/.

7. An alternative to Encore+, Vucavu, also launched in 2017 with support from the Canada Council for the Arts, a federal funding agency, whose remit includes theater, creative writing, music, and the visual arts. Vucavu curates and rents to user via its streaming platform "45 years of Canadian film and video arts." Vucavu's holdings do not receive broad commercial theatrical or television release unlike Encore+, which has a clear commercial intent of seeking to unlock value in Canadian content via YouTube. Both services despite their vastly different scales and business models seek to preserve access to Canadian media content, and reward media creator and license holders with revenue; they provide a study in contrast between attempts by artist collectives to maintain a media library on built from scratch streaming platform versus relying on a ready made transglobal social media platform to curate Canadian content. See "Canadian Film + Video." VUCAVA, accessed August 23, 2020. https://vucavu.com/en/home. Both entities arguably could not exist without federal funding and support.

8. The University of British Columbia's Human Research Ethics committee approved this project application numbered H19–02232 on May 19, 2019.

9. Ian Milligan, *History in the Age of Abundance: How the Web Is Transforming Historical Research* (Montreal and Kingston: McGill-Queen's, 2019).

10. CTV is the acronym for the Canadian Television Network, which is a major linear commercial television broadcaster owned by the Canadian Media conglomerate Bell Media that owns the streaming video service Crave that licenses mainly new American content for Canadian viewers. See http://bellcanada.ca/.

11. "Shirley Show CTV." YouTube, https://www.youtube.com/results?search_query=Shirley+Show+ctv.

12. AmazingFilmsNS. *The Shirley Show, Canadian TV, 1995*, accessed Sept 30, 2017. https://www.youtube.com/watch?v=mMI-Xxk12zQ&t=707s.

13. W. Hui Kyong Chun. "The Enduring Ephemeral, or the Future is Memory." *Critical Inquiry.* 35, no. 1 (2008): 148.

14. Kate Taylor. "For CBC Fans, TV History's just out of Reach: The Broadcaster Has Announced the Costly Digital Preservation of Its Old Recordings, but most Canadians May Never Get to See Them." *The Globe and Mail*, June 3, 2017, R4.

15. *The New Beachcombers*. Encore+. Director Brad Turner. September 3, 2018. https://www.youtube.com/watch?v=sDIew5MHAtE.

16. Mary Jane Miller, "Archive from the Point of View of the Scholarly User: or, if I Died and I Went to a Platonic Archetype of a Sound and Moving Images Archive This Is What I'd Find." *Documents that Move and Speak: Audiovisual Archives in the New Information Age*. Proceedings of a Symposium organized for the International Council of Archives by the National Archives of Canada. Ottawa: National Archives of Canada, 1990;

Michelle Byers, and Jennifer VanderBurgh. "Trafficking (in) the Archive: Canada, Copyright, and the Study of Television." English Studies in Canada 36, no. 1 (2010): 109–26.

Serra Tinic. "No Rerun Nation: Canadian Television and Cultural Amnesia." *FlowTV* 10, no 1 (June 12, 2009). http://www.flowjournal.org/2009/06/no-rerun-nation-canadian-television-and-cultural-amnesia-serra-tinic-university-of-alberta/.

17. Byers and Vanderburg, "Trafficking," 109–110.

18. One of the first articles on YouTube as an uneven repository of hard to find media content that does not deliver on the promise of a proper archive is Lucas Hilderbrand, "YouTube: Where Cultural Memory and Copyright Converge." *Film Quarterly* 61, no. 1 (2007): 48–57. Accessed September 30, 2020. doi:10.1525/fq.2007.61.1.48.

19. For an overview of discussions of Canadian media archival sovereignty in the 1990s see John D, Jackson, "Production, Preservation, and Access: The Struggle to Retain

Audiovisual Archives." *Canadian Journal of Communication* 26, no. 2 (2001), https://www.cjc-online.ca/index.php/journal/article/view/1219/1182.

20. Task Force on the Preservation and Enhanced Use of Canada's Audio-Visual Heritage. *Fading Away: Strategic Options to Ensure the Protection of and Access to Our Audio-Visual Heritage*. National Archives Canada, June 1995: 16.

21. Simon Doyle. "Arts and Culture Cuts Not Playing Well in Quebec, Could Affect Quebec Area: Opposition." *The Hill Times*, September 8, 2008: 1. ProQuest.

22. Laura Miller, "Coming Up with Plan B: Considering the Future of Canadian Archives." Archivaria [Online], 77 (2014): 105. 11 Oct. 2019. https://archivaria.ca/index.php/archivaria/article/view/13485.

See also Joy Palmer, "Archives 2.0: If We Build It, Will They Come?" Ariadne 60 (July) (2009), http://www.ariadne.ac.uk/issue/60/palmer/.

23. Miller, "Coming" 111.

24. Rick Prelinger, "Archives and Access in the 21st Century," *Cinema Journal* Spring, 46, no. 3 (Spring, 2007), 118.

25. Isto Huvila, "Participatory Archive: towards Decentralised Curation, Radical User Orientation, and Broader Contextualisation of Records Management." *Archival Science* no. 8 (2008): 15–36. https://doi-org.ezproxy.library.ubc.ca/10.1007/s10502-008-9071-0.

26. Abigail De Kosnik, *Rogue Archives: Digital Cultural Memory and Media Fandom* (Boston: Massachusetts Institute of Technology, 2016), 18.

27. De Kosnik, *Rogue* 18.

28. Isto, "Participatory."

29. The acronym CRTC stands for the Canadian Radio-Television and Telecommunication Commission, like the FCC in the United States it commissions licenses and regulated radio, television, Internet and phone providers. See https://crtc.gc.ca/eng/home-accueil.htm.

30. Jordan Pinto, "OTT Revenues Continue to Gain Significant Ground on TV: CRTC" *Media in Canada*. March 1, 2019. http://mediaincanada.com/2019/03/01/ott-revenues-continue-to-gain-significant-ground-on-tv-crtc/.

Additionally see Catherine Phillips, "Ad Spending in Canada to Reach $11.52 Billion in 2018: Report." *Media in Canada*. May 8, 2018. https://mediaincanada.com/2018/05/08/ad-spending-in-canada-to-reach-11-52-billion-in-2018-report/#:~:text=Total%20media%20ad%20spending%20in,exceed%20%2414%20billion%20by%202022.

31. For discussion of the vexed politics of the Canadian federal government managing the expectation of Canadian cable operators and those of international SVOD players in the Canadian mediascape, see these articles that detail how Netflix sought to pre-empt grumpy nationalist Canadian media producer by pledging to fund half a billion dollars towards the creation of content produced cheaply in Canada:

Daniel Leblanc, "Ottawa to Unveil Netflix Deal as Part of Cultural Policy Overhaul." *Globe and Mail*, September 28, 2017.

Kate Taylor, "The Netflix Chill," *Globe and Mail*. 5 November 2016. R8.

Corrie Wright. "What Netflix's Half a Billion CAD Investment in Canada Is Really about." *Netflix Media Center*. 10 October 2017. https://media.netflix.com/en/company-blog/what-netflixs-half-a-billion-cad-investment-in-canada-is-really-about.

Daniel Leblanc, "PM Rejects Streaming Tax to Help Fund Media Sector." *The Globe and Mail*, June 16, 2017, *ProQuest*. accessed September 30, 2019.

Encore+ operates as an intriguing footnote to this nationalist debate as no journalists have questioned the efficacy of the CMF using YouTube to reach the world rather than creating a bespoke made-in-Canada platform like the National Film Board of Canada's streaming rental platform. I agree with my interview subjects that the NFB platform would likely not have had the same success that Encore+ has enjoyed with YouTube. For evidence to support this hypothesis, one can look at the ill-fated partnership called Canada Screen (https://canadascreens.ca) that offered to rent on the NFB platform newly released Canadian content and ceased operation in spring 2019. This website in March 2021 no longer exists.

32. Alex Ballingall, and Alex Boutilier, "Canada Urged to Respond Faster as Digital Landscape Evolves." *Toronto Star*. October 12, 2018. https://www.thestar.com/politics/federal/2018/10/12/canada-urged-to-respond-faster-as-digital-landscape-evolves.html.

33. Ballingall and Boutilier, "Canada."

34. Catalina Briceño, interview June 2, 2020.

35. This section of the paper is developed from interviews and e-mails with Paulina Abarca-Cantin, current Chief of Programming and Operations for Encore+, Deborah Drisdell and Catalina Briceño, who both aided in the creation of Encore+ hammering out the legal framework for Encore+ and Susan Kudrenshi at digital transfer company ByDeluxe and Kealy Wilkinson with the Canadian Broadcast Museum Foundation. I thank them all.

36. Taylor, "For"

37. Simon Houpt, "A Visit to the CBC Archives, on the Eve of Destruction." *Globe and Mail.* 12 September 2018.

Kealy Wilkinson, "CBC Must Stop Destruction of a Vital Part of Canada's Broadcast History." *ACTRA.* 18 April 2018. https://www.actra.ca/press-releases/2018/04/cbc-must-stop-destruction-of-a-vital-part-of-canadas-broadcast-history/

Kealy Wilkinson, "Friendly Giant Faces Firing Squad." *ACTRA.* 2 May 2018. https://www.actra.ca/press-releases/2018/05/friendly-giant-faces-firing-squad/.

38. Wilkinson, Kealy. "personal e-mail," September 6 2019.

39. ImagineNative Film + Media Playlist. Encore+, https://www.youtube.com/playlist?list=PLXssjYeUyJVELPg7GObyF4o2_GvBxK_Jw.

40. CBC. "Canada's Public Broadcaster Launches CBC GEM Streaming Service with More than 4000 Hours of Live and On-Demand Programming Available for Free." *CBC Media Centre* December 11, 2018,

https://www.cbc.ca/mediacentre/press-release/cbc-gem-streaming-service-launches-with-more-than-4000-hours-of-free conten#:~:text=December%2011%2C%20 2018%E2%80%93%20CBCtoday%20announced%20the%20launch%20of,hours%20of%20 live%20and%20on-demand%20programming%20for%20free.

41. Paulina Abarca-Cantin. Interview August 30, 2019. The irony that this return of Canadian heritage is via large multinational tech companies' platform is not lost on me. The risks of locating heritage with a private company that lacks a mandate for preservation and is driven by a profit incentive via monetizing user data is one I return to in the conclusion.

42. Google, *Copyright Strikes Basics.* https://support.google.com/youtube/answer/2814000?hl=en.

43. YouTube, *Content Identification.* https://support.google.com/youtube/answer/2797370?hl=en.

44. Briceño, interview June 2, 2020.

45. *The Lotus Eater,* directed by Paul Shaprio, written by Peggy Thompson, Rave Films, 1993. Available on Encore+ https://www.youtube.com/watch?v=-2rc16Hm1L4&t=570s.

46. Hanna B. Hölling, *Paik's Virtual Archive: Time, Change, and Materiality in Media Art.* Oakland, CA, U of California P, 2017.

47. Wilkinson. "Friendly."

48. See Encore+'s playlists at https://www.youtube.com/channel/UCH9jfFz0VzO-sqfh_TLVT7A/playlists.

49. This focus accords well with a report on YouTube use by Canadians that determined 70% of Canadians use YouTube for education.

Irene, S Berkowitz, Charles Davis, and Hanako Smith. *Watchtime Canada: How YouTube Connects Creators & Consumers.* May 22, 2019. Ryerson Faculty of Communication & Design: Audience Lab. https://drive.google.com/file/d/1frDtTaR-y7qHQuECH-4M83zOhfBk-t2Z/view.

50. John N. Smith, *Prairie Giant: The Tommy Douglas Story.* CBC. 2006. https://www.youtube.com/watch?v=p9SNHt6lRCE, accessed March 1, 2021.

51. Staff affiliated with BBTV refused to be interviewed for this chapter citing client confidentiality.

52. Jerry Circcoritti, *Deadly Friends a.k.a. The Death and Life of Nancy Eaton*, Indian Grove Productions, 2003. https://www.youtube.com/watch?v=HGzwoPfFmM4&t=1s, accessed March 1, 2021. Note when I accessed this property in March 1, 2020, it had over 700 comments. On November 11, 2021, 629 comments are available; perhaps BBTV, the

social media managers for Encore+ have removed some older entries since no posts older than 3 years are available, proving the point, to paraphrase the 6th century BCE Greek philosopher Heraclitus, YouTube users never steps into the same digital stream twice.

53. Isto, "Participatory."

54. Leon Marr. *Dancing in the Dark*. Brightstar films, 1983. https://www.youtube.com/watch?v=WHaXBAnMVxI, accessed March 1, 2021.

55. "Martha Henry: Revisiting Dancing in the Dark." *Encore+*. May 23, 2020. https://www.youtube.com/watch?v=HI4DCSuvufU.

56. Bill Brioux, "Canadian TV Gold Shines Once More with Encore+." Brioux.tv. November 9, 2019. https://brioux.tv/blog/2017/11/09/canadian-tv-gold-shines-once-more-with-encore/.

Canada Press. "Encore+ YouTube Channel Hosts Decades of Canadian TV and Film Time for some Old-school "Degrassi" and "Mr. Dressup."" *Huffington Post*, November 11, 2017.

https://www.huffingtonpost.ca/2017/11/09/encore-youtube-channel-hosts-decades-of-canadian-tv-and-film_a_23272513/.

John Doyle, "Click, Click, Click: Three Hot Canadian online Shows." *Globe and Mail*. November 17, 2017. L1.

Regan Reid. "CMF."

57. Sally Springs, *Madeleine Is*, Spring Productions, 1971. https://www.youtube.com/watch?v=ARxXVqaxPjU.

58. *ImagineNative Film + Media Arts Festival Playlist*, https://www.youtube.com/watch?v=j7HQQjHPS-s&list=PLXssjYeUyJVELPg7GObyF4o2_GvBxK_Jw

59. Terry Pedwell, "400 Million Rescue Plan for Canadian Media Would Tax Google, Facebook and Rein in CBC." *Canadian Press* and *Guelph Mercury* January 26, 2017. https://www.guelphmercury.com/news-story/7086919--400-million-rescue-plan-for-canadian-media-would-tax-google-facebook-and-rein-in-cbc/.

60. PewDiePie. *YouTube*. https://www.youtube.com/channel/UC-lHJZR3Gqxm24_Vd_AJ5Yw, accessed November 11, 2021. See Jenni Hokka,"PewDiePie, Racism and YouTube's Neoliberalist Interpretation of Freedom of Speech." *Convergence* 27, no. 1 (2020/2021): 142–160.

61. A year and month after the initial launch of Encore+, CTV-Bell Media launched a video on demand [VOD] streaming service called Throwback that offers older commercial broadcast American television serials like ABC's *T.J. Hooker* (1982–1986), NBC's *Diff'rent Strokes* (1978–1986), *TBS's 10 items of Less* (2006–2009) and older Hollywood movies. With these older American programs, presumably rights can be attaining cheaply and the content can still attract the nostalgic or curious viewers with the content filled in with commercials. While Encore+ presents itself as a public facing archive driven by user demand to unlock forgotten and or overlooked analogue Canadian content that might be lost forever, Throwback frames its audience as a commodity. CTV Throwback, https://www.ctv.ca/throwback, accessed February 26, 2021.

62. NFDC. *Cinemas of India*, 2022. https://www.cinemasofindia.com, accessed November 11, 2021.

63. Taiwan Ministry of Culture. "Short Films of Taiwan's Indigenous Peoples from the Japanese Colonial Period: Formosa, Japanese Police Patrol 'Savage' Villages, Taichūshū Takasago Tribes Tour Japan, Sketches of the Takasago Tribes," *Taiwan Culture Toolkit>Cinema.>Film List*, 2022, https://toolkit.culture.tw/en/filminfo_62_465.html, accessed November 11, 2021.

64. Catalina Briceño, interview June 2, 2020.

Works Cited

AmazingFilmsNS. *The Shirley Show, Canadian TV, 1995*. https://www.youtube.com/watch?v=mMI-Xxk12zQ&t=707s, accessed September 1, 2017.

Ballingall, Alex, and Alex Boutilier. "Canada Urged to Respond Faster as Digital

Landscape Evolves." *Toronto Star.* October 12, 2018. https://www.thestar.com/politics/federal/2018/10/12/canada-urged-to-respond-faster-as-digital-landscape-evolves.html, accessed March 1, 2021.

Berkowitz, Irene, S., Charles Davis, and Hanako Smith. *Watchtime Canada: How YouTube Connects Creators & Consumers.* May 22, 2019. Ryerson Faculty of Communication & Design: Audience Lab. https://drive.google.com/file/d/1frDtTaR-y7qHQuECH-4M83zOhfBk-t2Z/view, accessed March 1, 2021.

Brioux, Bill. "Canadian TV Gold Shines Once More with Encore+." Brioux.tv. November 9, 2019. https://brioux.tv/blog/2017/11/09/canadian-tv-gold-shines-once-more-with-encore/, accessed March 1, 2021.

Canada Press. "Encore+ YouTube Channel Hosts Decades of Canadian TV and Film Time for some Old-school 'Degrassi' and 'Mr. Dressup.'" *Huffington Post,* November 11, 2017. https://www.huffingtonpost.ca/2017/11/09/encore-youtube-channel-hosts-decades-of-canadian-tv-and-film_a_23272513/, accessed September 1, 2020.

Canada Screens. https://canadascreens.ca. accessed August 23, 2020. No longer accessible.

"Canadian Film + Video." VUCAVA, accessed August 23, 2020. https://vucavu.com/en/home, accessed March 1, 2021.

Canadian Radio-Television and Telecommunications Commission, https://crtc.gc.ca/eng/home-accueil.htm, accessed March 1, 2021.

CBC. "Canada's Public Broadcaster Launches CBC GEM Streaming Service with More than 4000 Hof Live and On-Demand Programming Available for Free." *CBC Media Centre* December 11, 2018, https://www.cbc.ca/mediacentre/press-release/cbc-gem-streaming-service-launches-with-more-than-4000-hours-of-freeconten#:~:text=December%2011%2C%202018%E2%80%93%20CBCtoday%20announced%20the%20launch%20of,hours%20of%20live%20and%20on-demand%20programming%20for%20free. Accessed September 12, 2020.

Chun, W. Hui Kyong. "The Enduring Ephemeral, or the Future is Memory." *Critical Inquiry* 35, no. 1 (2008): 148–171.

Circcoritti, Jerry. *Deadly Friends a.k.a. The Death and Life of Nancy Eaton*, Indian Grove Productions, 2003. https://www.youtube.com/watch?v=HGzwoPfFmM4&t=1s, accessed March 1, 2021.

CTV. http://bellcanada.ca/, accessed March 1, 2021.

CTV Throwback. https://www.ctv.ca/throwback, accessed February 26, 2021.

De Kosnik, Abigail. *Rogue Archives: Digital Cultural Memory and Media Fandom.* Boston: Massachusetts Institute of Technology, 2016.

Doyle, John, "Click, Click, Click: Three Hot Canadian Online Shows." *Globe and Mail.* November 17, 2017. L1.

Doyle, Simon. "Arts and Culture Cuts Not Playing Well in Quebec, Could Affect Quebec Area: Opposition." *The Hill Times*, September 8, 2008: 1. ProQuest.

Encore+. Homepage. https://www.youtube.com/channel/UCH9jfFz0VzO-sqfh_TLVT7A/featured, accessed March 1, 2021.

Encore+. Playlists. https://www.youtube.com/channel/UCH9jfFz0VzO-sqfh_TLVT7A/playlists accessed March 1, 2021.

"Encore+ YouTube Channel Reaches 100,000 Subscribers and 25 Million Views Milestone." CMF, last modified August 18, 2020, https://www.cmf-fmc.ca/en-ca/news-events/news/august-2020/encore-youtube-channel-reaches-100-000-subscribers, accessed March 1, 2021.

Ferreira, André. "Encore+ YouTube Channel Research 150,000 subscribers and 40 M Views Milestone." CMF, last modified July 2, 2021. https://cmf-fmc.ca/news/encore-youtube-channel-reaches-150000-subscribers-and-40m-views-milestones/.

Google, *Copyright Strikes Basics.* https://support.google.com/youtube/answer/2814000?hl=en, accessed March 1, 2021.

Hilderbrand, Lucas. "YouTube: Where Cultural Memory and Copyright Converge." *Film Quarterly* 61, no. 1 (2007): 48–57. doi:10.1525/fq.2007.61.1.48, accessed September 30, 2020.

Hokka, Jenni. "PewDiePie, Racism and YouTube's Neoliberalist Interpretation of Freedom of Speech." *Convergence* 27, no. 1 (2020/2021): 142–160.

Hölling, Hanna B. *Paik's Virtual Archive: Time, Change, and Materiality in Media Art.* Oakland: University of California Press, 2017.
Houpt, Simon. "A Visit to the CBC Archives, on the Eve of Destruction." *Globe and Mail.* 12 September 2018.
Huvila, Isto. "Participatory Archive: towards Decentralised Curation, Radical User Orientation, and Broader Contextualisation of Records Management." *Archival Science* no. 8 (2008): 15–36. https://doi-org.ezproxy.library.ubc.ca/10.1007/s10502-008-9071-0.
ImagineNative *Film + Media Arts Festival Playlist. Encore+.* https://www.youtube.com/playlist?list=PLXssjYeUyJVELPg7GObyF4o2_GvBxK_Jw, accessed October 9, 2019.
Jackson, John D. "Production, Preservation, and Access: The Struggle to Retain Audiovisual Archives." *Canadian Journal of Communication* 26, no. 2 (2001), https://www.cjc-online.ca/index.php/journal/article/view/1219/1182, accessed March 1, 2021.
Leblanc, Daniel. "Ottawa to Unveil Netflix Deal as Part of Cultural Policy Overhaul." *Globe and Mail,* September 28, 2017.
Leblanc, Daniel, "PM Rejects Streaming Tax to Help Fund Media Sector." *The Globe and Mail,* Jun 16 2017, *ProQuest,* accessed September 30, 2019.
Marr, Leon. *Dancing in the Dark.* Brightstar films, 1983. https://www.youtube.com/watch?v=WHaXBAnMVxI, accessed March 1, 2021.
"Martha Henry: Revisiting Dancing in the Dark." *Encore+.* May 23, 2020. https://www.youtube.com/watch?v=HI4DCSuvufU, accessed March 1, 2021.
Millar, Laura. "Coming Up with Plan B: Considering the Future of Canadian Archives." *Archivaria* 77 (2014): 103–139. https://archivaria.ca/index.php/archivaria/article/view/13485, accessed September 7, 2021, accessed October 11, 2019.
Milligan, Ian. *History in the Age of Abundance: How the Web Is Transforming Historical Research.* Montreal and Kingston: McGill-Queen's, 2019.
NFDC. *Cinemas of India,*2022, https://www.cinemasofindia.com, accessed November 11, 2021.
Palmer, Joy. "Archives 2.0: If We Build It, Will They Come?" *Ariadne* 60 (July) (2009), http://www.ariadne.ac.uk/issue/60/palmer/, accessed September 7, 2021.
Pedwell, Terry. "400 Million Rescue Plan for Canadian Media Would Tax Google, Facebook and Rein in CBC." *Canadian Press* and *Guelph Mercury* January 26, 2017. https://www.guelphmercury.com/news-story/7086919--400-million-rescue-plan-for-canadian-media-would-tax-google-facebook-and-rein-in-cbc/.
PewDiePie. *YouTube.* https://www.youtube.com/channel/UC-lHJZR3Gqxm24_Vd_AJ5Yw, accessed November 11, 2021.
Phillips, Catherine. "Ad Spending in Canada to Reach $11.52 Billion in 2018: Report." *Media in Canada.* May 8, 2018. https://mediaincanada.com/2018/05/08/ad-spending-in-canada-to-reach-11-52-billion-in-2018-report/#:~:text=Total%20media%20ad%20spending%20in,exceed%20%2414%20billion%20by%202022, accessed March 1, 2021.
Pinto, Jordan. "OTT Revenues Continue to Gain Significant Ground on TV: CRTC" *Media in Canada.* March 1, 2019. http://mediaincanada.com/2019/03/01/ott-revenues-continue-to-gain-significant-ground-on-tv-crtc/, accessed September 7, 2021.
Prelinger, Rick. "Archives and Access in the 21st Century," *Cinema Journal* Spring, 2007, 46, no. 3 (Spring, 2007), 114–118.
Reid, Regan. "CMF Unveils Its Cancon YouTube Channel." *Playback* November 8, 2017. http://playbackonline.ca/2017/11/08/cmf-unveils-its-cancon-youtube-channel/, accessed September 7, 2021.
Shapiro, Paul and Peggy Thompson. *The Lotus Eater,* Rave Films, 1993. *Encore+* https://www.youtube.com/watch?v=-2rc16Hm1L4&t=570s, accessed September 7, 2021.
"Shirley Show CTV." YouTube, https://www.youtube.com/results?search_query=Shirley+Show+ctv, accessed March 1, 2021.
Smith, John, N. *Prairie Giant: The Tommy Douglas Story.* CBC. 2006. https://www.youtube.com/watch?v=p9SNHt6lRCE, accessed March 1, 2021.
Springs, Sally. *Madeleine Is,* Spring Productions, 1971. https://www.youtube.com/watch?v=ARxXVqaxPjU, accessed March 1, 2021.
Taiwan Ministry of Culture. "Short Films of Taiwan's Indigenous Peoples from the

Japanese Colonial Period: Formosa, Japanese Police Patrol 'Savage' Villages, Taichūshū Takasago Tribes Tour Japan, Sketches of the Takasago Tribes," *Taiwan Culture Toolkit>Cinema.>Film List.* 2022. https://toolkit.culture.tw/en/filminfo_62_465.html, accessed November 11, 2021.
Task Force on the Preservation and Enhanced Use of Canada's Audio-Visual Heritage. *Fading Away: Strategic Options to Ensure the Protection of and Access to Our Audio-Visual Heritage.* National Archives Canada, June 1995.
Taylor, Kate. "The Netflix Chill," *Globe and Mail.* 5 November 2016. R8.
Wilkinson, Kealy. "CBC Must Stop Destruction of a Vital Part of Canada's Broadcast History." *ACTRA.* 18 April 2018. https://www.actra.ca/press-releases/2018/04/cbc-must-stop-destruction-of-a-vital-part-of-canadas-broadcast-history/, accessed September 7, 2021.
Wilkinson, Kealy. "Friendly Giant Faces Firing Squad." *ACTRA.* 2 May 2018. https://www.actra.ca/press-releases/2018/05/friendly-giant-faces-firing-squad/. Accessed September 7, 2021.
Wilkinson, Kealy. "Personal e-mail," September 6 2019.
Wright, Corrie. "What Netflix's Half a Billion CAD Investment in Canada Is Really about." *Netflix Media Center.* 10 October 2017. https://media.netflix.com/en/company-blog/what-netflixs-half-a-billion-cad-investment-in-canada-is-really-about, accessed March 1, 2021.
YouTube, "Content Identification." https://support.google.com/youtube/answer/2797370?hl=en, accessed March 1, 2021.

Opting Out of the Streaming Wars

Second and Third Tier SVODs

Alexa Scarlata *and* Andrew Lynch

On the periphery of the loud and attention-hoarding "streaming wars" playing out between the likes of Netflix, Hulu, Apple, Amazon, Disney, WarnerMedia and NBCUniversal, there operates a substantial collection of streaming video-on-demand (SVOD) services that have quietly and (for the most part) successfully avoided direct competition with the major players, and even with each other. While the mainstream, or what we will call here, "first tier" SVODs are spending and charging significant amounts of money to adopt a generalist "conglomerated niche"[1] approach that tries to cater to every viewer and ensure that "your Netflix is not my Netflix," these niche services employ a range of specialist strategies and approaches to SVOD. They vary so significantly that it is difficult to construct a workable taxonomy of niche SVODs based on their strategies alone. However, Catherine Johnson has shown that while the 'online TV industry is inherently "messy," there is value in mapping it according to both its "business origins" and 'core businesses.'[2] As such, we argue that grouping SVODs in tiers according to their ownership status provides a useful and illuminative framework for analysis.

We define "second tier" SVODs as offshoots or subsidiaries of larger corporations with major media interests. These tend to be genre specific, playing the role of a "one-stop-shop" for distinct interest groups by either aggregating non-exclusive content or exploiting dust-gathering back catalogues owned by a parent company. Examples include Hayu (NBCUniversal), Acorn TV, Shudder and Sundance Now (AMC), Crunchyroll (WarnerMedia), and BritBox (BBC). "Third tier" SVODS are independent or marginal services, like MUBI, Nobudge, Full Moon Features, iwonder, ConTV, Dove Channel and Screambox, which operate separately from major media conglomerates.

This essay will consider multinational second tier players Hayu (reality TV) and Acorn TV (British drama) and examine third tier services Full Moon Features (exploitation and horror) and Nobudge (independent film). These services have largely escaped academic inquiry, despite their strategic diversity and surprising commercial resilience, making them worthwhile objects of investigation. Each has been able to carve out a viable existence in the larger streaming ecosystem, where they serve to complement the first tier SVODs, rather than compete with them directly. Analyzing these and other SVODs through a lens of ownership offers useful insights into the ways in which audiences are being configured, assessed and engaged by a complex and symbiotic videoscape of both expanding and increasingly concentrated "platform empires"[3] and the comparatively small-fry but tenacious auxiliary services that surround them.

A Tiered Approach to SVOD

The study of subscription video-on-demand platforms is well under way. While often part of a larger analysis of the emergence of a "post-network" period[4] and the rise of "portals,"[5] "platforms"[6] or "online TV,"[7] significant time and attention has been paid to the technological and industrial impacts of this distribution model. As a result, most of the recent academic work on internet-distributed television and SVOD more specifically has naturally gravitated towards multi-national market leaders such as Netflix and Amazon Prime Video.[8] While these services were early disrupters of the industry status quo, as Tom Evens and Karen Donders explained in *Platform Power and Policy in Transforming Television Markets*, the increasingly consolidated television landscape is evolving into a series of platform empires controlled by broadcasters/networks, studios and other IT/technology players. They posit that "the expansion of platform companies into vertical 'silos' that span multiple consumer products/services and operate under the principles of cross-subsidization and customer lock-in make it hard for standalone services to complete effectively with platforms."[9]

While this development is certainly significant and concerning, focusing solely on the "platformisation"[10] of major players overlooks the resilience of an array of comparatively small but sustainable SVOD services with very different aims and therefore definitions of success. Catherine Johnson's[11] approach to mapping the online TV industry by both business origins (TV natives, online natives and content natives) and core businesses (content or technology) is comprehensive and instructive here. This strategy explores the "competencies, dependencies and controlling points at work" and enables "analysis of the contextual factors that might shape the ways in which different players around the globe are enacting power within this particular segment of the contemporary media industries."[12]

Here we look beyond what Neil Landau[13] described as "The Big Three" sector—that is, the main providers of SVOD services (at the time of writing, Netflix, Amazon Prime and Hulu). We respectfully simplify Johnson's elegant approach to organize the dogged niche SVODs that remain according to their ownership. In so doing we can identify the myriad inventive ways these have been able to complement the space, rather than complete within it. Some of these subsist within the integrated ecosystem; others are contingent on their independence. Whatever the case, the findings of our tiered platform analysis confirm how this "highly volatile industry [is] made up of organizations operating multiple different [SVOD] business models which exist in dynamic and often dependent interrelationships with each other."[14] Our second and third tier SVODs may not garner vast or lucrative subscriber bases, but theirs are loyal, active and engaged communities.

Second Tier SVODs: Small but Mighty

We classify second tier SVODs as offshoots or subsidiaries of larger corporations with major media interests. Examples include Hayu (NBCUniversal/Comcast), Acorn TV, Shudder and Sundance Now (AMC), Crunchyroll (WarnerMedia), and BritBox (BBC). These services utilize very different strategies than those employed by their first-tier relatives. Namely, second tier SVODs tend to be genre specific, playing the role of a "one-stop-shop" for distinct interest groups by either aggregating non-exclusive content or exploiting dust-gathering back catalogues owned by a parent company. The increased integration Evens and Donders[15] envisaged is currently playing out, with more studios and networks announcing direct-to-consumer services, and first tier SVODs acquiring and subsuming competitors. This will no doubt threaten the resilience of the second tier going forward, but this makes a timely consideration of the effective ways in which they have invoked a sense of subscriber community all the more imperative.

Hayu

The NBCUniversal (Comcast) reality TV-focused SVOD Hayu claims to have experienced significant success.[16] It launched simultaneously in the United Kingdom, Ireland and Australia in March 2016 as the first all-reality TV streaming service of its kind, "curated and fully integrated with social media."[17] With a clear 18–34 female demographic or "tribe" of reality "super fans,"[18] a relatively low price point of AU$6.99 per month (initially AU$5.99), and various access deals with IPTV and pay-tv providers in its first years of operation, it increased its local weekly streaming audience in Australia, for example, by 500 percent in 2017.[19] AMPD Research[20] estimated a local paying subscriber base of 300,000 (and viewership of 800,000) there in 2019. Hayu in now available in 27 territories, including Canada, much of Scandinavia and Europe, and the Philippines, Hong Kong and Singapore.[21]

Interestingly, most of Hayu's more than 8000 episodes of content are not exclusive to the service, with many programs available via broadcast and cable providers with concurrent rights. It also diversified its NBCUniversal content proposition more recently, acquiring content from third parties with deals with A&E, Viacom and independent producers. Rather than compete directly with the growing popularity of reality television and develop its own content, Hayu welcomes what it considers to be the whetting of an appetite for the genre by commercial broadcasters[22] and instead functions solely as an aggregator and distributor. This flies in the face of the logic of the first tier SVODs, which typically market themselves based on the exclusivity of their branded content.

Hayu is marketed as a convenient location for the reality TV connoisseur: as Manning[23] put it, the key to its apparent success has been the combination of "Kardashians, Kost and Konvenience." According to NBCUniversal's senior vice-president of branded on-demand and managing director of Hayu, Hendrik McDermott, "It's a different proposition … we are a genre-based service focused on providing the best possible reality environments that you can have."[24] To this end, Hayu capitalizes on the size and scope of the NBCUniversal brand and its suite of assets (in the SVOD space alone this includes a stake in Hulu and the recently launched Peacock). It combines a familiar and intuitive user interface design and categorization strategies, as well as inclusive marketing to unabashedly cater directly to an audience too often chastened for their reality TV proclivities.

Acorn TV

Like Hayu, Acorn TV similarly focuses on one specific, albeit broadly defined, genre: British (and English-language) drama, crime and mysteries. The brand has had a presence and loyal customer base in the United States market for more than two decades: the Acorn Media Group has distributed British television to American fans since 1994 via VHS tapes via catalogue and later DVD and Blu-ray media. Acorn TV was launched as a standalone SVOD there in 2013, but the RLJ Entertainment (AMC)-owned platform expanded into thirty new territories in 2018.

As with the numerous documentary SVODs (for example, DocPlay, Curiosity Stream and Discovery+) that operate relatively harmoniously because they are available in disparate regions, Acorn TV initially had a regional monopoly on its genre, competing directly with the BBC's own anglophile SVOD BritBox only in the United States and Canada. However, in 2020 BritBox announced plans (and has slowly begun) to roll out to a further 25 countries worldwide.[25] Typical of second tier services, Acorn TV has a low price point that positions it as a complementary service rather than first tier competitor (AU$6.99 per month/AU$69.99 per year), and a carefully curated library of non-exclusive fan favorites from specific niche genres. Like AMC's other specialty SVODS, Shudder, Sundance Now and ALLBLK, Acorn TV has also licensed and commissioned original content (no doubt aided substantially by RLJ's 64 percent stake in Agatha Christie Limited).

As with Hayu, Acorn TV utilizes a now familiar user interface design but its ability to categorize and recommend titles is limited by its relatively small catalogue (of between 150–300 titles, depending on your location). This limitation must be weighed against the highly curated nature of Acorn TV's content, which skews towards newer titles and expediting the availability of new seasons of content, as well as its community-focused engagement with fans. In October 2021 *Variety* confirmed that the service, once dubbed "Netflix for the Anglophile" by NPR,[26] now has "more than 1 million subscribers in the U.S and Canada, as well as viewership in the U.K., Australia, New Zealand and Latin America."[27] President of global direct-to-consumer at AMC Miguel Penella described the SVOD as having led the way for streamers focused on a specialized audience: "Acorn TV's strong momentum ... underscores that the special interest SVOD market is growing and has vast potential, including some meaningful advantages over general interest SVOD."[28]

Third Tier SVODs: More Than MUBI

We define the remaining independent or marginal services that are not owned by major media conglomerates as third tier SVODS. This category covers a range of platforms that offer their users a much greater variety of services than either first or second tier SVODs. These services also demonstrate a wider range of business practices and commercial models than their upper-tier cousins, highlighting the respective limitations associated with scale.

In terms of reach, MUBI (The Auteurs until 2010) is likely the most commercially successful third tier SVOD. Operating out of London since 2007, MUBI has more than ten million subscribers[29] across 195 countries.

It has been described as the "anti–Netflix"[30] because it features a rotating library of only thirty art-house and classic films at a time, available for AU$9.99 per month. Furthering this hyper-curation model, MUBI justifies its selections through an online magazine *Notebook* as well as detailed editorial copy and biographical details for each film. Because of its long-standing success and visible central author and chief curator Efe Çakarel, MUBI has featured in a number of scholarly investigations,[31] but it is worth reconsidering under this tiered framework not as a maverick anomaly (as too easily fits its highbrow branding) but as one of a number of SVOD services operating outside of the first tier streaming wars and thus working with and towards different markers of viability, competition and ultimately, success. For example, in their discussion of MUBI's changing approach to internet video, Smits and Nikdel argue that by moving away from its initial goal to compete with first tier services and their large catalogues, "MUBI developed a new and innovative online business model that deviates in various ways from the dominant discourse of audience empowerment, enhancement of choice and the democratization of access that characterizes the common perception of the digital landscape."[32] We reframe this deviation as not just a move away from the first tier of SVODs, but also as a move into line with other third tier services. Many within this third-tier category demonstrate just as much innovation as MUBI, if not as wide a reach.

Some third tier SVODs cater to specialist audiences such as Dove channel, a U.S. based, family-friendly, conservative Christian service which spun out of the Dove Foundation. The foundation was founded in the early 1990s to inform Evangelical Christian consumers about the content of feature film releases. Owing to the organization which birthed it, Dove Channel allows users to sort through its library of "Dove Approved" films and TV series via a "five-point rating system ranking programming in six key criteria, including sexuality, language, violence, drug and alcohol use, and nudity."[33] Other third tier SVODs follow the well-worn approach of single genre, specialist cable channels (and second tier SVODs) and target a particular genre or type of content. Examples include iwonder and Screambox, which specialize in documentary features and horror films respectively.

However, the real significance of the third tier is arguably in their diversity of experimental approaches to SVOD. With the exception of the short-lived first tier Quibi, which experimented with short form serialized TV, major SVODs have largely followed conventional models for distributing film and TV content. Because of their smaller size and (usually) more modest business models, third tier SVODs are able to more directly engage their users as fans, encouraging the creation of fan communities which both consume the films and TV on offer, but also increase the value for other users by engaging in dialogue about the content and creating a sense of belonging and identity associated with these smaller platforms.

Full Moon Features

Describing itself as a "virtual ticket to a mind blowing three-ring circus of horror, sci-fi, fantasy & cult movie entertainment, retro favorites and lost classics!,"[34] Full Moon Features (FMF) is another third tier SVOD service, but one that differs vastly from MUBI in terms of content, scale and strategy. Launching in 2014 (as Full Moon Streaming), the service is owned and operated by Full Moon Studios, an independent, low-budget movie studio operating since 1988, and specializes in the production of what Jeffrey Sconce called "paracinema"[35]: original and licensed horror, sci-fi, fantasy and soft-core pornography. The service is available for AU$6.95 per month through a standalone website and app internationally, but also as one of Amazon Prime Video's add-on "channels" in the U.S., the U.K. and Germany.

Like MUBI, FMF is centered around a primary authorial figure, in this case the company's founder Charles Band, well-known to cult film fans for producing and directing horror films throughout the 1980s under the Empire International Pictures label and 1990s under Full Moon Productions. Band is named in promotional material for the SVOD and appears in person on several behind-the-scenes featurettes and introductions available in its catalogue.

FMF's streaming catalogue is mostly comprised of feature films—such as *Puppet Master* (Schmoeller 1989) and *Castle Freak* (Gordon 1995) produced by Full Moon and its various subsidiaries over the last three decades, as well as acquisitions from the libraries of other cult film companies such as Blue Underground which specializes in European horror and exploitation cinema. For several years, it also included films from Band's softcore pornography imprint Surrender Cinema which focused "on erotica made for singles and couples."[36] In 2021, the more explicitly pornographic films in Band's catalogue were spun off into new dedicated SVOD named Exotic Movie House. FMF also houses a limited range of TV series produced by Full Moon, but which originally aired elsewhere, including *William Shatner's Halloween Fright Nights* (SyFy 2002) and *Elvira's 10 Nights of Halloween* (Hulu 2014). Unlike MUBI, which orients its business model around a brand of careful curatorship, Full Moon Features offers something of a "kitchen-sink" cult media catalogue and exists as a supplementary service for movie and TV viewers already interested in the larger Full Moon brand. It also drives further engagement with other aspects of the larger company, such as their transaction video-on-demand service Full Moon Direct, as well as an extensive merchandising arm which offers figurines, clothing and other collectable merchandise to its engaged fanbase.

We consider FMF to be a "cult" SVOD service. This term works as a classifier for culturally marginalized media genres, including sci-fi, horror and fantasy, which have gained a loyal subcultural following, because of either textual attributes or industrial and cultural circumstances.[37] These fans actively and enthusiastically participate in identity construction using cult media. Matt Hills problematizes the "authentic" relationship between cult media and its fans by arguing "cult fans have become one niche market amongst others to be surveyed, understood, and catered for."[38] Mainstream media may have co-opted the potential of cult fandom, but in terms of its small scale and hyper-niche appeal, FMF might be as far from mainstream and as authentically subcultural a platform as the contemporary U.S. commercial media landscape allows. FMF's status as a cult SVOD is reflected in the ways in which it addresses and engages its small but loyal user base.

Unlike the first tier SVODs, both second and third tier SVODs have (for the most part) not prioritized the commissioning of dedicated original productions, due to the inherent costs in such an enterprise. Instead, their value to consumers has been in curation. This is where Full Moon's history as an independent, low-budget production company makes it a particularly experimental and innovative third tier portal because it *does* produce original content, albeit within a low-budget scope. Full Moon's *Deadly Ten* project is an example of this more experimental tendency: "ten original new Full Moon features will be filmed back-to-back all over the world and fans will have an exclusive, all-access virtual pass to watch them being produced here, LIVE in real time."[39] Most of the ten proposed films (a number of which have already been completed and released) are either remakes of films produced by Band under previous iterations of Full Moon such as *Necropolis: Legion* (2020) or sequels such as *Puppet Master* spinoff *Blade: The Iron Cross* (2020) and *Sorority Babes in the Slimeball Bowl-O-Rama 2* (2020). By live streaming the production and post-production of these films, all the while engaging with fans via its message boards, FMF is adopting an approach not unlike MUBI's engagement with its cinephile audience. FMF has almost entirely escaped academic enquiry. In a forthcoming article for the journal *Senses of Cinema*, we further examine how the SVOD invokes the auteur status of Band himself to attract patronage from its fans/subscribers.

While FMF is accessible wherever the Microsoft, Amazon Fire, Roku, iTunes, and Google Play stores are available, its number of subscribers is unclear. It is likely a fraction of MUBI's ten million. However, like many third tier SVOD services, its viability rests not with a goal of mainstream popularity or even niche supremacy, but simply as a supplementary revenue stream that capitalizes on an already existing catalogue of content.

Nobudge

Third tier SVOD Nobudge collects low-budget, no-budget and DIY indie filmmaking and invites both aspiring and professional filmmakers to submit their work (for a small fee, US$25–$45) for release via the platform. The site hosts hundreds of short and feature films, with the only stipulation being that the films were budgeted under US$100,000. The site first launched in 2011 as a Tumblr film blog and later became a free streaming site in 2015 (with users encouraged to contribute to the site via "crowd-patronage platform"[40]). Nobudge releases several new films per week and publishes film analysis and interviews with directors. The name "Nobudge" itself is an abbreviation of "no-budget" but also suggests the no-compromise approach of indie filmmaking.[41] Like many third tier SVODs, Nobudge is a small-scale operation, the sole work of founder Kentucker Audley. In 2021 Audley launched a more traditional monthly subscription platform, Nobudge^2 ("Nobudge Squared"), which features exclusive content[42] for US$5.99 per month. Despite this shift to a subscription model for Nobudge^2, the original site (now called Nobudge^1) remains free. In this way Nobudge actually operates in a similar way to mixed-model first tier SVODs which offer premium memberships to avoid advertising. But whereas subscribers to those service are paying for convenience, Nobudge members are largely paying for the implied "cultural capital"[43] associated with supporting artistic endeavors, with 60 percent of profits from Nobudge^2 going to the filmmakers whose work it hosts.[44] Nobudge subscribers are further incentivized with merchandise including membership cards and buttons, as well as reduced fees for submitting their own films for consideration, inviting them to become part of the independent film community themselves. Nobudge also hosts in-person screenings in Brooklyn, New York, where the business is based. As such, like other third tier SVODs including Full Moon Features, Nobudge invokes the idea of community creation through membership and support of the platform. This sense of an inclusive fan community is given a tongue in cheek twist by Audley's other business, a playful clothing label called "Movies Brand," through which he sells hats embroidered with the words "movies," "arthouse garbage" and "documentaries." The brand's website ironically describes it as "[t]he industry leader in putting the word movies on hats & more."[45] Nobudge and Movies Brand frequently cross promote one another, and members of the American indie film scene enthusiastically endorse both on their own personal social media accounts.

Like MUBI, Nobudge is highly curated and explicitly authored, but to an even greater degree. All decisions as to what plays on the site are made by Audley himself. As *Guardian* writer Guy Lodge notes, "viewers and film-makers alike are subject to one man's critical sensibility."[46] Audley himself is an active part of the American Indie filmmaking scene, directing and acting in a number of "mumblecore" films including *Team Picture* (Kentucker Audley 2007), *Queen of Earth* (Alex Ross Perry 2015) and *She Dies Tomorrow* (Amy Semietz 2020). Geoff King describes mumblecore as a growing corpus of recent American independent films defined by a "shared minimal-budget low-key naturalism ... and the vocal hesitancies of non-professional performers."[47] Nobudge hosted the online premier of prominent mumblecore director Joe Swanberg's new film *Build the Wall* (2020). Swanberg is best known for films including *Drinking Buddies* (2013), *Digging for Fire* (2015) and his Netflix series *Easy* (2016–2019). As such, Audley's taste, which directly informs the site's catalogue, tends towards films which follow in the mumblecore aesthetic tradition. However, it also includes more experimental work as well as films from outside the U.S. Along with choosing which films will be available on the platform, Audley also curates subcategories within the portal's library, highlighting particular groups of films with shared characteristics. These "playlists" are frequently updated and thus reflect contemporary topics. For example, "New Black Voices" reflects the current global focus on the Black Lives Matter racial justice movement. Likewise, "On Isolation" collects short films that speak thematically or formally to the state of isolated lockdown many nations are suffering due to the Covid-19 pandemic. Jennifer Hessler describes MUBI's shift from a large on-demand catalogue to its current rotation of thirty films at a time, as a move from "participation to patronage" guided primarily by market forces.[48] We argue that in a very real sense, Nobudge represents a complex model of participation *and* patronage. Both Audley and Nobudge's viewers and subscribers are participating patrons. Audley relies on contributors submitting films for the platform to maintain a steady release schedule, but at the time those contributors are at the mercy of Audley's critical judgment of their work as worthy for Nobudge. Likewise, viewers of the site rely on Audley's taste for their viewing pleasure, but without their subscriptions, it is unlikely Nobudge could operate in its current form, as a "home for movies that don't have another home."[49]

In summary, as third tier SVODs, Full Moon Features and Nobudge share two key characteristics: they have a clear, identifiable authorial force curating their libraries, and they invoke ideas of community when addressing their audiences. Generally lacking the budgets of first and second tier SVODs, these third-tier portals instead rely on a sense of audience participation through discourse with and a meaningful affinity for the platforms' authors. Whereas first and second tier SVOD viewers understand their monthly contribution is a drop in the proverbial bucket, third tier SVODs and their audiences have a mutual understanding that every subscription counts.

Widening the Scope of SVOD Analysis

Adopting Johnson's approach to mapping online TV according to business interests and ownership widens the scope of SVOD analysis by highlighting the complex and varied range of symbiotic services that are often overshadowed by the size and reach of large multinational services. Compared to first tier services, the individual reach of these second and third tier SVOD players is certainly insignificant (after all, Disney+ signed up ten million customers worldwide on its first *day* of operation[50]), but the strategies they have used to not just withstand but welcome the fragmentation of viewers across services offer useful insights into their resilience. These strategies have helped them carve out a viable place in the larger streaming ecosystem where they are complementary to the first tier SVODs, rather than competitive.

The big players are battling it out in an over-crowded space that is "indisputably heading for big consolidation,"[51] so what will ultimately determine the future of niche SVODs is their ownership status. As media pundits like Bylykbashi[52] have prognosticated, while the major media players continue to expand globally, Hayu, Acorn TV and other second tier subsidiaries stand to be subsumed into increasingly powerful first tier services, becoming at best mere "channels," or at worst shuttered and their libraries absorbed. Just as the "middle" fell out of the movie industry, so too might the second tier soon fall out of the SVOD market. However, these offer useful insights into the motivations and limitations of first tier services and their conglomerated niche strategies. Additionally, if third tier services like Full Moon Features and Nobudge continue to maintain their independence, specialty status and community loyalty, they stand to avoid the major conflicts of the so-called streaming wars altogether.

Notes

1. Amanda D. Lotz, *Portals* (Ann Arbour: University of Michigan Press, 2017).
2. Catherine Johnson, *Online TV* (London; New York: Routledge, 2019), 54.
3. Tom Evens and Karen Donders, *Platform Power and Policy in Transforming Television Markets* (Cham: Palgrave Macmillan, 2018), 255.

4. Michael Strangelove, *Post-TV: Piracy, Cord-Cutting, and the Future of Television* (Toronto: University of Toronto Press, 2015).

5. Lotz, *Portals*.

6. Evens and Donders, *Platform Power and Policy in Transforming Television Markets*.

7. Johnson, *Online TV*.

8. See for example: Mareike Jenner, *Netflix and the Re-invention of Television* (Cham: Palgrave Macmillan, 2018); Ramon Lobato, *Netflix Nations: The Geography of Digital Distribution* (New York: NYU Press, 2018); Lotz, *Portals*; Kevin McDonald and Daniel Smith-Rowsey, *The Netflix Effect* (New York: Bloomsbury, 2016); Michael L. Wayne, "Netflix, Amazon, and branded television content in subscription video on-demand portals," *Media, Culture & Society* 40, no. 5 (2018): 725–741.

9. Evens and Donders, *Platform Power and Policy in Transforming Television Markets*, 116.

10. Evens and Donders, *Platform Power and Policy in Transforming Television Markets*.

11. Johnson, *Online TV*.

12. Johnson, *Online TV*, 55.

13. Neil Landau, *TV Outside the Box: Trailblazing in the Digital Television Revolution* (New York: Focal Press, 2016).

14. Johnson, *Online TV*, 74–75.

15. *Platform Power and Policy in Transforming Television Markets*.

16. Josh McDonnell, "Hayu: Australia's 'local reality content isn't competition," *Ad News*, April 2, 2019, http://www.adnews.com.au/news/hayu-australia-s-local-reality-content-isn-t-competition.

17. Leo Barraclough, "NBCUniversal Launches Reality Streaming Service Hayu in U.K., Ireland, Australia," *Variety*, February 11, 2016, https://variety.com/2016/digital/global/nbcuniversal-reality-streaming-service-hayu-uk-ireland-australia-1201703166/.

18. Lindsay Bennett, "Hayu touts 'next generation' SVOD service," *Ad News*, February 26, 2016, http://www.adnews.com.au/news/hayu-touts-next-generation-svod-service.

19. Zoe Samios, "Hayu signals content expansion as Australia's average weekly streaming 'grows by 500%,'" *Mumbrella*, March 12, 2018, https://mumbrella.com.au/hayu-signals-content-expansion-australias-average-weekly-streaming-grows-500-504071.

20. AMPD Research, *Australia: SVOD Study*, July, https://www.media-partners-asia.com/files/mpa/262/AustraliaSVODStudy.pdf.

21. *Mediaweek*, "hayu celebrates five years in Australia and launches new brand campaign," May 20, 2021, https://www.mediaweek.com.au/aana-announces-that-facebook-has-agreed-to-fund-advertising-self-regulation/.

22. Pippa Chambers, "Hayu not threatened by free-to-air reality rivals," *Ad News*, May 14, 2018, http://www.adnews.com.au/news/hayu-not-threatened-by-free-to-air-reality-rivals.

23. James Manning, "Streaming anniversary: hayu goes global after NBCU's Aussie launch," *MediaWeek*, March 25, 2019, https://www.mediaweek.com.au/streaming-anniversary-hayu-goes-global-after-nbcus-aussie-launch/.

24. Zoe Samios, "Hayu 'to survive with big players,'" *The Australian*, June 24, 2019, 26.

25. Naman Ramachandran, "BritBrox Set for Global Expansion in 25 Countries," *Variety*, July 27, 2020, https://variety.com/2020/tv/news/britbox-global-expansion-1234716939/.

26. *Mumbrella*, "Streaming platform Acorn TV expands Australian offering," September 17, 2019, https://mumbrella.com.au/streaming-platform-acorn-tv-expands-australian-offering-598489

27. Manori Ravindran, "Jodie Comer and Stephen Graham Drama 'Help' Sells to U.S. Streamer Acorn TV (EXCLUSIVE)," *Variety*, October 11, 2021, https://variety.com/2021/tv/global/jodie-comer-stephen-graham-help-acorn-us-1235086620/.

28. Jon Lafayette, "AMC Streamer Acorn TV Tops 1M Subscriber Total," *Next TV*, September 19, 2019, https://www.nexttv.com/news/amc-streamer-acorn-tv-tops-1m-subscriber-total#:~:text=Acorn%20TV%2C%20AMC%20Networks'%20streaming,and%20Canada%2C%20the%20company%20said.

29. Michael Rosser, "Independent VoD players in focus: Mubi," *Screen Daily*, August 2, 2021, https://www.screendaily.com/features/independent-vod-players-in-focus-mubi/5161811.article.

30. Nathan McAlone, "The 'anti-Netflix' is worth $125 million—and it's already moving into China to capitalise on the booming movie market," *Business Insider Australia*, March 3, 2016, https://www.businessinsider.com.au/mubi-indie-movie-streaming-startup-worth-125-million-as-it-moves-into-china-2016-3.

31. See for example: Daniel Herbert, "From Art House To Your House: The Distribution of Quality Cinema on Home Video," *Canadian Journal of Film* 2, no. 2 (2011): 2–18; Chuck Tryon, *On-demand culture: Digital delivery and the future of movies* (New Jersey: Rutgers University Press, 2013); Jennifer Hessler, "Quality You Can't Touch: MUBI Social, Platform Politics, and the Online Distribution of Art Cinema," *The Velvet Light Trap* 82 (Fall 2018): 3–17; Roderik Smits and E.W. Nikdel, "Beyond Netflix and Amazon: MUBI and the curation of on-demand," *Studies in European Cinema* 16, no. 1 (2019): 22–37; Mattias Frey, *MUBI and the Curation Model of Video on Demand* (Cham: Springer, 2021).

32. Smits and Nikdel, "Beyond Netflix," 26.

33. Todd Spangler, "Cinedigm Launches Dove Channel SVOD Service That Strips Out Sex, Drugs and Violence," *Variety*, September 16, 2015, https://variety.com/2015/digital/news/cinedigm-dove-channel-launch-1201595074/.

34. John Squires, "Full Moon Launches Brand New Streaming App 'Full Moon Features,'" *Bloody Disgusting*, August 8, 2019, https://bloody-disgusting.com/movie/3577518/full-moon-launches-brand-new-streaming-app-full-moon-features/.

35. Jeffrey Sconce, "'Trashing' the Academy: Taste, Excess and an Emerging Politics of Cinematic Style," *Screen* 36, no. 4 (1995): 371–393.

36. Karina Michael Field, "Charles Band of 'Full Moon Features': The Power of Flexibility; How I Was Able To Pivot To A New Exciting Opportunity Because Of The Pandemic." *Authority Magazine*, January 25, 2021, https://medium.com/authority-magazine/charles-band-of-full-moon-features-the-power-of-flexibility-how-i-was-able-to-pivot-to-a-new-d80d952423c6.

37. See for more on this: Stacey Abbott, ed., *The Cult TV Book: From Star Trek to Dexter, New Approaches to TV Outside the Box* (Berkley: Soft Skull Press, 2010); Steffen Hantke, "Cult horror cinema," in *The Routledge Companion to Cult Cinema*, eds. Ernest Mathijs and Jamie Sexton (Milton: Routledge, 2020); Matt Hills, *Fan Cultures* (London; New York: Routledge, 2002); David Lavery, ed., *The Essential Cult TV Reader* (Lexington: University Press of Kentucky, 2010); Ernest Mathijs and Jamie Sexton, eds., *The Routledge Companion to Cult Cinema* (Milton: Routledge, 2020).

38. Matt Hills, "Mainstream Cult," in *The Cult TV Book: From Star Trek to Dexter, New Approaches to TV Outside the Box*, ed. Stacey (Berkley: Soft Skull Press, 2010), 69.

39. *Deadly Ten*, October 24, 2021, https://deadlyten.com

40. Jon Swords, "Crowd-patronage—intermediaries, geographies and relationships in patronage networks," *Poetics* 64 (2017): 63–73.

41. Glenn Kenny, "NoBudge, a One-Man Independent Film Factory," *The New York Times*, March 2, 2018, https://www.nytimes.com/2018/03/02/movies/nobudge-a-one-man-independent-film-factory.html.

42. Kate Erbland. "Kentucker Audley's Microbudget Discovery Site NoBudge Launches Subscription Service," *Indiewire*, April 19, 2021. https://www.indiewire.com/2021/04/nobudge-streaming-platform-subscription-1234628286/

43. Pierre Bourdieu, *Distinction: a social critique of the judgement of taste* (Cambridge: Harvard University Press, 1984).

44. Caleb Hammond. "NoBudge Founder Kentucker Audley Launches New Streaming Service That Shares Majority of Profits With Moviemakers," *Moviemaker*, January 19, 2021. https://www.moviemaker.com/nobudge-kentucker-audley-interview-short-films/

45. *Movies Brand*. October 24, 2021. https://www.moviesbrand.com/about.

46. Guy Lodge, "NoBudge: a one-man passion project," *The Guardian*, June 3, 2018, https://www.theguardian.com/film/2018/jun/03/kentucker-audley-nobudge-film-streaming-micro-budget.

47. Geoff King, *Indie 2.0: change and continuity in contemporary American indie film* (London& New York: I.B. Taurus, 2013), 122.

48. Hessler, "Quality You Can't Touch," 10.

49. Audley cited in Kate Erbland. "Kentucker Audley's Microbudget Discovery Site NoBudge Launches Subscription Service," *Indiewire*, April 19, 2021. https://www.indiewire.com/2021/04/nobudge-streaming-platform-subscription-1234628286/

50. Lauren Feiner, "Disney+ surpasses 10 million sign-ups since launch," *CNBC*, November 13, 2019, https://www.cnbc.com/2019/11/13/disney-surpasses-10-million-sign-ups-since-launch.html.

51. Evens and Donders, *Platform Power and Policy in Transforming Television Markets*, 244.

52. Kaltrina Bylykbashi, "Will 2019 mark the end of niche SVOD?," *Television Business International*, January 21, 2019, https://tbivision.com/2019/01/21/will-2019-mark-the-end-of-niche-svod/.

Works Cited

Abbott, Stacey, ed. *The Cult TV Book: From Star Trek to Dexter, New Approaches to TV Outside the Box*. Berkley: Soft Skull Press, 2010.

AMPD Research. *Australia: SVOD Study*. July. https://www.media-partners-asia.com/files/mpa/262/AustraliaSVODStudy.pdf.

Barraclough, Leo. "NBCUniversal Launches Reality Streaming Service Hayu in U.K., Ireland, Australia." *Variety*, February 11, 2016. https://variety.com/2016/digital/global/nbcuniversal-reality-streaming-service-hayu-uk-ireland-australia-1201703166/.

Bennett, Lindsay. "Hayu touts 'next generation' SVOD service." *Ad News*, February 26, 2016. http://www.adnews.com.au/news/hayu-touts-next-generation-svod-service.

Bourdieu, Pierre. *Distinction: A Social Critique of the Judgement of Taste*. Cambridge: Harvard University Press, 1984.

Bylykbashi, Kaltrina. "Will 2019 mark the end of niche SVOD?" *Television Business International*, January 21, 2019. https://tbivision.com/2019/01/21/will-2019-mark-the-end-of-niche-svod/.

Chambers, Pippa. "Hayu not threatened by free-to-air reality rivals." *Ad News*, May 14, 2018. http://www.adnews.com.au/news/hayu-not-threatened-by-free-to-air-reality-rivals.

Deadly Ten. October 24, 2021, https://deadlyten.com.

Erbland, Kate. "Kentucker Audley's Microbudget Discovery Site NoBudge Launches Subscription Service," *Indiewire*, April 19, 2021. https://www.indiewire.com/2021/04/nobudge-streaming-platform-subscription-1234628286/.

Evens, Tom and Karen Donders. *Platform Power and Policy in Transforming Television Markets*. Cham: Palgrave Macmillan, 2018.

Feiner, Lauren. "Disney+ surpasses 10 million sign-ups since launch." *CNBC*, November 13, 2019. https://www.cnbc.com/2019/11/13/disney-surpasses-10-million-sign-ups-since-launch.html.

Frey, Mattias. *MUBI and the Curation Model of Video on Demand*. Cham: Springer, 2021.

Hammond, Caleb. "NoBudge Founder Kentucker Audley Launches New Streaming Service That Shares Majority of Profits With Moviemakers," *Moviemaker*, January 19, 2021. https://www.moviemaker.com/nobudge-kentucker-audley-interview-short-films/.

Hantke, Steffen. "Cult horror cinema." In *The Routledge Companion to Cult Cinema*, edited by Ernest Mathijs and Jamie Sexton, 50–58. Milton: Routledge, 2020.

Herbert, Daniel. "From Art House To Your House: The Distribution of Quality Cinema on Home Video." *Canadian Journal of Film* 2, no. 2 (2011): 2–18.

Hessler, Jennifer. "Quality You Can't Touch: MUBI Social, Platform Politics, and the Online Distribution of Art Cinema." *The Velvet Light Trap* 82 (Fall 2018): 3–17.

Hills, Matt. *Fan Cultures*. London; New York: Routledge, 2002.

Hills, Matt. "Mainstream Cult." In *The Cult TV Book: From Star Trek to Dexter, New Approaches to TV Outside the Box*, edited by Stacey Abbott, 67–73. Berkley: Soft Skull Press, 2010.

Jenner, Mareike. *Netflix and the Re-invention of Television*. Cham: Palgrave Macmillan, 2018.

Johnson, Catherine. *Online TV.* London; New York: Routledge, 2019.

Kenny, Glenn. "NoBudge, a One-Man Independent Film Factory." *The New York Times*, March 2, 2018. https://www.nytimes.com/2018/03/02/movies/nobudge-a-one-man-independent-film-factory.html.

King, Geoff. *Indie 2.0: Change and Continuity in Contemporary American Indie Film.* London & New York: I.B. Taurus, 2013.

Lafayette, Jon. "AMC Streamer Acorn TV Tops 1M Subscriber Total." Next TV, September 19, 2019. https://www.nexttv.com/news/amc-streamer-acorn-tv-tops-1m-subscriber-total#:~:text=Acorn%20TV%2C%20AMC%20Networks'%20streamingand%20Canada%2C%20the%20company%20said.

Landau, Neil. *TV Outside the Box: Trailblazing in the Digital Television Revolution.* New York: Focal Press, 2016.

Lavery, David, ed. *The Essential Cult TV Reader.* Lexington: University Press of Kentucky, 2010.

Lobato, Ramon. *Netflix Nations: The Geography of Digital Distribution.* New York: NYU Press, 2018.

Lodge, Guy. "NoBudge: A one-man passion project." *The Guardian*, June 3, 2018. https://www.theguardian.com/film/2018/jun/03/kentucker-audley-nobudge-film-streaming-micro-budget.

Lotz, Amanda D. *Portals.* Ann Arbour: University of Michigan Press, 2017.

Manning, James. "Streaming anniversary: hayu goes global after NBCU's Aussie launch." *MediaWeek*, March 25, 2019. https://www.mediaweek.com.au/streaming-anniversary-hayu-goes-global-after-nbcus-aussie-launch/.

Mathijs, Ernest and Jamie Sexton, eds. *The Routledge Companion to Cult Cinema.* Milton: Routledge, 2020.

McAlone, Nathan. "The 'anti–Netflix' is worth $125 million—and it's already moving into China to capitalise on the booming movie market." *Business Insider Australia*, March 3, 2016. https://www.businessinsider.com.au/mubi-indie-movie-streaming-startup-worth-125-million-as-it-moves-into-china-2016-3.

McDonald, Kevin, and Daniel Smith-Rowsey. *The Netflix Effect.* New York: Bloomsbury, 2016.

McDonnell, Josh. "Hayu: Australia's 'local' reality content isn't competition." *Ad News*, April 2, 2019. http://www.adnews.com.au/news/hayu-australia-s-local-reality-content-isn-t-competition.

Mediaweek. "hayu celebrates five years in Australia and launches new brand campaign." May 20, 2021, https://www.mediaweek.com.au/aana-announces-that-facebook-has-agreed-to-fund-advertising-self-regulation/.

Michael Field, Karina. "Charles Band of 'Full Moon Features': The Power of Flexibility; How I Was Able To Pivot To A New Exciting Opportunity Because Of The Pandemic." *Authority Magazine*, January 25, 2021, https://medium.com/authority-magazine/charles-band-of-full-moon-features-the-power-of-flexibility-how-i-was-able-to-pivot-to-a-new-d80d952423c6.

Movies Brand. October 24, 2021. https://www.moviesbrand.com/about.

Mumbrella. "Streaming platform Acorn TV expands Australian offering." September 17, 2019. https://mumbrella.com.au/streaming-platform-acorn-tv-expands-australian-offering-598489.

Ramachandran, Naman. "BritBrox Set for Global Expansion in 25 Countries." *Variety*, July 27, 2020. https://variety.com/2020/tv/news/britbox-global-expansion-1234716939/.

Ravindran, Manori. "Jodie Comer and Stephen Graham Drama 'Help' Sells to U.S. Streamer Acorn TV (EXCLUSIVE)." *Variety*, October 11, 2021. https://variety.com/2021/tv/global/jodie-comer-stephen-graham-help-acorn-us-1235086620/.

Rosser, Michael. "Independent VoD players in focus: Mubi." *Screen Daily*, August 2, 2021. https://www.screendaily.com/features/independent-vod-players-in-focus-mubi/5161811.article.

Samios, Zoe. "Hayu signals content expansion as Australia's average weekly streaming 'grows by 500%.'" *Mumbrella*, March 12, 2018. https://mumbrella.com.au/hayu-signals-content-expansion-australias-average-weekly-streaming-grows-500-504071.

Samios, Zoe. "Hayu 'to survive with big players.'" *The Australian*, June 24, 2019. 26.
Sconce, Jeffrey. "'Trashing' the Academy: Taste, Excess and an Emerging Politics of Cinematic Style." *Screen* 36, no. 4 (1995): 371– 393.
Smits, Roderik and E.W. Nikdel. "Beyond Netflix and Amazon: MUBI and the curation of on-demand." *Studies in European Cinema* 16, no. 1 (2019): 22–37.
Spangler, Todd. "Cinedigm Launches Dove Channel SVOD Service That Strips Out Sex, Drugs and Violence." *Variety*, September 16, 2015. https://variety.com/2015/digital/news/cinedigm-dove-channel-launch-1201595074/.
Squires, John. "Full Moon Launches Brand New Streaming App 'Full Moon Features.'" *Bloody Disgusting*, August 8, 2019. https://bloody-disgusting.com/movie/3577518/full-moon-launches-brand-new-streaming-app-full-moon-features/.
Strangelove, Michael. *Post-TV: Piracy, Cord-Cutting, and the Future of Television*. Toronto: University of Toronto Press, 2015.
Swords, Jon. "Crowd-patronage—intermediaries, geographies and relationships in patronage networks." *Poetics* 64 (2017): 63–73.
Tryon, Chuck. *On-Demand Culture: Digital Delivery and the Future of Movies*. New Jersey: Rutgers University Press, 2013.
Wayne, Michael L. "Netflix, Amazon, and branded television content in subscription video on-demand portals." *Media, Culture & Society* 40, no. 5 (2018): 725–741.

Disney+

Legacy Media Strikes Back

Jason Scott

The launch of Disney+, the video streaming service from the Walt Disney Company, has been noted as heralding the increased competition between the legacy media conglomerates, each including a Hollywood film studio and interests in television and a range of other media and businesses, and the market leading digital companies that have grown the market, particularly Netflix but also Amazon Prime Video. This essay will explore the significance of Disney+, to the conglomerate but also the evolving and contested streaming market. For Disney this encompasses the major change to the conglomerate's business model, with its reorganization emphasizing this new focus on the global direct-to-consumer market. Disney+ is the culmination of developments during the Bob Iger franchise era, most notably the acquisitions of Pixar, Marvel, Lucasfilm, Fox and BamTech.[1] The service also combines practices from the established subscription video streaming services with the company's strategies associated with its historic pre-eminence in home entertainment. Hence, Disney+ brings to streaming a combination of the legacy media companies' focus on content (particularly branded and franchised) coupled with distributor power, and the digital business model focused on data that enables personalization, aggregating taste cultures through an intuitive interface. Disney+ aims to disrupt the disruptors.

This continues Disney's longstanding focus on strategies of synergy, globalization, franchising as well as exploiting new technology and revenue streams, that underpinned the company's growth into a global media conglomerate in the 1990s and continued under the leadership of Iger.[2] Disney continues in the distribution business, renewing, extending and exploiting its intellectual property, yet it has also pivoted or morphed into a direct-to-consumer company, integrating its content streaming and content warehousing, its franchises and branded studios, into its global platform (or expansive walled garden, keeping customers within the Disney conglomerate ecosystem).[3] Kevin Mayer, who was the first chairman of the new Direct-to-Consumer and International division of Disney, identified "a fundamental shift in the marketplace and growing consumer demand for streaming services … a tremendous opportunity for [Disney] given the unparalleled strength of [its] brands" and intellectual property. He noted the "number of direct-to-consumer subscriptions globally, which is growing by 37% annually to top 800 million by the end of next year." Alongside these subscriber numbers, there was "significant rise in content consumption on these services. From a total of 20 million hours a day in 2010 to an expected 1.2 billion hours a day in 2020, that implies an annual growth rate of 50% per year over this 10-year period."[4] Significantly, this period of growth aligns with Netflix first demonstrating a viable market for subscription video streaming services, and its subsequent domination of the domestic market and global growth, particularly from 2016, as well as the period during which the Disney owned ad-supported streaming service Hulu was operating. Entering the global video streaming market thus constituted an opportunity for international growth for Disney, enabled by lower entry costs for digital products for new markets (that don't require significant staffing in each territory, nor shipping or warehousing costs). Competing with Netflix was also enticing given that Netflix had benefited from licensing Disney content, initially sublicensed from Starz Entertainment in 2008,[5] and then from 2012 with a direct deal that ran until 2018. Disney would now be able to fully exploit the value of its library via streaming, including access to the data generated by viewers of their content. Disney+ also followed Disney's previous attempts at developing its own proprietary video streaming service, in the form of transactional video on demand with Disney Movies Online, then Disney Movies Anywhere, and the United Kingdom trialed Disney Life subscription streaming service.

Theorizing the Discursive and Business Practices of Streaming Services

Several recent studies of video streaming services have shared a similar methodological approach, for instance a combination of political economy and discourse analysis.[6] In particular, applying discourse analysis to "keynote addresses, advertisements, P.R. initiatives, platform interfaces, social media accounts, and interviews with company executives" and "promotional materials, executive and talent interviews, and responses from trade presses and critics,"[7] "spokespeople," as well as "platform-produced texts."[8] This methodological allegiance may result from a growing interest in media industry studies, and the acknowledged influence of a paper advocating critical media industry studies,[9] or else subsequent co-authored work by its authors focused on streaming. This discursive focus is also found in work on HBO, around distinctions of quality,[10] which has influenced streaming services.[11]

I will follow this proposed

> critical media industry studies [that] examines the business culture of the media industries; how knowledge about texts, audiences, and the industry form, circulate, and change; and how they influence textual and industrial practices. Second ... how particular media texts arise from and reshape mid-level industrial practices.[12]

Significantly, I will adopt Barker and Brooks' conception of discourse analysis as structured investigation of language and how it embodies or refers "to wider social processes, conceptualisations, assumptions, ways of thinking." I also follow their focus on recurrent discourses, and caveats that such analysis should be transparent, productive (adding to our understanding), and defensible, that is substantiated (by triangulation).[13] In relation to the discourses around Disney+, then, I will prioritize "repetitions: discursive features which recurred, and particularly if they recurred in different contexts suggesting some independent force," for instance those carried from institutional discourses to publicity and critical responses; "connections: any feature which appeared linked or combined, with particular attention to trying to identify the nature of the link or connection," so the semantic fields mobilized around Disney+; and, amongst other features, distinctions; key concepts; and structural absences/omissions.[14] This essay will consider the micro level of the Disney+ interface and content, alongside "macro-level issues such as control, ownership, and integration."[15] So my focus will be the business model and strategies of the Disney company, how these are reflected and effected through discourses (press release, interviews, public statements), and practices at the levels of production/programming choices, platform interface, and promotional and publicity paratextual materials. A number of studies of subscription streaming services have combined, to various degrees, these twin perspectives, albeit with the particular lens of "political–economic perspective that emphasizes macrolevel structural issues" inflected by the technological or technological determinist, especially of Netflix as disruptor, or conversely of the dangers of big data.[16]

The focus on Netflix has nonetheless considered the changing nature of the company, with significant transitions from its origins as a DVD rental service, disrupting the Blockbuster business model, into primarily a streaming service from 2007, with focus on its recommendation algorithm, whereas from 2011 its focus was original content.[17] The company further shifted, into a global platform from 2016.[18] Within this evolution, scholars disagree about its driver of growth in subscribers, whether original content or personalization through its use of data, or both.[19] A Netflix blog identifies the company's business model with personalization "to maximize member satisfaction and month-to-month subscription retention."[20] Cox cites a Netflix document attributing their subscription surge in 2017 "fuelled by our original content slate," whilst conceding Autoplay and recommendation "maintain users with their ecosystem."[21]

Within the literature, a number of key concepts have been developed or applied to frame the growing significance and evolving nature of the streaming sector and Netflix. These might be categorized as concerning digital media and platforms, economic, adopted from accounts of premium television services, or specific to Netflix. So those accounts that prioritize the disruptive nature of streaming, particularly Netflix, or focus on the platform's self-framing, distinguish streaming services as portals or platforms, and develop data and algorithms as important to the company and other streaming services. Hence global, personalized "services like Netflix, Amazon Prime Video, and Hulu present themselves as 'portals' that act as generalized viewing platforms for subscribers."[22] Further stressing the technology and intermediary nature of platforms, Secular explores the companies responsible for constructing and maintaining these, including Bamtech who developed Disney+.[23] As he explains, a key feature of these technologies is the use of data, combined with algorithmic systems to provide a "personalized" service, through recommendation and other means, albeit balanced with wider popularity, "trending" or "popular," in interfaces.[24] In this respect algorithms are deemed "mechanisms of both distribution *and* valuation," and "pure new media," so distinct from previous subscription-based television.[25] Particularly in relation to Netflix, critical accounts question the projected benefits of their algorithms, which support an "illusion of plenitude and personalization," or the Netflix PR focus on taste clusters and personalized recommendation system aligned with "uniquely powerful data analytics."[26] Personalization is thus primarily a promotional discourse, and form of service branding.[27] Literature on Netflix therefore divides between those who recognize algorithmic culture and personalization as intrinsically significant to Netflix, including informing their production and releasing decisions,[28] or exaggerated by the company to distinguish their brand. Company accounts suggest the use of data and personalization/recommendation systems retains subscribers, or reduces marketing spend,[29] or in the case of Amazon Prime Video keeps subscribers within the Amazon ecosystem.[30] It is this privileged discourse of personalization, aligning data, algorithms and "auto-curation," across the video streaming sector, but most pronouncedly with Netflix's notion of taste cultures or clusters,[31] that warrants attention to the power of framing a discourse "that privileges specific ways of understanding the media and their place in people's lives."[32] One specific practice of Netflix that was purportedly motivated by data analytics, adopted by other streaming services, is the simultaneous release, "instant mode" or drop, of series with all episodes available at once, linked to the phenomenon of binge watching.[33]

In contrast, the (political) economic framing of streaming focuses on the business models, strategies, and corporate scope of "streaming media platforms as internationally scaled services with global user bases and financial interests stretching across territories."[34] The global reach of Netflix, particularly following its global "switch on" in 2016,[35] thus conforms to wider accounts of globalization. In this last respect, the growth in Netflix subscriber numbers has to be broken down into "domestic" U.S. (and Canada), early territories, and then from 2016 sudden massive scaling. This takes advantage of the economies of scale and scope, and affordances of digital globalization—reduced need for physical presence, reduced costs of logistics and distribution, but also deregulation around where profits are accounted for and hence taxes paid, as enjoyed by the FAANG U.S. digital technology giants. For Netflix, this resulted in 2019 subscriber numbers of 158.4 million, breaking down to "67.1M (million) subscribers in North America; 47.4M in Europe, the Middle East, and Africa; 29.4M in Latin America; and 14.5M in the Asia Pacific."[36] With subscriber growth slowed in the U.S., although with the "highest average monthly revenue per subscriber,"[37] Netflix not only presents itself as a global service, economically it is dependent on international markets for future growth (that in turn enables investment in Originals and licensed content).

With the increasing number of international, conglomerate funded streaming services, their differing business models have been considered, as well as whether the wider array of streamers are in competition or have complementary business models "as a result of different underlying industrial strategies" (and provide consumers complementary services).[38] So Petruska identifies the distinct business model for Prime Video, whilst Kompare distinguishes Hulu's ad-supported model, that "gathers users for their advertisers." Initial discussion of Disney+ and other "Netflix killers" "assert these services are quite different in aim and strategy and are building services to leverage an existing library of intellectual property."[39]

I will suggest a dual motivation, for Disney+, but possibly also for the other legacy media conglomerate streaming services, to exploit their content library, whilst also adding to its value, alongside the opportunity to grow a global, scalable digital business model. Furthermore, Disney+ shares strategies with the likes of Amazon, whose Prime Video is amongst benefits that "situate customers within its corporate ecosystem more fully, firmly and inescapably."[40] Similarly, Disney+, particularly with the company's longstanding strategy of synergy, aims to keep customers consuming within its ecosystem, or walled garden. Discussing CBS All Access, Johnson also distinguishes the franchise strategy for conglomerate IP Library streamers, associated with flagship productions and exclusivization. This "franchise strategy thus increases the value of library access to the parent series," and is a motive for "library series" revival. Quoting Cynthia Littleton, conglomerate streamers value programming for "how much it will contribute to the ... platform as part of a library of shows available en masse for years to come."[41] The franchise strategy links to Disney's established approach in cable using brands as a reliable means of "holding onto viewers, of ensuring that they watched in Disney's preferred (i.e., fully monetized) settings."[42] The Disney+ organization around its branded studios, and hence franchises such as *Star Wars* or those of the Marvel Cinematic Universe, correlates with the company's franchising strategy.

Scholarly accounts of Netflix, Hulu, and Amazon have stressed the notion of original productions, aligned with quality TV and exclusivity, albeit acknowledging HBO's earlier exploitation of these practices.[43] For Netflix, investment in Originals also follows from their competition for exclusive rights to programming with Showtime and HBO.[44] Santo suggests the institutional imperatives "continuously to attract new subscribers while keeping churn to a minimum" prompted original programming, for which they owned the rights, associated with discourses of quality and exclusivity, to differentiate the HBO brand. For Santo, following Lotz, this is concentrated on a few flagship programs, such as *The Sopranos*, but nonetheless balanced by the need to exploit syndication markets through recognizable (not too new) forms of television.[45] As Barker notes, like Netflix, and Hulu, Amazon invested in "original series production to supplement its growing library of licensed film and television content."[46]

The Mandalorian

As the (globally) exclusivized flagship series for the launch of Disney+, *The Mandalorian* was always going to be important to establishing the appeal of the service, beyond core Disney fans. Due to the impact of Covid-19, increasing interest in video streaming services whilst simultaneously delaying production and hence streaming of original and exclusive content, it has grown more significant, the key exemplar of must-watch

Disney+. Notably the Marvel series *The Falcon and the Winter Soldier,* planned for Disney+ for August 2020 and promoted in a Super Bowl ad, was delayed until March 2021. With standalone (cross-generational) appeal to non-fans of *Star Wars*, including for global markets where the franchise is less established, and high budget of $15 million an episode, the series has been designed as family friendly quality TV, an entry point into the saga.[47] Trade discourses, particularly responding to the opening episode, acknowledge the blend of novel and familiar, the look and feel of the *Star Wars* Universe, an "all-new story in the Star Wars universe," but again qualifying it as new, not too new.[48] "The Mandalorian is set after the fall of the Empire and before the emergence of the First Order." The series combines this wider appeal, and markers of quality, with fan interest generating buzz at events like Comic-Con, Celebration and D23. Its setting in the saga relates to the recent sequel trilogy, but more prominently the original trilogy (embodied in the parallels with the Mos Eisley Cantina). And it offers Easter Eggs for fans—the eponymous Mandalorian, (baby) Yoda, bounty hunters like IG11, an Ugnaught, his Blurrg mounts, the dark saber, and with Season 2 more prominent characters Ahsoka and Boba Fett.

The Mandalorian, then, combines the renewal of franchise intellectual property, in the form of flagship quality television, to engage new subscribers, and with both the *Disney Gallery: The Mandalorian* behind the scenes series and upcoming season 2 aims to reduce churn and maintain subscribers.[49] Its staggered, weekly release, maintained with *Disney Gallery*, also discouraged churn, by limiting binge viewing and cancellation, similarly to the cessation of free trials of Disney+ coinciding with *Hamilton*. This is dependent on a framing discourse of quality, combined with exclusivity, live-action *Star Wars* television for all, and from one of the five branded studios of the service. This goal for Disney+, with flagship and exclusive content, is outlined by CEO Robert Chapek: "one of the biggest things in terms of subscriber acquisition is having new hot tentpole content to bring to the service," but aligning with Johnson's account he adds, "new content tends to bring in new subscribers, but catalog increases engagement and helps us retain subscribers."[50] Combining these goals, in a way that is repeated across Disney+, *The Mandalorian* offers must-see viewing whilst also adding value, through guiding viewers to other *Star Wars* content on the service including the films but also animated series: the "franchise strategy thus increases the value of library access to the parent series" and other iterations.[51]

Quality television has been identified with "authorial freedom," "lattitude to tell stories differently … without having to compromise," and "smart writing, compelling stories told in an innovative way, high production values and a unique creative vision behind each project."[52] With the caveat that quality television is discursively framed, by promotional discourses stressing creativity and vision, commonly around the showrunner and their freedom or autonomy provided by a brand like HBO or Netflix,[53] *The Mandalorian* adheres to this, despite differing from the more adult themed and edgy quality TV of HBO such as *The Sopranos* or *Game of Thrones*. It nonetheless follows a cycle of fantasy/horror/sci-fi series, particularly sci-fi adaptations, as original and exclusive series for streaming services such as *The Man in the High Castle* (Amazon Prime Video) or *The Handmaid's Tale* (Hulu), that have been "increasing[ly] dominant" in quality television.[54] Whilst *The Mandalorian* deviates with its family-friendly focus, it combines "never-ending or continuous themes or plotlines within series that rely on self-contained episodes," and "the producer's successful negotiation" of the genre and quality TV format through "character development, structural complexity, reflexivity, [and] aesthetic innovation."[55] To demonstrate the discursive positioning of *The Mandalorian* as quality TV, and consequently the framing of the Disney+ service as having potential opportunities for creatives, and with that a notion of plusness, it is necessary to interrogate the paratexts used to discursively frame the series, for fans, or within trade and popular publications.

Most prominently, the creative autonomy of showrunner Jon Favreau, as writer, with "latitude" to tell a different kind of story, is stressed by Favreau both in relation to long form storytelling, but particularly in the context of freedom in the relationship with Disney to override the merchandising potential of "Baby Yoda" to keep this as a revelation in the series. Alongside this, the delegated creative autonomy and collaboration by the directors of each "chapter" [episode] is stressed in the *Disney Gallery* spin-off. This might equally result from the positioning of Lucasfilm (alongside Marvel Studios, Pixar and Walt Disney Animation studios after the Pixar acquisition) as having creative autonomy—particularly for directors—valorized by Robert Iger in repeated annual reports that position these as creative engines.[56]

Aesthetic innovation in the series has been more widely promoted and recognized, as successfully recreating the *Star Wars* universe for live-action television, particularly through the use of new technologies, albeit alongside practical effects, puppets, and miniatures with motion-control that align with the tradition in *Star Wars* films. The blend of these with StageCraft, ILM's new production technology combining the Unreal game engine with real time effects, including virtual lighting of location shot material and the cast in the volume, was widely publicized, initially in specialist sources and then in the *Disney Gallery*. Wider recognition of high production values for the series came with Emmy wins for cinematography, production design, sound editing, sound mixing, and visual effects. Furthermore, nominations in a number of categories including Outstanding Drama suggest the series won critical and industry acclaim beyond technical contributions.

Casting for the series could also be read as positioning the series in relation to established quality TV, notably Giancarlo Esposito as Moff Gideon (best known from *Breaking Bad*), as well as Pedro Pascal's previous role in *Game of Thrones*. Alongside the generically hybrid mix of the Western and sci-fi, this suggests morally grey, if not necessarily complex, characters (and follows on from the lawless Outer Rim setting, and intertextual links to the Mos Eisley cantina). Chapter headings such as "The Gunslinger," "The Prisoner," "The Reckoning" and "Redemption" also evoke earlier generic influences signaled in the media kit: "we follow the travails of a lone gunfighter in the outer reaches of the galaxy." In animation, Executive Producer Filoni has directed a generically hybrid *Star Wars*. The *Seven Samurai* set-up of "The Sanctuary" episode previously featured in *Clone Wars* Season 2 episode 17 "Bounty Hunters." Favreau also situates the series in relation to the Saga, departing from the focus of the films, but as a continuation "draw[n] from all over Star Wars." Alongside new stories (in a new medium and format) from the *Star Wars* universe, much of the focus of official materials has been creativity, storytelling, and the energy or passion of those producing the series. Favreau has noted new "opportunities" with streaming "able to tell a story on a scale and in chapters" [only possible] "in this format," with the chance to "explore these characters beyond" the program later.[57] Yet economically, *The Mandalorian* continues Iger's franchise strategy of content streaming—as noted in terms of behind the scenes programming, but also animated spin-offs. Disney+ transposes this franchise and brand focus, as a reliable means of "holding onto viewers,"[58] but can still participate in Disney's wider synergies, with coordinated releasing of *The Mandalorian* just prior to *Star Wars: The Rise of Skywalker*, or for instance the platform "makeover" of all *Star Wars* content to celebrate May 4.

"Exclusive Disney+ Originals"

As noted *The Mandalorian* led the roll-out of Disney+, signaling the quality as well as exclusivity of Disney+ originals. This exemplified the company's approach to exclusivity:

> "We have to take our content and make it as exclusive as we can to our service.... Ultimately our direct-to-consumer service is going to be the only place you can find that content."[59]

The lesson from Disney Life, which lacked exclusivity of content due to licensing Disney films on Sky,[60] was to focus on exclusivity, and with *The Mandalorian* not available in any other form (syndication to cable or broadcast, release on Blu-ray), this suggests a strict exclusivity at least for the flagship *Mandalorian*, and other originals, not simply exclusive to SVOD or first pay window. This contrasts with the flexible exclusivity of Netflix with Blu-ray or DVD releases of *The Irishman* or *Roma*, Amazon's release of *Annihilation*, and the syndication/partner model of HBO (which pioneered the strategy of exclusivity).[61] It also contrasts territorially limited exclusivization in the case of *Star Trek: Discovery*, although Netflix's licensing of non–U.S. rights "paid for" the production costs of that series.[62] Whether this strict exclusivity, at least for the originals, will continue is moot, but Disney has clearly chosen to invest more in exclusive content, particularly from its branded studios Disney, Marvel Studios, Pixar, *Star Wars* and National Geographic, but also DisneyNature. Disney has even more reason to maintain exclusivity, at least as it grows its global subscriber base and manages churn, to bolster its walled garden of magical content. Hence, to "elevate the experience and enhance the value to consumers" Iger promised a "constant pipeline of exclusive new content."[63] This informed the plan for the "first year over 30 exclusive original series and over 15 exclusive original movies and specials produced by the Company's film and television studios."[64] Whilst the delays to production caused by Covid-19 impacted this, original content on launch, like *Lady and the Tramp*, has been shored up by rerouting presold films as originals: *Artemis Fowl* and *Hamilton* were "more watched in July than anything on Netflix."[65] However, the majority of originals for the service conformed more closely to the Disney brand, "true to the values of what a Disney live-action film offers" as Sean Bailey WD Studio outlined a space for "holiday comedies, kid-centric capers and true-life adventures" now excluded from theatrical release,[66] which would encompass *Noelle*, *Timmy Failure*, *Stargirl*, and *Togo*, and continue the strategy of Disney Channel original movies. Hence, besides the few flagship titles from Lucasfilm and Marvel Studios, the majority of original scripted content comprised adaptations and reimaginings that fit, but also renew the Disney brand amongst "original movies, TV shows, short-form content and other Disney-branded exclusives."[67]

Disney has spent $24 billion on originals (for Disney+, Hulu, and ESPN+), responding to Netflix's increasing annual investment in original productions that "has skyrocketed from $2.4B (billion) in 2013 to $5B in 2015, $9B in 2017, $12B in 2018, and $15B in 2019."[68] Netflix content chief Spangler says 85 percent of new spending is on originals, resulting in 371 new television shows and movies in 2019, a 55 percent increase over its output of 240 in 2018.[69] Whilst Netflix's original production is more global in scope, with focus on a number of localized productions, the service is still identified with isolated flagships like *The Crown* or slightly cheaper *Stranger Things*.[70] Disney, like the other conglomerates entering streaming, in contrast promotes a degree of exclusivity around its library. Most notably, the Disney Vault, "the entire 13 film signature collection will all be available on day 1 of the U.S. launch of Disney+."[71] This emulated Disney Life, that previously made the iconic animated features available without temporal restriction, ending the practice of limited release periods for the films on VHS, DVD and Blu-ray, "under the 'Classic Movies' banner on the home screen of the app—we're not moving those off."[72] Disney also heralded the exclusive (SVOD) nature of *Captain Marvel* and subsequent Marvel films, and Jennifer Lee noted "Disney+ will also be the exclusive home of Frozen 2 by the summer of 2020 following its theatrical and traditional home entertainment releases."[73]

The Mandalorian is not only exclusive, bringing the *Star Wars* Universe to television, with a discourse of differentiation around cinematic production values, but as noted also linked to new long form storytelling for branded IP, by Favreau as well as Kathleen Kennedy. Kennedy closely paralleled Marvel's Kevin Feige on the new opportunity Disney+ offered Lucasfilm and Marvel respectively (in a discourse that might be seen as aimed dually at fans of those branded studios' films, but also within Disney, stressing the contribution they could make to the service with their creative cultures and evergreen, global IP). In this respect Disney+ further develops content streaming, around transmedia and the recent trend for fan-oriented programs accompanying quality TV.

Plussing Disney

As well as renewing Disney titles, Disney+ also promised expansion of the Marvel and Lucasfilm storyworlds in new forms, as well as new shorts and non-fiction series from Pixar and Walt Disney Animation. For Marvel the (planned) expanded transmediality was the opportunity offered by Disney+: for the MCU "it is growing it, it is expanding it" and "bring[ing] together the MCU into one place," said Feige.[74] Again with antecedents in home entertainment, where Marvel's Cinematic Universe expanded, in the form of value-added exclusive content, in the Marvel One Shots on Blu-ray. Now, rather than motivating the purchase of a Blu-ray disk, Marvel's exclusive transmedial content will encourage subscription. Delayed by Covid-19, Feige's plan for Marvel, like Favreau's, is "to tell new longform stories in ways that we've never done before." But distinctly providing "major storylines set in the MCU with ramifications that will be felt both through the other Disney+ we're producing and our features on the big screen."[75] This notably distinguishes these plans from the earlier largely one-way transmedia links between the MCU and *Agents of Shield*, and likewise suggests parity between the television series and films in terms of canonical status. Hence, audiences would "meet" *Ms. Marvel* on Disney+, before MCU movies, whilst *WandaVision* would lead to events in *Doctor Strange in the Multiverse of Madness*, thus developing the franchise strategy to motivate subscription for the "television" component and encourage, as well as cross-promote, theatrical box-office. This notion of Disney+ enabling extension and expansion of storyworlds, through new formats, was echoed by Kathleen Kennedy, to "continue to expand the *Star Wars* universe." Similarly, Walt Disney Animation and Pixar were also linked to the idea of extension, in new forms. Both character extension, to "extend our stories with characters our audiences know and love," as well as original animated shorts to "explore new types of storytelling and animation with emerging filmmakers and show it all exclusively on Disney+."[76] For Pixar extension was planned with *Monsters at Work* and the Bo-Peep short *Lamp Life*, but from day one comprised shorts, the "Forky Asks a Question" lo-fi series a spin-off around the character introduced in *Toy Story 4*.

Alongside these extensions, Disney+ also continued the company's focus on value-added content, the supplementary materials and extensions previously offering hybrid consumption or industrial intertextuality through the *Disneyland* television series in the 1950s, the Disney Channel and video from New Disney, and each subsequent iteration of Disney branded home entertainment, through to Disney Life with "shorts, extras and spin-offs, some not available anywhere else."[77] Parallel to Marvel's development from One Shots on Blu-ray and transmedia storytelling with ABC's *Agents of S.H.I.E.L.D.* and *Agent Carter* transferring onto the platform, the Disney Home Entertainment focus on value-added content, which differentiated special edition VHS, Laser Disc, Blu-ray, and Disney Movies Anywhere, now gathered together inhouse, lower budget "unscripted" behind the scenes programs on Disney+. The focus remained on flagship behind-the-scenes content, "to bring you exclusive content you can't see anywhere else," most notably *Disney Gallery: Behind the Mandalorian*, and *Into the Unknown Making Frozen 2* that "showcases our collaborative environment in a way we have never shared before,"[78] as well as the documentary on *Hamilton*, "Hamilton: History Has Its Eyes on You," featuring the ABC *Good Morning America* presenter Robin Roberts interviewing the cast. This exclusive value-added content also includes National Geographic's *Magic of the Animal Kingdom*, shot at Disney's Animal Kingdom and Epcot Seabase

Aquarium, and series like *The Imagineering Story, Disney Insider* and *One Day at Disney,* further suggesting the continued hybrid consumption and transparent synergies with the wider Disney ecosystem. Topical inclusion of a repurposed ABC Special, "Chadwick Boseman: A Tribute of a King" or "The Undefeated Present Hamilton in Depth," partnered with this ESPN initiative suggests Disney+ will draw content from other Disney subsidiaries, and can relax its exclusivity for content shared with these.

New Business Model

Disney+ and the Disney's Direct-to-consumer and International division (with its global remit), marked "an entirely new growth strategy for the Company, one that takes advantage of the incredible opportunity that changing technology provides us to leverage the strength of our great brands."[79] Thus, the platform as megabrand becomes a conduit of compelling experiences straight to its global subscribers. The more marked difference from the Disney and Pixar focused homegrown Disney Life service trialed in the UK is the Disney+ aggregation "Disney+ = Disney + Pixar + Marvel + Star Wars + National Geographic," one dimension of plusness. Each brand is claimed to "attract a 4-quadrant audience, adults and children, males and females" across generations and geographies, and to contribute to the "ever-growing slate of original content … as well as recently released films and iconic content from our extensive libraries."[80]

This aggregation of branded studios and the mutually revaluating relationship of original and library content are embodied in the platform interface: beneath a carousel of emerging titles, the central "brand tiles … showcase the very best of that particular brand." The Marvel "iconic comic book flip" leads to an "epic collection that includes Captain Marvel … at launch." Each title page provides "trailers, extras and behind-the-scenes footage."[81] So value-added content is built into the interface, one means for continuing the experience. The design and many features of the Disney+ interface, not markedly different from other streaming services, are themed around the Disney brands and characters, and stress a family friendly set-up—avatar/profiles for family members and parental controls, as well as anytime/anywhere, multiple users with downloadable content. Besides privileging Disney+ originals, the "recommended for you" section, and "browse by brand, by genre or in any other curated collection," the sequencing of titles on the interface is personalized, based on "individual's unique viewing history," emulating Netflix. Thus Bamtech's "data analytic tools and deep machine learning allows us to better serve consumers by delivering a highly personalized experience."[82] The Disney Plus privacy policy terms and conditions similarly link data collection to "personalize[d] content and experiences." Yet Bamtech is notably described by the company as using "consumer data to provide a better user experience, while giving us the ability to grow revenue and increase the effectiveness of our digital marketing efforts."[83]

However, Iger contrasts Disney+ with the algorithm-led, established streaming services of Netflix and Amazon Prime Video, and emerging services from other legacy media conglomerates, with its "treasure trove of long-lasting valuable content.... The Disney+ platform is being built on that foundation, one that no other content or technology company can rival."[84] Foregrounding the continuing strategy of content warehousing, with 7500 series and 500 movies from the "Company's library,"[85] he further elucidates Disney's historical tradition of success in home entertainment, in relation to evergreen content creating value. Iger notes the "evergreen appeal" of *Snow White* or *Cinderella*, "designed to entertain people of all ages. And they're still entertaining people today, passed on from generation to generation to generation, because they hold their relevance, having touched audiences in profound, heartfelt and deeply entertaining ways." He further elaborates the logic of Disney "Plus": "Pixar, Marvel and Star Wars films share that same powerful characteristic, and they're all going to populate Disney+. Now we will of course augment those treasures with an array of quality storytelling from our strong, successful, creative engines and an unprecedented collection of talent." So Disney+ is founded on the library of evergreen content, combined with these creative engines to produce a pipeline of exclusive, quality content.[86] Again, this discourse of quality storytelling, and the evergreen qualities of the Disney library, recur in the welcome page for the desktop version of Disney+ "From hit movies to timeless classics and new originals—there's something for everyone." Likewise, the promotion for Disney+ heralds "The greatest stories, all in one place" illustrated with characters from the branded studios: Iron Man, Woody, Kylo Ren and Elsa.

Disney+ then also reflects Iger's focus "to create great content and to distribute it in innovative ways."[87] The three key strategies during the Iger era, creativity, technology and global expansion, are encapsulated in the new corporate strategy "to deliver the highest quality branded entertainment franchises on all relevant platforms, employing the most effective technology in service of our customers around the world."[88] They are also reflected in the company vision, that valorizes "the power of unparalleled storytelling, reflecting the iconic brands, creative minds and innovative technologies that make ours the world's premier entertainment company."[89]

Disrupting the disruptors, "after watching Netflix build an empire in part on the back of Disney's own library, it's striking back."[90] On terminating its deal with Netflix, Disney set out "to take back control of our content."[91] Adapting the digital business model—data, personalization, aggregating taste cultures, through an intuitive interface—but incorporating its integrated legacy media conglomerate model: synergy, quality, renewing/revaluating its library, and hybrid consumption. The resulting digital integrated service, conglomerate Disney 2.0 "transition[ed] from traditional distribution models into the walled garden of direct-to-consumer services."[92]

Significantly "Disney+ is obviously a global product with universal appeal" said Mayer, achieved through Bamtech's scalable infrastructure, and bolstered with the acquisition of 21st Century Fox and the Hotstar service in India.[93] The company expects "between 60 million and 90 million subscribers around the world by the end of fiscal 2024," with ⅓ from the U.S. and ⅔ international.[94] Initial figures suggest this target is modest, as subscribers hit 60.5 million by September 2020. This successful growth of subscriber numbers is also associated with the four "quadrant appeal of our brands."[95]

But enticing these global subscribers is part of the business model. "Disney+ provides viewers of all ages, an unrivaled living, breathing ecosystem of content. Through Disney+, subscribers will deepen their relationships with our beloved characters and worlds, while forging new connections to new worlds brought to life on the service." With this "ecosystem of storytelling founded on talent, wanting to tell their stories, using our IP, characters and brands."[96] It is the synergistic benefits of this ecosystem, or walled garden, that motivate Disney+, with average revenue per family held as more important than average revenue per subscription, paralleling the Amazon ecosystem.[97]

Disney+ synergizes the strategies of content streaming and content warehousing, from its franchises, Disney Vault and branded studios, into its proprietary global platform—an expansive walled garden, keeping customers within the Disney conglomerate ecosystem through hybrid consumption. Viewers may engage with the platform, with the value-added content that underpinned the DVD. Or they may experience coordinated and expanded transmediality between the service and the theatrical box-office, as through Marvel's plans of coordinated and scheduled tie-ins of *WandaVision* with the *Doctor Strange* sequel, or around *Ms Marvel*. Or when necessary, they company can create or reroute presold films as original content, as with *Lady and the Tramp*, *Stargirl*, *Artemis Fowl*, and *Hamilton*, to build subscribers and reduce churn through a "constant pipeline of exclusive new content."[98]

Notes

1. See Jason Scott 'Disney+ : It all adds up,' *In Media Res*, 15 March 2020 at: http://mediacommons.org/imr/content/disney-it-all-adds.
2. See Jason Scott "Disneyizing Home Entertainment Distribution," in *DVD, Blu-ray*

and Beyond eds. Jonathan Wroot & Andy Willis (Cham, Switzerland: Palgrave Macmillan, 2017), 15–33.

3. On Streaming Services as an enclosed ecosystem, or keeping customers within the parent company ecosystem, on Netflix see Christopher Cox, "Programming—Flow in the convergence of digital media platforms and television," *Critical Studies in Television*, 13, no. 4 (2018): 449. On Amazon see Karen Petruska, "Amazon Prime Video: Where Information is Entertainment" in *From Networks to Netflix*, ed. Derek Johnson (Oxford & New York: Routledge, 2018): 358. On Netflix, Amazon, Apple, Disney and Comcast see Gary R. Edgerton, "Silicon Valley + Hollywood = Convergence 2.0," 31 Jan. (2020), https://cstonline.net/silicon-valley-hollywood-convergence-2-0-by-gary-r-edgerton/.

4. Disney, "Disney Investor Day webcast," 11 April 2019, https://thewaltdisneycompany.com/the-walt-disney-companys-2019-investor-day-webcast/. These figures align with those for domestic and international growth for online video subscriptions given in the MPAA Annual Report for 2019.

5. Edward Jay Epstein, "Why Netflix Won't Be the HBO of the 21st Century," *The Gawker*, 15 February 2010, https://gawker.com/5471943/why-netflix-wont-be-the-hbo-of-the-21st-century?skyline=true&s=i.

6. Evan Elkins, "Algorithmic cosmopolitanism: on the global claims of digital entertainment platforms," *Critical Studies in Media Communication*, 36 no. 4 (2019); Chuck Tryon, "TV Got Better: Netflix's Original Programming Strategies and Binge Viewing," *Media Industries Journal* 2(2) (2015); Cory Barker, "'Great Shows, Thanks to You': From Participatory Culture to 'Quality TV' in Amazon's Pilot Season," *Television & New Media*, 18, no. 5 (2017).

7. Elkins, "Algorithmic cosmopolitanism," 377; Barker, "Great Shows," 441.

8. Elkins, "Algorithmic cosmopolitanism," 377,378.

9. Timothy Havens, Amanda D. Lotz & Serra Tinic, "Critical Media Industry Studies: A Research Approach," *Communication, Culture & Critique*, 2 (2009).

10. Applying notions from Pierre Bourdieu, Avi Santo, "Para-television and discourses of distinction: The culture of production at HBO," in *It's not TV: watching HBO in the post-television era*, eds. Cara Louise Buckley, Marc Leverette and Brian L. Ott (London, New York: Routledge, 2008). See also Janet McCabe and Kim Akass "It's not tv, it's HBO's original programming," in Cara Louise Buckley, Marc Leverette and Brian L. Ott, *It's Not TV.*

11. Daniel Herbert, Amanda D Lotz and Lee Marshall, "Approaching Media Industries comparatively: A case study of streaming," *International Journal of Cultural Studies* 22(3) (2019): 355.

12. Havens, Lotz & Tinic, "Critical Media Industry Studies," 237.

13. Barker, Martin and Kate Brooks, *Knowing Audiences: Judge Dredd, its friends, fans and foes* (Luton: University of Luton Press, 1998), 117–8.

14. Barker and Brooks, *Knowing Audiences*, 52.

15. Amanda D. Lotz, Ramon Lobato, and Julian Thomas, "Internet-Distributed Television Research: A Provocation," *Media Industries* 5(2) (2018).

16. Havens, Lotz, & Tinic, "Critical Media Industry Studies," 234.

17. Tryon, "TV Got Better," 108; Amanda D. Lotz, "Netflix dossier" March (2017), https://www.global-internet-tv.com/netflix-country-reports/united-states/; Edgerton "Silicon Valley" dates Original content to 2013.

18. Ramon Lobato, *Netflix Nations: The Geography of Digital Distribution* (New York: New York University Press, 2019); Elkins "Algorithmic cosmopolitanism"; also Edgerton "Silicon Valley."

19. Content as factor: Cox "Programming," 445. Data: Elkins, "Algorithmic cosmopolitanism"; Blake Hallinan and Ted Striphas, "Recommended for you: The Netflix Prize and the production of algorithmic culture," *new media & society* Vol. 18(1) (2016); Edgerton, "Silicon Valley." Both data and content: Timothy Havens, "Netflix: Streaming Channel Brands as Global Meaning Systems," in Derek Johnson, *From Networks to Netflix.*

20. Xavier Amatriain and Justin Basilico, "Netflix Recommendations: Beyond the 5 stars (Part 1)," *Netflix Technology Blog*, 6 Apr 2012, https://netflixtechblog.com/netflix- recommendations-beyond-the-5-stars-part-1-55838468f429.

21. Cox, "Programming," 445, 449.
22. Michael L. Wayne, "Global Portals in National Markets: Branding Netflix in Israel," *Cinema and Media Studies*, 59 (3) (Spring 2020): 149.
23. Steven Secular, "Games without Frontiers: Streaming Sports and the Evolution of Digital Intermediaries," *Media Industries* 5(2) (2018), https://quod.lib.umich.edu/m/mij/15031809.0005.209/--games-without-frontiers-streaming-sports-and-the-evolution?rgn=main;view=fulltext
24. David Hesmondhalgh and Amanda D. Lotz, "Video Screen Interfaces as New Sites of Media Circulation," *International Journal of Communication* 14 (2020), http://ijoc.org; Elkins, "Algorithmic cosmopolitanism"; Hallinan and Striphas, "Recommended"; Edgerton, "Silicon Valley"; Daniel Chamberlain, "Television Interfaces," *Journal of Popular Film and Television*, Summer (2010); Secular "Games."
25. T Gillespie, "#trendingistrending: When algorithms become culture," in *Algorithmic cultures: Essays on meaning, performance, and new technologies*, eds. R. Seyfert & J. Roberge (New York, NY: Routledge, 2016), 53; Lobato, *Netflix Nations*, 43.
26. Tryon, "TV Got Better"; Elkins, "Algorithmic cosmopolitanism," 383.
27. Havens, "Netflix."
28. Hallinan and Striphas, "Recommended."
29. Cox, "Programming"; Mattias Frey, "The Internet Suggests: Film, Recommender Systems, and Cultural Mediation," *Journal of Cinema and Media Studies*, 59, no. 1 (2019).
30. Petruska, "Amazon Prime Video."
31. Havens, "Netflix"; Elkins, "Algorithmic cosmopolitanism."
32. Havens, Lotz & Tinic, "Critical Media Industry Studies."
33. Hallinan and Striphas, "Recommended," 129; Tryon, "TV Got Better," 106; Cox, "Programming," 450; Herbert, Lotz and Marshall "Approaching Media Industries"; on Amazon see Barker, "Great Shows."
34. Elkins, "Algorithmic cosmopolitanism"; also Havens, "Netflix"; Ramon Lobato and Amanda Lotz, "Imagining Global Video: The Challenge of Netflix," *Cinema and Media Studies* Spring 2020, 59 (3); Herbert, Lotz and Marshall "Approaching Media Industries."
35. Lobato, *Netflix Nations*.
36. Edgerton, "Silicon Valley" citing Natalie Jarvey, "Netflix Under Pressure," *Hollywood Reporter*. 7 August 2019.
37. Natalie Jarvey, "Netflix's Subscriber Growth Story: Focus Overseas: Asia Pacific is the streamer's fastest-growing region," *Hollywood Reporter*, Dec 19, Vol. 425 Issue 42, 2019.
38. Lotz, Lobato and Thomas, "Internet-Distributed Television," 39.
39. Petruska, "Amazon Prime Video"; Derek Kompare, "Adverstreaming: Hulu Plus," *Flow*, 24 Feb 2020; Lobato and Lotz, "Imagining Global Video"; Lotz, Lobato and Thomas, "Internet-Distributed Television."
40. Petruska, "Amazon Prime Video," 358.
41. Derek Johnson, "CBS All Access: To boldly franchise where no one has subscribed before," in *From Networks to Netflix*, ed. Derek Johnson (2018), 398, 399.
42. Kyra Hunting and Jonathan Gray, "Disney Junior: Imagining Industrial Intertextuality" in *From Networks to Netflix*, ed. Derek Johnson (2018).
43. Barker, "Great Shows."
44. Tryon, "TV Got Better."
45. Santo, "Para-television," 20, 31,19; see also Epstein, "Why Netflix Won't."
46. Barker, "Great Shows," 441.
47. Maureen Ryan and Cynthia Littleton, "TV Series Budgets Hit the Breaking Point as Costs Skyrocket in Peak TV Era," *Variety* 26 Sep (2017), https://variety.com/2017/tv/news/tv-series-budgets-costs-rising-peak-tv-1202570158/.
48. Daniel Fienberg, "The 'Plus TV' Era Is Upon Us," *Hollywood Reporter*, 20 Nov., Vol. 425, Issue 38 (2019).
49. Johnson "CBS All Access," 396.
50. Disney, "Walt Disney Q3 FY20 Earnings Conference Call," 4 August (2020), https://thewaltdisneycompany.com/app/uploads/2020/08/q3-fy20-earnings-transcript.pdf.
51. Johnson, "CBS All Access," 398.

52. McCabe and Akass, "It's not tv," 87, 89.
53. Santo "Para-television"; McCabe and Akass "It's not tv"; Barker "Great Shows," 450.
54. D. Hassler-Forest, "*Game of Thrones*: The Politics of World-Building and the Cultural Logic of Gentrification," in *The politics of adaptation: media convergence and ideology*, eds. Hassler-Forest, D. & Nicklas, P. (Basingstoke: Palgrave Macmillan 2015), 189–190.
55. Santo, "Para-television," 29; Hassler-Forest, "*Game of Thrones*," 189–190.
56. Disney, Annual Report (2015) Pixar, Marvel and Lucasfilm identified with "creative energy"; Disney, Annual Report (2013) a "creative resurgence" from Pixar; Disney, Annual Report (2012) acquisitions generated "creative potential" across company.
57. Disney, "Disney Investor Day webcast"; Carolyn Giardina, "Whatever You Imagine, You Can Bring to Audiences," *Hollywood Reporter*, 4 Dec., Vol. 425, Issue 40 (2019).
58. Hunting and Gray, "Disney Junior," 3.
59. Mayer in Natalie, Jarvey, "The Deal Closing Still Keeps Me Up at Night," *Hollywood Reporter*, Vol. 424, Issue 41, 2019.
60. Disney, "question and answer session held by The Walt Disney Company on December 14, 2017," (2017) https://www.sec.gov/Archives/edgar/data/1308161/000095015717001616/form425.htm.
61. Santo, "Para-television."
62. Elaine Low, "Netflix 'Star Trek' Deal Helps CBS Chief Les Moonves Sleep At Night." *Investors Business Daily*, 20 September (2016).
63. Daniel Frankel, "Battling Netflix Won't Be Cheap for Disney+," *Multichannel News*, Nov. 26, Vol. 35, Issue 25 (2018), 22.
64. Disney, Annual Report (2019).
65. Scott Mendelson, "These Smaller-Scale Movies Are Putting The 'Plus' In Disney+." *Forbes.com*, 18 August (2020) https://www.forbes.com/sites/scottmendelson/2020/08/18/great-movies-on-disney-plus-mulan-magic-camp-one-and-only-ivan-hamilton-stargirl-beyonce/#6b66f4113c1c.
66. Disney, "Disney Investor Day webcast."
67. Disney, "The Walt Disney Company to Acquire Majority Ownership of BAMTech" 8 August (2017), https://thewaltdisneycompany.com/walt-disney-company-acquire-majority-ownership-bamtech/.
68. Max Löffler, "Netflix's Global Reach: By the Numbers," *Hollywood Reporter*, August 2019: 63; Jarvey, "Netflix Under Pressure," 52; in Edgerton, "Silicon Valley."
69. Melody Hahm, "Eye-Popping Chart Shows How Much Original Content Netflix Is Creating," *Yahoo Finance*. 17 December 2019. https://finance.yahoo.com/news/netflix-original-content-disney-and-apple-plus-230418533.html; Edgerton, "Silicon Valley."
70. Havens, "Netflix," 330; Ryan & Littleton "TV Series Budgets."
71. Disney, "Disney Investor Day webcast."
72. Matt Kamen "DisneyLife aims to be Disney's all-in-one streaming platform," *Wired*, 6 Jan (2016), https://www.wired.co.uk/article/disney-life-interview; Scott, "Disneyizing Home Entertainment," 19.
73. Disney, "Disney Investor Day webcast."
74. Disney, "Disney Investor Day webcast."
75. Disney, 2020; Kevin Fiege, Disney, "Disney Investor Day webcast."
76. Kennedy and Jennifer Lee, in Disney, "Disney Investor Day webcast."
77. Kamen, "DisneyLife."
78. Jennifer Lee, in Disney, "Disney Investor Day webcast."
79. Iger, in Disney, "The Walt Disney Company to Acquire Majority Ownership of BAMTech."
80. Mayer, in Disney, "Disney Investor Day webcast."
81. Mayer, in Disney, "Disney Investor Day webcast."
82. Michael Paull, President of Disney Streaming Services, in Disney, "Disney Investor Day webcast."
83. Disney. "Quarterly 4 FY17 Investor Conference Call," 9 Nov. (2017), https://thewaltdisneycompany.com/app/uploads/q4-fy17-earnings-transcript.pdf.
84. Iger, in Disney "Disney Investor Day webcast."

85. Iger, in Disney, Annual Report (2019).
86. Iger, in Disney "Disney Investor Day webcast."
87. Iger, in Disney "Disney Investor Day webcast."
88. Iger, in Disney "Disney Investor Day webcast."
89. https://thewaltdisneycompany.com/about/.
90. Steven Zeitchik, "Three big questions Disney+ streaming presentation will address." *Washington Post*, 10 Apr. (2019).
91. Disney, "question and answer session."
92. Cynthia Littleton, "A Stream Of Questions," *Variety*, 29 Jan., Vol. 342, Issue 17 (2019).
93. Disney, "Disney Investor Day webcast."
94. Disney, "Disney Investor Day webcast."
95. Rebecca Campbell, Chairman of Walt Disney Direct-to-Consumer and International, in Disney, "Disney Plus Continues International Expansion," 15 Sept (2020) https://dtcimedia.disney.com/news/disney-plus-continues-international-expansion; Disney, "Walt Disney Company (DIS) Q1 2020 Earnings Call Transcript," 28 Oct. (2019), https://www.fool.com/earnings/call-transcripts/2020/02/04/walt-disney-company-dis-q1-2020-earnings-call-tran.aspx.
96. Agnes Chu, in Disney "Disney Investor Day webcast."
97. Matthew Ball, "Nine Reasons Why Disney+ Will Succeed (And Why Four Criticisms are Overhyped)," 17 March (2019), https://redef.com/original/nine-reasons-why-disney-will-succeed-and-why-four-criticisms-are-overhyped+&cd=1&hl=en&ct=clnk&gl=uk.
98. Iger, in Frankel, "Battling Netflix."

Works Cited

Amatriain, Xavier, and Justin Basilico. "Netflix Recommendations: Beyond the 5 stars (Part 1)," *Netflix Technology Blog*, 6 Apr 2012, accessed October 14, 2020 https://netflixtechblog.com/netflix-recommendations-beyond-the-5-stars-part-1-55838468f429.

Ball, Matthew. "Nine Reasons Why Disney+ Will Succeed (And Why Four Criticisms are Overhyped)," 17 March (2019), https://redef.com/original/nine-reasons-why-disney-will-succeed-and-why-four-criticisms-are-overhyped+&cd=1&hl=en&ct=clnk&gl=uk.

Barker, Cory. "'Great Shows, Thanks to You': From Participatory Culture to 'Quality TV' in Amazon's Pilot Season." *Television & New Media*, 18, no. 5 (2017): 441–458.

Barker, Martin, and Kate Brooks, *Knowing Audiences:* Judge Dredd, *Its Friends, Fans and Foes*. Luton: University of Luton Press, 1998.

Brinker, Felix. "Transmedia Storytelling in the 'Marvel Cinematic Universe' and the Logics of Convergence-Era Popular Seriality," in *Make Ours Marvel: Media Convergence and a Comics Universe*, ed. Matt Yockey, Austin: University of Texas Press (2017): 207–233.

Chamberlain, Daniel. "Television Interfaces." *Journal of Popular Film and Television*, Summer (2010): 84–88.

Cox, Christopher. "Programming—Flow in the convergence of digital media platforms and television." *Critical Studies in Television*, 13, no. 4 (2018): 438–454.

Disney. "Disney Investor Day webcast," 11 April 2019. https://thewaltdisneycompany.com/the-walt-disney-companys-2019-investor-day-webcast/.

Disney. "Disney Plus Continues International Expansion." 15 Sept 2020. https://dtcimedia.disney.com/news/disney-plus-continues-international-expansion.

Disney. "Quarterly 4 FY17 Investor Conference Call." 9 Nov. 2017. https://thewaltdisneycompany.com/app/uploads/q4-fy17-earnings-transcript.pdf.

Disney. "Question and answer session held by The Walt Disney Company on December 14, 2017." https://www.sec.gov/Archives/edgar/data/1308161/000095015717001616/form425.htm.

Disney. "The Walt Disney Company to Acquire Majority Ownership of BAMTech." 8 August 2017, https://thewaltdisneycompany.com/walt-disney-company-acquire-majority-ownership-bamtech/.
Disney. "Walt Disney Company (DIS) Q1 2020 Earnings Call Transcript," 28 Oct. (2019). https://www.fool.com/earnings/call-transcripts/2020/02/04/walt-disney-company-dis-q1-2020-earnings-call-tran.aspx.
Disney. "Walt Disney Q3 FY20 Earnings Conference Call," 4 August 2020. https://thewaltdisneycompany.com/app/uploads/2020/08/q3-fy20-earnings-transcript.pdf.
Edgerton, Gary R. "Silicon Valley + Hollywood = Convergence 2.0." *CST Online,* 31 January 2020. https://cstonline.net/silicon-valley-hollywood-convergence-2-0-by-gary-r-edgerton/.
Elkins, Evan. "Algorithmic cosmopolitanism: on the global claims of digital entertainment platforms." *Critical Studies in Media Communication,* 36 no. 4 (2019): 376–389.
Epstein, Edward Jay. "Why Netflix Won't Be the HBO of the 21st Century," *The Gawker,* 15 February 2010. https://gawker.com/5471943/why-netflix-wont-be-the-hbo-of-the-21st-century?skyline=true&s=i.
Fienberg, Daniel. "The 'Plus TV' Era Is Upon Us." *Hollywood Reporter,* 20 Nov., Vol. 425, Issue 38 (2019).
Frankel, Daniel. "Battling Netflix Won't Be Cheap for Disney+." *Multichannel News,* Nov. 26, Vol. 35, Issue 25 (2018), 22.
Frey, Mattias. "The Internet Suggests: Film, Recommender Systems, and Cultural Mediation." *Journal of Cinema and Media Studies,* 59, no. 1 (2019): 163–169.
Giardina, Carolyn. "Whatever You Imagine, You Can Bring to Audiences," *Hollywood Reporter,* 4 Dec., Vol. 425, Issue 40 (2019).
Gillespie, T. "#trendingistrending: When algorithms become culture," in *Algorithmic Cultures: Essays on Meaning, Performance, and New Technologies,* eds. R. Seyfert & J. Roberge. New York: Routledge, 2016, 52– 75.
Hahm, Melody. "Eye-Popping Chart Shows How Much Original Content Netflix Is Creating," *Yahoo Finance.* 17 December 2019. https://finance.yahoo.com/news/netflix-original-content-disney-and-apple-plus-230418533.html.
Hallinan, Blake, and Ted Striphas. "Recommended for you: The Netflix Prize and the production of algorithmic culture," *new media & society* Vol. 18(1): 117–137, 2016.
Hassler-Forest, D. "*Game of Thrones*: The Politics of World-Building and the Cultural Logic of Gentrification" in Hassler-Forest, D. & Nicklas, P. (2015) *The Politics of Adaptation: Media Convergence and Ideology,* Basingstoke: Palgrave Macmillan.
Havens, Timothy. "Netflix: Streaming Channel Brands as Global Meaning Systems," in Derek Johnson (2018) *From Networks to Netflix*: 321–331.
Havens, Timothy, and Amanda D. Lotz, and Serra Tinic. 'Critical Media Industry Studies: A Research Approach' *Communication, Culture & Critique,* 2: 234–253, 2018.
Herbert, Daniel, Amanda D. Lotz, and Lee Marshall. "Approaching Media Industries Comparatively: A Case Study of Streaming," *International Journal of Cultural Studies* 22(3), 349–366, 2019.
Hesmondhalgh, David, and Amanda D. Lotz. "Video Screen Interfaces as New Sites of Media Circulation," *International Journal of Communication* 14 (2020), Available at http://ijoc.org.
Hunting, Kyra, and Jonathan Gray. "Disney Junior: Imagining Industrial Intertextuality" in Johnson, Derek (2018) *From Networks to Netflix,* Oxford and New York: Routledge: 197–207.
Jarvey, Natalie. "The Deal Closing Still Keeps Me Up at Night," *Hollywood Reporter.* Vol. 424, Issue 41, 2019.
Jarvey, Natalie. "Netflix's Subscriber Growth Story: Focus Overseas: Asia Pacific is the streamer's fastest-growing region," *Hollywood Reporter.* 19 Dec. 2019, Vol. 425 Issue 42, p. 34.
Jarvey, Natalie. "Netflix Under Pressure," *Hollywood Reporter.* 7 August 2019: 50–53.
Johnson, Derek "CBS All Access: To boldly franchise where no one has subscribed before" in Derek Johnson (2018) *From Networks to Netflix*: 395–407.

Johnson, Derek. *From Networks to Netflix*, Oxford & New York: Routledge, 2018.
Kamen, Matt "DisneyLife aims to be Disney's all-in-one streaming platform." *Wired*, 6 Jan 2016 https://www.wired.co.uk/article/disney-life-interview.
Kompare, Derek "Adverstreaming: Hulu Plus." *Flow* 24 Feb. 2020.
Littleton, Cynthia. "A Stream of Questions." *Variety*, 29 Jan., Vol. 342, Issue 17, 2019.
Lobato, Ramon. *Netflix Nations: The Geography of Digital Distribution*. New York: New York University Press, 2019.
Lobato, Ramon, and Amanda Lotz. "Imagining Global Video: The Challenge of Netflix." *Cinema and Media Studies* Spring 2020, 59 (3).
Löffler, Max. "Netflix's Global Reach: By the Numbers." *Hollywood Reporter*, August 2019: 63.
Lotz, Amanda D. "Netflix dossier," March 2017, https://www.global-internet-tv.com/netflix-country-reports/united-states/.
Lotz, Amanda D., and Ramon Lobato, and Julian Thomas "Internet-Distributed Television Research: A Provocation," *Media Industries* 5(2) (2018).
Low, Elaine "Netflix 'Star Trek' Deal Helps CBS Chief Les Moonves Sleep at Night." *Investors Business Daily*, 20 September (2016).
McCabe, Janet, and Kim Akass. "It's not tv, it's HBO's original programming," in Leverette, Marc, Brian L. Ott and Cara Louise Buckley (2008) *It's Not TV: Watching HBO in the Post-Television Era*, London & New York: Routledge.
Mendelson, Scott. "These Smaller-Scale Movies Are Putting The 'Plus' In Disney+." *Forbes.com*, 18 August (2020) https://www.forbes.com/sites/scottmendelson/2020/08/18/great-movies-on-disney-plus-mulan-magic-camp-one-and-only-ivan-hamilton-stargirl-beyonce/#6b66f4113c1c.
Palmeri, Christopher "Disney's Iger Plots Online Future with a Little *Star Wars* Help," Bloomberg.com, 8 November 2018 at: https://www.bloomberg.com/news/articles/2018-11-08/disney-earnings-buoyed-by-theme-parks-film-studio-strength.
Petruska, Karen. "Amazon Prime Video: Where Information is Entertainment" in Derek Johnson (2018) *From Networks to Netflix*: 355–364.
Ryan, Maureen, and Cynthia Littleton "TV Series Budgets Hit the Breaking Point as Costs Skyrocket in Peak TV Era." *Variety* 26 Sep 2017. https://variety.com/2017/tv/news/tv-series-budgets-costs-rising-peak-tv-1202570158/.
Santo, Avi "Para-television and discourses of distinction: The culture of production at HBO" in Cara Louise Buckley, Marc Leverette, Brian L. Ott (2008) *It's Not TV: Watching HBO in the Post-Television Era*. London, New York: Routledge.
Scott, Jason. "Disney+: It all adds up," *In Media Res*, 15 March 2020 at: http://mediacommons.org/imr/content/disney-it-all-adds.
Scott, Jason. "Disneyizing Home Entertainment Distribution" in Wroot, Jonathan & Andy Willis (2017) (eds.) *DVD, Blu-ray and Beyond: Navigating Formats and Platforms within Media Consumption*, Cham, Switzerland: Palgrave Macmillan.
Secular, Steven. "Games without Frontiers: Streaming Sports and the Evolution of Digital Intermediaries" *Media Industries* 5(2) 2018. https://quod.lib.umich.edu/m/mij/15031809.0005.209/--games-without-frontiers-streaming-sports-and-the-evolution?rgn=main;view=fulltext.
Spangler, T. "Netflix content chief says 85% of new spending is on originals." 2018. https://variety.com/2018/digital/news/netflix-original-spending-85-percent-1202809623.
Tryon, Chuck. "TV Got Better: Netflix's Original Programming Strategies and Binge Viewing," *Media Industries Journal* 2(2) 2015.
Wayne, Michael L. "Global Portals in National Markets: Branding Netflix in Israel." *Cinema and Media Studies* Spring 2020, 59 (3).
Zeitchik, Steven. "Three big questions Disney+ streaming presentation will address." *Washington Post*, 10 Apr. 2019.

Part 3

Case Studies and Narrative Representations

Coherence Effects in Digital TV

The Case of Anthology Series

Patrick Gill

Introduction: Seriality and Teleology

At the turn of the 21st century, when networks still ruled the world of television, and DVD box sets were only just beginning to introduce viewers to the notion of "bingeing,"[1] it seemed that the template for a successful TV show had been set. The most fundamental characteristic of those TV shows of the noughties was that they employed "episodic forms under the influence of serial narration."[2] That is to say that there was "a shifting balance"[3] between story arcs extending over the course of a single episode and others extending over the course of a whole season. The aspect of serial narration was perhaps the more visible one in some of the most successful shows of the early 2000s, often characterized by a large ensemble cast, complex interwoven storylines, and a penchant for using flashbacks to fill in characters' back stories. More than anything, however, the phenomenon of seriality is epitomized by the cliffhanger, the introduction of a shocking twist or revelation at the very end of an episode. In the world of appointment viewing, this meant that audiences would spend a week waiting for the next episode to be broadcast, usually opening with a "Previously on ..." recap of the story thus far, while buyers of DVDs were obviously encouraged to move on immediately to the next episode.

For the purposes of this essay, which will inquire into the relation of anthology series and digital TV to argue that anthology shows are surprisingly adept at making use of the affordances provided by video streaming platforms, rather than contrasting the serial and the episodic, it is important to consider a specific *kind* of seriality featured in typical shows of the 2000s. After all, for all their complexity in terms of big casts and challenging timelines, what shows like *Lost* (ABC 2004–2010) or *Heroes*

(NBC 2006–2010) rely on more than anything in terms of their storytelling is a sense of teleology. The story being told here, it is suggested to viewers, is not a serial narration in the narrow sense of the "endlessly deferred openness of soap operas":[4] the stories being enjoyed in the case of these hit shows take their viewers toward a predefined goal or outcome. This narratological notion of a *telos* the shows are working toward is supported by an intradiegetic insistence on ideas of fate and prophecy, at least in the two cases referenced here. Where the *telos* becomes the dominant unifying feature of a TV show, it follows that attention is drawn to the sequence of events (as story and viewers are propelled toward the desired goal) and on causation: the emphasis of the storytelling—despite all the complexity, the introduction of flashbacks, the reliance on an impressive cast—is placed firmly on the idea of a chain of one thing causing another in the interest of leading to a result that may or may not have in fact been part of the plan of the show's creators all along. And for at least the first decade of the 2000s, that seemed to be the standard template for TV drama: complexity by means of large casts and multiple story arcs; and sustained viewer interest by means of a frequently unsustainable[5] teleology. In terms of storytelling coherence, it is the sequence of events and the promise that they lead somewhere that is hard at work in the case of these stories.

So dominant did this teleological recipe for complex drama and the forward momentum it gave the shows of the first decade of the new millennium become, even shows conceived as typical procedurals and thus strongly tending toward the episodic increasingly came to rely on overarching storylines imbuing them with a sense of teleology. *Monk* (USA Network 2002–2009) is an example of such a show in which the titular character solves 125 cases dispersed across eight seasons. What works perfectly well as a procedural, a typical case-per-week show modelled on the famous example of *Columbo* (NBC 1968–1978; ABC 1989–2003), is given a serial veneer, however, by the addition of Monk's continuous quest to find his wife's murderer. Similar examples of ostensible procedurals following the call for more seriality include *House, M.D.* (Fox 2004–2012)[6] and *Lie to Me* (Fox 2009–2011).

Not only were other forms of drama affected by the post-millennial vogue for seriality in televisual storytelling: it even bled into other genres. Sitcoms, traditionally equipped with episodic story arcs, where the prevailing order is disturbed at the start of an episode only to be restored by the end of it, suddenly started aligning themselves with drama series in their teleological quest. In most cases, that did not necessarily mean a complete rejection of the episodic structure of comedy—but it did mean a search for overarching structures that would suggest a teleology to audiences. NBC's *My Name Is Earl* (2005–2009) is structured around a list of past misdemeanors the titular character seeks forgiveness for, the implication being that when the list is done, Earl's quest is over. In a similar vein, the more recent *Two Broke Girls* (CBS 2011–2017) revolves around two friends doing odd jobs to save up for their own business, with a tally of the sum of their savings concluding every episode. The height of the habit of imbuing sitcoms with a sense of teleology was reached with shows retrospectively narrating their characters' past fates from a point in the supposed present. *The Increasingly Poor Decisions of Todd Margaret* (IFC and More4 2010–2016) is one such example. In that show's pilot episode, the titular character is arraigned in court on a list of hyperbolic-sounding charges, so that the rest of the series can tell us how he came to end up in this predicament. A more famous example is *How I Met Your Mother* (CBS 2005–2014), which embarks on a nine-season retrospective that was clearly not envisioned in that particular form by the show's creators from the start.

These developments show that the dominant template establishing itself before the rise of video streaming services was heavily reliant on ideas of seriality and teleology. Given the technical possibilities of streaming platforms as well as their principal business model of participating in the emergent attention economy, it was assumed that they would follow this model. And to some extent, they undeniably have, as the existence of the "Skip Intro" and "Next Episode" buttons on Netflix bears out. Based on these considerations of the supposed dominance of seriality and teleology in TV narratives of the early 2000s, the following looks at an alternative model of televisual storytelling and how it may relate to the rise of video streaming platforms.

Video Streaming Services and Anthology Series

The notion that if sustained attention is what video streaming services must be after, serial narratives would drive out other forms of storytelling has not turned out to be true. One interesting example of the serial template being broken is that of erstwhile Fox sitcom *Arrested Development* (2003–2006).[7] Its revival on Netflix (2013–2019) did not set out to reprise the original run's reliance on madcap seriality. Instead, season four, the first season made for Netflix, was structured around an elaborate version of the Rashomon effect, with every episode covering a near-identical timespan and successively adding different characters' perspectives to what viewers had found out thus far. What became more important than the sequence of events, to be followed in pursuit of some *telos*, was the viewer's ability to re-watch older episodes with relative ease to enjoy the multiplicity of perspectives on offer. In this instance, re-watchability was clearly more important than bingeability. There are two aspects of the fourth season of *Arrested Development* that are particularly instructive when considering coherence models of shows on video streaming services. The first is that *Arrested Development* had a life before moving to Netflix. Critically successful in its run on Fox and endowed with a devoted following up in arms at its—as they felt—premature cancellation, *Arrested Development* arrived at Netflix with a bankable recognizability. The second is that the material circumstances of the series' production directly impacted its narrative outlook: given the limited availability of the show's cast after a seven-year hiatus, the Rashomon narration provides ample opportunity to tell the same scene over and over again without having to have multiple lead actors in the same shot. While this could be considered a constraint on the shooting of *Arrested Development* in its fourth season, the close link between the materiality of production and the way stories are told can also be considered a core strength of anthology series.

An anthology series is one in which individual chapters are not immediately connected by means of obvious coherence markers such as an ongoing plot, recurring characters, or identical settings. Rather than presenting an ongoing narrative, then, an anthology series places several narratives of a similar nature side by side. Historically, the anthology format "was amply used in the 1950s and 1960s, but abandoned shortly after," while "[t]oday, *Black Mirror* appears to be one of the few embodiments of the traditional anthology series."[8] Written by Charlie Brooker for Britain's Channel 4 and broadcast from 2011, the show moved to Netflix from season three on. As a "traditional anthology series" in the vein of *The Twilight Zone* (original show 1959–1964 with several revivals), each episode introduces viewers to new characters, new locations, and new stories. Seriality and teleology simply do not link the episodes of this show with one another. What *is* a link, however, is *Black Mirror*'s persistent interest in technology and the harm it can do.

In contrast to *Black Mirror*'s pedigree in following the template set by a classic show of the 1950s and 60s, a different type of anthology series is that of "'seasonal anthologies,'"[9] i.e., shows which do not forego the causal linkage between individual episodes but do so between entire seasons, so that each season tells a coherent story from beginning to end, leaving viewers with a sense of closure, and then going on to begin the next season in a different locality, a different time period and with an entirely different cast of characters. One such seasonal anthology series is *Fargo*, created and for the most part written by showrunner Noah Hawley for the pay TV channel FX and broadcast from 2014. Even though, like *Black Mirror*, originally conceived for a more traditional TV channel, *Fargo* has arguably achieved its biggest audience numbers via streaming on demand services as in many territories outside the U.S. it is shown by Netflix with additional availability through Amazon Prime and Google Play. While *Black Mirror*'s move to Netflix was undertaken on the strength of the first two seasons, *Fargo* has a different type of pedigree to look back on, as it is based on the eponymous Oscar-winning movie by the Coen brothers (1996). That said, while the show is consistent with the movie in terms of tone, mood, and setting, there is very little causal linkage. As, at least superficially, there isn't within the TV series itself: while season one (2014) is set in January 2006, season two (2015) provides a prequel of sorts, with the action taking place in March 1979. Season three then returns to the more recent past with its action set in 2010. But as in the case of *Black Mirror*, the viewer's close attention will reveal several intricate linking strategies that turn all of the seasons of *Fargo* (and possibly other stories emanating from the world of the Coen brothers) into a coherent text. How both these series go about their work of effecting coherence is the subject of the following discussion.

Black Mirror

The degree to which the term *coherence* can be usefully applied to episodes of Charlie Brooker's *Black Mirror* may at first appear doubtful. The visuals alone suggest that viewers are witnessing distinct stories in distinct contexts, from the monochrome world of "Metalhead" (s04e05)[10] via the 1980s neon signs and hair-dos of "San Junipero" (s03e04) to the pastel ad-brochure charm of "Nosedive" (s03e01). But far beyond the distinctive visuals, there are multiple intra- and extradiegetic "centrifugal narrative forces," at work, i.e., "those strategies ... that try to disintegrate"[11] the unity of a composite text such as *Black Mirror*. Individual episodes are usually separated by setting, by the technological standard achieved in the world of each episode, and by an absence of through lines where plot and causality are concerned: to all intents and purposes, the stories seem to be set in separate worlds, freeing writers (although admittedly Charlie Brooker is the writer behind the vast majority of episodes) and directors from the need to neatly fit their ideas into extant strands of causality or even chronology in a shared storyworld. Changing directors and a changing cast along with different run times of episodes (at least since the move to Netflix) add to a sense of inconsistency and heterogeneity.

However, attentive viewers can identify "centripetal"[12] strategies at work in *Black Mirror*, whose role it is to signify shared concerns and even a shared universe between individual episodes. Most obvious is the consistent use of news channels on television screens. This may at first strike viewers primarily as a reminder that they are witnessing a near future in which everyone is constantly kept abreast of the latest developments by means of news crawls. On closer inspection, the news stories featured in these media frequently refer to past or future episodes of *Black Mirror*, and their employment as a linking device is introduced from the second season on. Thus "The National Anthem" (s01e01) and "The Waldo Moment" (s02e03) feature shots of the news channel displaying identical headlines, linking the events of both stories in chronological terms. References to the Victoria Skillane case abound even outside of "White Bear" (s02e02), the episode primarily concerned with the fate of that particular person, as do references to Michael Callow, the Prime Minister humiliated in the show's very first episode: having been blackmailed into committing an act of bestiality in his own story, we soon read "Callow to Divorce" on a news website in "Shut Up and Dance" (s03e03), while a barely legible news crawl in "Black Museum" (s04e06) reads "PM Callow marries pig." The value of these texts—besides the rough chronology they allow viewers to establish between episodes—is that they represent a playful connection between various series and episodes and encourage viewers to look out for further linkages.

There are tentative overlaps in terms of plot and personnel as well, not to the extent that characters from different episodes interact, but in a way that makes viewers believe they *could*: a job interview at the beginning of "The Entire History of You" (s01e03) mentions a technology that is at the center of "Arkangel" (s04e02), and one of the detectives in "Hated in the Nation" (s03e06) served on the Skillane case mentioned above. But while these minor intersections based on shared news or human connections are a pleasant find for fans of the show, they do little to mesh episodes together at first viewing. What really does connect the episodes in the minds of viewers are the more emotive objects so liberally peppered throughout the show. There is the futuristic-looking pregnancy test used with great poignancy in "Be Right Back" (s02e01) and "White Christmas" (s02e04). The same dating app is used in "Hang the DJ" (s04e04) and in "USS Callister" (s04e01); and there is a curious pictographic symbol that appears in the context of certain technologies in "White Bear," "Playtest" (s03e02), "White Christmas," and "Bandersnatch" (interactive special). These objects and graphic representations on the whole carry much more emotive weight than the on-screen writing of news crawls. Their emotional impact is perhaps only surpassed by the recurring musical connections, first and foremost versions of the Irma Thomas song "Anyone Who Knows What Love Is (Will Understand)," which appear in "15 Million Merits" (s01e02), "White Christmas," "Men Against Fire" (s03e05) and "Crocodile" (s04e03).

All these connections reach their apogee in "Black Museum," in which protagonist Nish is taken around an exhibition of technological artifacts by Rolo Hayes, the museum's owner. As the latter explains the back stories to some of the artifacts that the viewer is not as yet familiar with, they note in passing many objects that did have a destructive role to play in earlier episodes: the robotic bees from "Hated in the Nation," the smashed and bloodied tablet computer from "Arkangel," the laboratory mice named Hector and Kenny just like the main characters in "Shut Up and Dance": every object they pass, whether commented upon or not, has the potential to evoke key moments from previous episodes, and they now all find themselves in the museum's collection. As a kind of compilation album of the other episodes' most evocative objects, "Black Museum" already plays an important role in letting viewers know that the events of all episodes, disjointed as they may appear, take place in a shared reality. Beyond that, "Black Museum" allows viewers to construct an elaborate chronology: if the interactive Netflix special "Bandersnatch" is the only *Black Mirror* installment set in the past, and objects from all other episodes appear in "Black Museum," there is a *terminus a quo* and a *terminus ad quem*: the events contained in all the other episodes must have occurred on a timeline between these two points. While far from making it easy to reconstruct the exact temporal order in which all episodes occur, the mere implied existence of a joint chronology offers a sense of unity underlying the entire *Black Mirror* project.

More than the emotive recurrence of particular objects and songs, and even more than the idea of a shared chronology—what unifies *Black Mirror* episodes into a common project is the overarching theme of technology and the way the human mind falls prey to what must at first have appeared an easy fix for humanity's problems, or at least a desirable commodity. All of the horrors of technology that *Black Mirror* has made it its mission to drive home to us, exist in its fictional world (and to an as yet lesser degree in our own) because they answer some universal human need. And so, while technology is problematized and its use is shown in all its tragic consequences, *Black Mirror* episodes are unified by the idea that the root of these problems is not really technology itself but the combination of that technology with human desires. A superficial viewing of the show might result in an impression such as the following:

> You begin in one place, half- to two-thirds of the way through, you get either a twist or an unexpected escalation, and then, yep, that thing you suspected was not good at the start ends up being really, extra not good by the end. Once you've seen more than one or two episodes, you know the third-act revelation is coming.[13]

In fact, given its status as part of an anthology series, every episode of *Black Mirror* is fully aware that its viewers are familiar with the show's idiosyncrasies. Based on this prior knowledge, viewers may come to expect a twist. But given that these twists tend to be based on a multitude of human weaknesses, the audience will be surprised and affected by the exact nature of the twist confronting them in each new episode.

Fargo

In the course of the first three seasons of *Fargo*, viewers can detect obvious intradiegetic connections between them, such as a similarity of geographical setting in the Midwest, some (though relatively few) recurring characters, and a slew of lazy and incompetent police chiefs. What unites these seasons beyond such superficial intradiegetic features is the overall atmosphere viewers expect from the series based on their familiarity with the 1996 movie on which it is based. That influence of the original movie on the spin-off series extends from the title music to Stavros, a character in season one, finding the money buried by Carl at the end of the movie. The most literal borrowing the show makes from the film, though, is to be found in its use of a sequence of intertitles at the beginning of each episode which copy a textual sequence shown on screen in the opening scene of the movie: "This is a true story. The events depicted in this film took place in Minnesota in 1987.[14] At the request of the survivors, the names have been changed. Out of respect for the dead, the rest has been told exactly as it occurred." This repetition at the beginning of each episode creates a strong bond between the movie and the show.

On an explicit level, it reminds viewers that they are watching a continuation of a movie once nominated for multiple Academy Awards. Implicitly, what it does is to drive home the idea that both movie and show are interested in similar phenomena, and one of the strongest, though perhaps subtler, shared properties within the franchise is a persistent interest in questions of truth and story, and along with that, of objective reality and individual perception. This is played out on many levels. For one, the show highlights the idea of various intertexts, real or imagined, as when "The Narrow Escape Problem" (s03e04) opens with the introduction to Sergei Prokofiev's *Peter and the Wolf*, associating the various characters of that symphonic fairy tale and their musical cues with the characters in that season. In a similar vein, "The Castle" (s02e09) introduces viewers to a made-up *History of True Crime in the Mid West* written by the fictional Barton Brixby, a book that begins: "The events depicted in this book took place in Minnesota, Wisconsin, Iowa, Nebraska, and North and South Dakota from 1825 to the present. At the request of the survivors, the names have been changed. Out of respect for the dead, the rest has been told exactly as it occurred."[15] Even beyond extended narratives in whose terms viewers are invited to frame events in *Fargo*, the show is absolutely riddled with stories intended by one character to drive home a point to another, but really serving as foils for the viewer to compare and contrast events in the show with. From Molly's story of the man who lost a glove in "Morton's Fork" (s01e10) to Varga's recapitulation of the 2008 Lehman Brothers collapse in "The Lord of No Mercy" (s03e06): "This is a true story. A 150-year-old bank with $60 billion in assets collapses overnight. Its stock price drops 93% in eight hours. One day it's solvent, the next it's worthless. Perception of reality becomes reality."

The show is saturated with anecdotes, fables, parables—stories that may not be literally true but are expressive of universal truths or concepts, thus begging the question in how far the insistence on a "true story" at the beginning of each episode actually represents a useful category. A separate aspect of this emphasized by Varga's narration of the collapse of Lehman Brothers is that perception may at times become indistinguishable from truth. Varga sees that at work on a societal level, but the show takes an equal interest in the individual and their perception, occasionally leading to what might be termed intermittent unreliable narration, i.e., the championing within a brief segment of an episode of one character's subjective (and sometimes deluded) view on things. The most obvious example is that of Peggy's occasional misreadings of situations as when she perceives her situation in "Palindrome" (s02e10) to be similar to that of the protagonists of a film she watches in "Loplop" (s02e08). In "The Gift of the Magi" (s02e05), the audience encounters Ronald Reagan at a urinal on the campaign trail where he proceeds to tell policeman Lou Solverson about his filming of the 1942 Paramount picture *Operation Eagle's Nest* as if that was the same as actually fighting in a war. The entire idea of unreliable narration present in every season of *Fargo* offers viewers one possible take on the supernatural events taking place within the show, from Malvo's unexplained disappearance from Lester's house in "The Crocodile's Dilemma" (s01e01) to the pivotal UFO sightings in season two and the bowling-alley scene representing the afterlife in "Who Rules the Land of Denial?"(s03e08).

These supernatural occurrences can also be linked to two other strands present in all three seasons of *Fargo*: a penchant for biblical imagery as well as ideas of an existentialist nature. In terms of allusions to the bible in particular and religious texts in general, the most persistent allusion *Fargo* makes is based on its portrayal of sibling rivalry, mirroring the jealous relationship between Cain and Abel. This is already present in a subplot in season one, in which perpetually downtrodden Lester Nygaard ultimately manages to frame his brother Chaz for a crime he didn't commit, thus taking revenge for the latter's successes in life. It is a more pronounced feature in season two, in which brothers Bear and Dodd vie for leadership of the family in the power vacuum created by their father Otto's stroke in "Before the Law" (s02e02). Their conflict will eventually result in Bear's son Charlie being incarcerated through Dodd's doing in "Rhinoceros" (s02e06), and Dodd's daughter Simone being murdered by Bear in "Did You Do This? No, You Did It!" (s02e07). The most prominent use of sibling rivalry as a catalyst for catastrophe is to be found in season three, throughout which brothers Ray and Emmit Stussy are entangled in an argument over their inheritance with bitter consequences for both.

Other biblical allusions can be found in the figure of season one's Lorne Malvo who, in "A Fox, a Rabbit and a Cabbage" (s01e09) says about some apple pie served to him by Lou Solverson, "I haven't had a piece of pie like that since the Garden of Eden," thus identifying himself as a satanic figure. This is further supported when, earlier in the same episode, he shoots three people in an elevator and when the doors open, we see him in front of the crudely wing-shaped blood stains on the elevator walls, marking him out as a vengeful angel. The purpose these biblical allusions frequently fulfill is not so much that of a precise parallel but a general matrix of familiar texts against which to make sense of events in *Fargo*. In more abstract terms, then, the biblical allusions tend to reinforce notions of good and evil, but they do so in contingent rather than in absolute terms: in a given situation, *Fargo*'s characters are capable of behaving in ways the audience has encountered in familiar stories.

The notion of contingent human behavior ties in with a principal concern of the Coen brothers' movies that also functions as a coherence marker within the show. Time and again, reference is made to "the loss of meaning and certainty in the modern world and the increasing sense of personal alienation in a society quickly losing its traditional values."[16] This existentialist perspective is reflected many times, from Malvo's contention that man is a predator and can only lead a worthwhile existence once he has accepted that (see s01e10); to open reference to Camus's *The Myth of Sisyphus* in one of the episode titles (s02e03) as well as within the dialogue (s02e10); to the questionable ontological status of Gloria Burgle, who is not just invisible to automatic doors and hand dryers but whose name elicits no response from an online search engine (s03e06). While connecting the individual seasons with one another, such thematic through lines also serve to embed them in the larger universe of the Coen brothers, echoing concerns, scenes, music and visuals from films such as *Barton Fink* (1991), *The Big Lebowski* (1998) and *The Man Who Wasn't There* (2001). The primary mechanism by which *Fargo* establishes coherence, then, is by locating itself and its constituent series within a vast web of intertextual relations, encompassing specifically the Coen *oeuvre* and the world of film noir (or "noir comedy"[17]) in general, and extending from concrete sacred texts to parables and sayings of less specific origin. The show even creates its own fictional texts (movies, regional histories) to which it can refer. Within that web of references, the idea of the "true story" is lost alongside that of the primacy of linear narrative: viewers of one season of *Fargo* can move on to an earlier or a later season at will, as they can take a sideways glance at the films of the Coens, or any number of other intertexts.

Conclusion: Anthology Series and Streaming Services

As we can see, *Black Mirror* and *Fargo* employ various means of creating a coherence that extends far beyond the cause-and-effect linearity, the sense of teleology often created in other kinds of series. That sense of seriality and teleology serves the purpose of keeping viewers hooked, rushing them on to the next episode. While that idea of seriality and teleology was dominant in TV narration immediately before the advent of video streaming services and seemed tailor-made for the purposes of these platforms, the discussion of *Fargo* and *Black Mirror* has shown that very different types of narrative models can also prosper in this environment. But what exactly makes these two shows a perfect fit for streaming services when their narration is so different from the norm? What they offer from the viewer's perspective is depth instead of pace, and that leads to a certain rewatchability. Rather than hurtling from event to event, cliffhanger to cliffhanger, these shows slowly build a fictional world with its own rules and expectations. It is common to refer to this as world-building, but in the present context I would prefer to think of it as the creation of a knowing audience. Having been educated in the search for meaningful patterns through previous episodes and seasons, such knowing audiences are interested in delving ever deeper, finding more layers of parallels and deviations. Given this need to make sense of complex stories by relating them to other stories within the same narrative world, viewers will require easy access to previous installments, and this is provided on streaming services to an even greater degree than in the case of box sets. But if the viewer's enjoyment of these series on streaming platforms can be explained by way of their elaborate world-building, what makes anthology shows an attractive proposition on the production side?

The first point that needs to be made here is that in buying or commissioning these shows, streaming platforms buy into notions that viewers are already familiar with (witness the tendency to commission work from established directors such as Martin Scorsese's 2019 film *The Irishman*).

To some extent, this is the equivalent of cinema's love of Marvel movies and sequels in general. As Strank points out, the love of the familiar is an undeniable factor in the commissioning process of video streaming services: "It is hardly surprising that nostalgia is one of the greatest market factors in a system so concerned with the preferences of its users.... Contemporary series culture is partly one of remixes and reboots, sequels and reimaginings."[18] *Black Mirror* was able to build on its cult status as a Channel 4 show, *Fargo* had the renown of the Coen brothers behind it. It was always likely that they would draw an audience to any broadcaster acquiring the rights to them. What goes for entire shows is equally true of individual seasons or episodes: while they may trace more or less independent storylines, their belonging to a larger world already familiar to viewers, to a kind of franchise,[19] so to speak, makes them much lower-risk products than if, for instance, every episode of *Black Mirror* had been produced independently of the *Black Mirror* label, as hour-long standalone movies. Risk averse platforms interested in giving viewers what they already know they want (i.e., what they have a sense of familiarity with), will find that anthology series make attractive acquisitions.

What helps the establishment of such a franchise is the presence of familiar faces, and anthology series facilitate the casting of famous actors. Billy Bob Thornton, Martin Freeman, Kirsten Dunst, Ewan McGregor in *Fargo*; Miley Cyrus, Maxine Peak, Kelly Macdonald, Bryce Dallas Howard in *Black Mirror*—these are not commonly thought of as TV actors, and they would have been unlikely to sign contracts obligating them to take part in the filming of several seasons of a traditional sitcom or drama series. The casting of famous actors comes with increased costs, a problem further exacerbated by the need for new sets. If, as is the case in *Black Mirror*, each episode is supposed to be set in what feels like a different world, with its own aesthetics and idiosyncrasies, having your show made by a streaming platform financed through viewer subscriptions across the globe, or at least selling the rights to transmit your show on such platforms becomes a very useful prospect indeed.

In the final analysis, we can see anthology series employing very different means than traditional series interested in seriality and teleology. Rather than vying for attention based on the principle of a sequence of events (although that phenomenon is also present in seasonal anthologies such as *Fargo*), anthology series set out their stall by gradually educating audiences as to their own rules and traditions, so that they can subsequently adhere to or deviate from established patterns. The accruing of ever greater series knowledge on the part of viewers in turn affords an anthology series ever greater freedom to play with established expectations. By thus implicitly or explicitly referring to previous installments, anthology series garner a different kind of attention on the part of the viewer: they encourage slower consumption but also frequent rewatching of previous seasons and episodes. Given their modes of production, they can call upon a more famous cast as well as a more varied backdrop, playing on familiar patterns that give viewers a sense of being part of an exclusive club while never excluding anyone—after all, previous seasons and episodes are always available, and there's no need to watch them in sequence to get the overall gist. The development of "alternative consumption patterns in which viewers binge on series, catch up from earlier seasons after starting midway through, and frequently rewatch episodes"[20] has gone hand in hand with the development of alternative narrative forms, and with more freedom to decide when and how to watch, it would appear that viewers are interested in taking on more responsibility when it comes to making sense of narratives and establishing connections between them.

Notes

1. James Poniewozik, "Go Ahead, Binge-watch That TV Show," *Time*, July 10, 2012, https://entertainment.time.com/2012/07/10/go-ahead-binge-watch-that-tv-show/
2. Jason Mittell, *Complex TV: The Poetics of Contemporary Television Storytelling* (New York: New York UP, 2015), 18.
3. Mittell, *Complex TV*, 18.
4. Mittell, *Complex TV*, 22.
5. For a discussion of *Lost*'s limited success in convincing viewers of the credibility of its final season, see Mittell, *Complex TV*, 323–324.
6. For *House, M.D.* in particular, the case can be made that its ongoing storyline is at least as important as the individual cases negotiated in each successive episode. That does not take away from the fact that the show is conceived as quintessentially episodic, presenting a new case every week.
7. For a discussion of *Arrested Development*'s narrative strategies, see: Gill, Patrick. "'I swore I'd not go reality': The Bluths through the Lens of Genre." In *A State of* Arrested Development*: Critical Essays on the Innovative Television Comedy*, ed. Kristin M. Barton (Jefferson: McFarland, 2015), 197–210.
8. Veronica Innocenti and Guglielmo Pescatore, "Changing Series: Narrative Models and the Role of the Viewer in Contemporary Television Seriality," *Between* 4, no. 8 (2014): 4, http://dx.doi.org/10.13125/2039-6597/4
9. Innocenti and Pescatore, "Changing Series," 4.
10. While references will primarily be made by episode title, initial mention of any episode is additionally accompanied by a numerical identifier.
11. Rolf Lundén, "Centrifugal and Centripetal Narrative Strategies in the Short Story Composite and the Episode Film," *Cycles, Recueils, Macrotexts*, special issue of *Interférences littéraires/Literaire interferenties* 12 (2014): 50.
12. Rolf Lundén, "Centrifugal and Centripetal," 49.
13. Kathryn Vanarendonk, "The Case Against *Black Mirror*," *Slate*, October 25, 2016, https://slate.com/culture/2016/10/the-case-against-black-mirror.html
14. The date and place given will vary depending on when and where the respective season of the show is set.
15. In both cases, the casting emphasizes the point of storytelling as a powerful creator

of coherence: the opening sequence of *Peter and the Wolf* is read by Billy Bob Thornton, while the fictional Barton Brixby is voiced by Martin Freeman, two of the leads in the show's first season.

16. Jeffrey Adams, *The Cinema of the Coen Brothers: Hard-Boiled Entertainments* (New York: Columbia UP, 2015), 110.

17. Jeffrey Adams, *The Cinema of the Coen Brothers*, 108.

18. Willem Strank, "Status Quo Ante: Music in (Post)Quality TV," *American Music* 37, no. 4 (winter 2019): 465.

19. See Strank, "Status Quo Ante," 463: "Netflix and Amazon Prime Video … tend to prefer franchises and branding to proper innovation."

20. Jason Mittell, *Complex TV*, 165.

Works Cited

Adams, Jeffrey. *The Cinema of the Coen Brothers: Hard-Boiled Entertainments*. New York: Columbia University Press, 2015.

Gill, Patrick. "'I swore I'd not go reality': The Bluths through the Lens of Genre." In *A State of* Arrested Development*: Critical Essays on the Innovative Television Comedy*, ed. Kristin M. Barton. Jefferson, NC: McFarland, 2015, 197–210.

Innocenti, Veronica, and Guglielmo Pescatore. "Changing Series: Narrative Models and the Role of the Viewer in Contemporary Television Seriality." *Between* 4, no. 8 (2014): 1–15. http://dx.doi.org/10.13125/2039-6597/4.

Lundén, Rolf. "Centrifugal and Centripetal Narrative Strategies in the Short Story Composite and the Episode Film." *Cycles, Recueils, Macrotexts*, special issue of *Interférences littéraires/Literaire interferenties* 12 (2014): 49–60.

Mittell, Jason. *Complex TV: The Poetics of Contemporary Television Storytelling*. New York: New York University Press, 2015.

Poniewozik, James. "Go Ahead, Binge-watch That TV Show." *Time*, July 10, 2012. https://entertainment.time.com/2012/07/10/go-ahead-binge-watch-that-tv-show/.

Strank, Willem. "Status Quo Ante: Music in (Post)Quality TV." *American Music* 37, no. 4 (winter 2019): 458–471.

Vanarendonk, Kathryn. "The Case Against *Black Mirror*," *Slate*, October 25, 2016. https://slate.com/culture/2016/10/the-case-against-black-mirror.html.

Joshua Marston's *Come Sunday* (2018)

Biopic in the Streaming Era

Despoina Triantafyllidou

In this essay, I will analyze Josh Marston's *Come Sunday* based on theoretical tools with the aim of concluding that the movie is a *biopic*. The biopic is one of the earlier film genres which appeared during the silent cinema. Rick Altman called it a "major" genre, alongside the western and the musical.[1] The characteristics and conventions of the biopic film genre were identified in 1992 by George F. Custen, who examined a corpus of 291 biographies of the classic Hollywood period (1927–1960). Custen defines the biopic as a movie that "depicts the life of a historical person, past or present."[2] He also refers to the silent era in which a major development for the biopic took place. Specifically, in 1902 "fame was democratized" with Edwin S. Porter's short film *The Capture of The Biddle Brothers*.[3] The brothers Jack and Ed Biddle were two criminals imprisoned in Pittsburgh, Pennsylvania, who managed to escape thanks to the actions of the guard's wife, Katherine Soffel.[4] So, biopics no longer narrated the lives of already known historical figures, but also focused on people, "headliners," as Custen calls them, who occupied the "print media," the newspaper pages.[5]

Joshua Marston's *Come Sunday* depicts a "headliner," a person whose story became widely known to the American public through a different type of media, the radio. Also, the film is part of a tendency that emerged in the biopic during the mid–1990s, in which the number of films narrating the lives of "people of color" increased.[6] Taking into account Jason Mittel's view that television "genres are cultural categories that surpass the boundaries of media texts and operate within industry, audience, and cultural practices"[7] and the methods of *The New Film History*, *Come Sunday* will be examined according to textual and contextual analysis.[8] Mittel underlined that genres are "categories of texts" and that "textual analysis"

> cannot examine media genres as they operate at the categorical level—there are texts that are categorized by genres, but their textual sum does not equal the whole of the genre. Instead, we must separate the practice of analyzing generically labeled texts from analyzing genre as a cultural category. Analyses of generic texts are certainly worthwhile, but they do not explain how genres themselves operate as categories.[9]

Applying the methods of *The New Film History* this paper will focus on "critical examination of primary sources, both filmic and non-filmic,"[10] examining all the stages of the production of the movie.

Pre-Production

The film is based on the 304th episode titled *Heretics* of the weekly public radio program and podcast *This American Life*. The episode aired on December 16, 2005, and by its official website we are informed that the program reveals "The story of Reverend Carlton Pearson, a rising star in the evangelical movement, who cast aside the idea of hell, and with it everything he'd worked over his entire life."[11] Ira Glass, the producer and host of the program, was also one of the film's producers. He wrote a short text on the same website, mentioning that *This American Life* was the first medium which brought to light Pearson's true story, the actors participating in the film and its Netflix streaming.[12] Glass also promoted the movie's verisimilitude by stating that

> (...) the stuff that Oral says to Carlton—even the stuff about his gay son—is stuff he really said in real life to Carlton. (Our screenwriter Marcus Hinchey spent hundreds of hours talking to Carlton.)[13]

In this way Glass assures the audience that everything depicted in the movie is the truth. It also presents a tactic of the major studios in the classical Hollywood era. Given the fact that "legal considerations were a factor controlling a biopic life,"[14] each production tried to avoid any reaction of the protagonist's relatives by hiring "them as paid consultants" or "obtain their approval."[15] As we are informed by the closing credits, Bishop Pearson was a consultant of the movie, thus making the story more believable.

The Filmic Text

The movie starts in medias res, using the real names of all the people involved in the biopic subject's story. It does not, therefore, narrate

Pearson's (Chiwetel Ejiofor) life as a whole, but only a part of it. After all, Custen underlines that few movies described a person's life from "cradle to the grave," from birth to the final moment.[16] So, starting in medias res, the plot presents Pearson as a priest who is loved and accepted by his flock, by his mentor Oral Roberts (Martin Sheen), by his close friend and collaborator Henry (Jason Segel) and by all those who support the Pentecostal church of Higher Dimensions.

Custen suggests that "almost every biopic" begins with "title cards that place the piece in context or with a voice-over narration that historically 'sets up' the film."[17] He names this "convention" of the biopic film genre "the introductory assertion of truth."[18] If a biopic didn't have this convention, other forms of "facticity," such as photos, songs, etc., appeared to certify to the public that the film depicted real people and events.[19] *Come on Sunday* has two "introductory assertions of truth." We are able to locate the first one before the main title appears. In the opening scene we see Pearson's left hand as he flips through his bible, which is full of notes. He is getting ready for another inspired speech in front of a new congregation, part of his spiritual tour in the U.S. The "introductory assertion of truth" is the Bible itself. The real subject of the biopic, Pearson, gave his own Bible to the production to use.[20] The Bible becomes a direct connection between the actor and the real person portrayed in the movie.

The second "introductory assertion of truth" is a title card which informs us that the story we are about to watch is *BASED ON ACTUAL EVENTS*. This card is "avowing," as Custen claims about title cards, "that the film that follows is true."[21] Then we conclude that the "flashback," which according to Custen is a "framing devise" of the biopic that informs the viewers of "the tale of success" of the protagonist, is not present here.[22] The movie's narration is linear, and it starts in 1998, when Pearson was on his tour around the country. This finding is not problematic, if we take in consideration that "one out of every five films" that Custen studied applied the flashback "framing device."[23]

Apart from the "introductory assertion of truth" and the "framing devices," Custen analyzes various "narrative components" of the biopic. He states that "family," "close friends and guides," "public reception of talent," "innovation," "the price of being different," "fortune and misfortune," "historical era depicted," "character demographics and ethnicity," and "social class"[24] are aspects of the genre that influence and shape its essence and evolution.

The story begins in 1998 when Pearson, who was born in 1953, was 45 years old. According to Custen, most of the biopics in his sample depicted their protagonists starting at the age of 19 years old or later in their life.[25] In this way

> Self-creation, the free development of talent through the will of an individual who is detached from a family, is the dominant biopic credo.[26]

Here the hero is presented at an age when he is not affected by the family environment. His new path is the result of his own choice and his own thoughts regarding religion and man and it was revealed to him one night while he was holding his little daughter in his arms. As he tried to put her to sleep the news talked about the humanitarian crisis in Rwanda. Watching all those children dying and suffering had an enormous impact in his religious views. He came to realize that God is not a "monster," showing His mercy only to those who accept Him, but He accepts even them in paradise. Pearson believes that God spoke to him at that moment, guiding him to a new path.

In Pearson's case self-creation finds him in a more mature age, which is pointed out by a scene that reveals the influence of the family and particularly of his mother in embracing of his previous views. After the funeral of his uncle, Quincy (Danny Glover), who committed suicide after Pearson refused to assist in his release from prison, Pearson talks with his mother (Charming Lee) in the kitchen. Their discussion informs us that his mother was the one who as a child instilled in him the fear of hell. But now the changing of his views will take place thanks to his free will and not to the influence of his family. Apart from this scene, Carlton's family is absent in the rest of the movie. According to Custen, "something must take the place of the family" when it is absent in a biopic, because "the biopic figure cannot be without some sources of human contact."[27] In the Hollywood Studio era biopics "heterosexual romance" and "friends" were the sources of human contact that replaced family relations.[28]

Oral is Pearson's mentor, guide, and a father figure to the young priest. Oral accepted him in his church and university and treats him as his successor. Henry is Carlton's close friend and collaborator. However, their support declines since Carlton openly disputes the existence of hell and supports the view that all people can be saved by God. Henry makes a last effort out of love to persuade him to recall what he said. The love between them is obvious even when Henry informs him that he will create a new church and later on, when the two meet again, he admits that the new church is doing very well in contrast to Carlton's, where the whole flock fits in a small room.

Usually, the friend of the famous figure is a guide, a "manager," a "moral gyroscope, reminding the great one of nonprofessional values like modesty, honesty, family, and, above all else, love," or "a representative of the larger public that acclaims the great man or woman."[29] Henry is a kind of manager. He treats the church not only as a place of prayer, but also as such a commercial transaction. Speaking with Carlton, he focuses on the number of believers who attend the Sunday Service, the promotion of Carlton's tour and the television broadcast of the service. Carlton is also interested in these parameters bypassing, as the movie promotes, the true message of faith.

But Henry's, and Oral's, influence on Carlton is not presented in depth. On the contrary his relationship with young Reggie (LaKeith Stanfield) is more substantial. Reggie, an organist in the church's band who suffers from a serious illness, becomes a true friend, reminding Carlton about the meaning of his profession. When the two disagree, Reggie decides to go away, and they do not meet for a whole year.

As far as the "heterosexual romance" is concerned, Pearson's relationship with his wife Gina (Condola Rashad) is present in the biopic. The viewer is informed that their marriage did not come from love, but was arranged. Pearson confesses to a total stranger whom he wishes to help that "I was raised to believe that having a family was a distraction from God. I struggled with it; I still do. Even though they are the most precious thing to me."

While the hero is at the top of his career, Gina is sidelined and criticized for her views. There is an obvious distance between the couple, which, although it causes conflicts, is gradually decreasing. When Carlton's fall begins Gina stays by his side, supporting him warmly. However, confused by what is happening, he does not realize that she is his most important supporter. Finally, he embraces the truth and Gina's love.

Analyzing the narrative component of the "public reception of talent," Custen refers to the "central conflict" of the biopic in which the protagonist, as he/she tries to achieve the "undoable" "the unconventional" and the impossible, "confronts the members of a given community" that does not agree with his/hers views of his/hers way of life.[30] So, we see Carlton trying to convince his followers as well as Henry, Oral, and all the representatives of the Pentecostal church that all men are children of God and that all can be "saved," even if they are not baptized or converted. Here the conflict culminates in a "trial-like scene." In the classic form of the biopic, one could come across a trial scene or a "trial-like scene" in which the subject of the movie expressed his/her views. This resulted in a shift of the community opinion and the acceptance of the subject's talent and personality. Carlton is called to apologize before the Joint Council of African-American Bishops. The scene evolves into a form of sacred examination, from which, however, Carlton does not emerge victorious. His superiors consider his views heretical, while Oral and Henry support that Carlton did not hear the voice of God, but the voice of Satan, who is trying to deceive him.

Meanwhile, innovation in the biopic can be expressed by making "the famous person relentlessly normal in other spheres" in addition to the quality that made him/her known. In the beginning of the movie Carlton is about to speak in front of an audience during his U.S. tour. The announcer (Gerard Catus) welcomes him with the following words:

> Ladies and Gentlemen. We are blessed to have with us a key man in the world today. One of the most beloved of the Pentecostal movement in America. God has chosen him. There is a destiny a work in him. He is prayed with presidents. Now, I know no one who ministers so tirelessly to so many. And he's been going non-stop this tour, and I thank God for giving him the strength to be with us before he flies back home to Tulsa. Ladies and Gentlemen put your hands together for the one, the only Bishop Carlton Pearson!

The crowd applauds and we realize that this man is an important person for the American Pentecostal Church, a bishop that has won the appreciation and respect of his congregation, a man of God. God has chosen him for a reason and that reason was up until that moment the spiritual guidance. So, Carlton appears as a strong and confident shepherd who did not question his faith and beliefs. But like all people, the biographical figure has weaknesses and vulnerabilities that portray him as "normal" in his personal life. He has difficulty in communicating with his wife and reaches a point he never thought he would reach. The "innovation" in this case is summarized in that an "enlightened" priest, as most people consider him, behaves like an ordinary person in his personal life. He faces family problems and dilemmas.

The fact that he dares to question key points of his faith relates to the "fortune and misfortune" that Custen pointed out. Carlton was at one point the successor of Oral, but suddenly fell into disfavor. His "misfortune" highlights the "lesson one learns from biopic vicissitudes (…): with an unusual gift comes unusual suffering."[31] In addition to the gift of a capable orator, he has the ability not only to be close to God and the well-dressed people who listen to him every Sunday, but to feel the deeper meaning of the love and the mercy of God. Saying in his sermon that God accepts in the kingdom of heaven even those who were not baptized in his name and those who did not hear the word of Christ, he automatically creates a gap between himself and his followers. His followers react strongly to the thought that a sinner who never knew God can be forgiven and accepted in paradise. The result is that Carlton must suffer for believing that God is merciful for all his children, regardless of religion, origin, and race. His gift, his open mind and compassionate heart, causes his suffering and gives a message to the viewer.

> As Lowenthal and Adorno suggested (…) the audience member viewing a misfortune in a popular film is reassured that a normal, obscure life is perhaps

> preferable to the proverbial price of fame; life as it is, not life as the movies show it, should be cherished.[32]

Although Carlton is treated as an outcast, his "salvation" comes in an "explanatory episode." Custen notes that the "episode can be a single case or instance that changes a life."[33] So, a year after the events that led him out of the church, he visits Reggie, whose illness has worsened. Reggie is surprised to see him after so long and the two men start to talk about God. Reggie tells him that being gay is not a choice, but who he is, and asks Carlton to save him from hell. Finally, Carlton realizes the meaning of the hard times he went through and the message he had to share with people. He may not have saved his uncle, but he gets his chance with Reggie, telling him that

> "You don't have to be saved (…) Look at me, Reggie. When the time comes you'll be with Him" (singing) Jesus loves me this I know. For the Bible tells me so (…)

Reggie is fighting not only with his condition but with his homosexuality, believing, as Carlton has told him, that he will only be saved if he does not "act as gay." His fear of death and hell has peaked when Carlton meets him again after a year apart. Away from his flock, Carlton has lost his way and he no longer preaches. He is waiting for something that will give meaning to his new views and will mean a new beginning to his call. Reggie brings this opportunity to him, this redemption. As the two men speak, Carlton has an epiphany, and everything clears up. Offering Reggie salvation and a relief from fear, Carlton saves himself in this "explanatory episode." After their conversation Carlton finds himself on the bank of a river. With a symbolic gesture, pouring water on his head, he is baptized again. The reborn hero returns to the church, but now preaches to "outcasts" like himself, people who really need him, welcoming into God's church all people, regardless of origin, sexual orientation, appearance, and color, and telling them that God is merciful. He talks to them in a small room, realizing that he has made the right choice. Only this time he knows that the message he conveys to the world is that of inclusion.

As for "historical era depicted," "character demographics and ethnicity," and "social class," the movie depicts the life of a living person, an African American bishop who managed to succeed in his life. His quote "The way it was back then, you either went to church or you went to jail," explains his choice to become a priest and enhances the success he enjoys at the beginning of the movie. His subsequent fall and the fact that he managed to get up again indicate his desire to find out if he could find God again.

Reception and Netflix Release

The movie's premiere took place on the 21st of January at the 2018 *Sundance Film Festival.* The following day senior movie critic for *Variety* Peter Debruge commented on the movie's release on Netflix:

> "Come Sunday" may be the perfect film for Netflix. Too fair-and-balanced to have come from the faith-based community and far too churchy to have gotten the blessing of any studio (…).[34]

He also noted that if it had been released in big city movie theaters it would have probably become a big failure. Inland moviegoers would have never experienced its screening, as a result of the possible lack of enthusiasm from the major markets. That is to say, Debruge pointed out what Tom Brueggemann expressed a year earlier, that

> (…) those concerned with the future of the medium, and of independent film in particular, need to embrace the way that Netflix is changing the business, because it might just end up saving it.[35]

So, Netflix, a popular and constantly developing video streaming service, becomes a "savior," as we might call it, for indie films. The following April Netflix subscribers, beginning in the U.S, had the opportunity to watch Marston's biopic. Just one day before its release, *The Guardian* published an interview of director Josh Marston and Bishop Carlton Pearson.[36] Marston notes the significance of telling Pearson's true story. Considering that we live in an era in which people hold strong to their opinions, he underlines that Pearson questioned openly and with bravery his faith and opinions.[37] Upon the movie's online streaming, Marston states that this way Netflix gives the opportunity to more people, and especially to those who live in small communities, the freedom to watch without hesitation or fear a story that concerns "a heretic."[38]

Glenn Kenny praised the actors' performances, especially Chiwetel Ejiofor's portrayal of Pearson, but characterized the movie as "bloodless," because the conflict between Pearson and his former associates is not as strong as it ought to be.[39] Ben Kenigsberg called the screenplay by Marcus Hinchey "occasionally too blunt," but concluded that the movie

> (…) accords sympathetic moments to all its characters—a strategy that gives this chronicle of religious convictions a conviction of its own.[40]

For Tim Grierson *Come Sunday* is a "reverential biopic" which respects the variety of contrasting opinions expressed in it. This is stated by the fact that though Hinchey and Marston agree with the main character's point of view, they are not focusing on promoting his religious beliefs but instead depicting how the faith of a single man can be both "personal and passionate."[41] Ejiofor's performance was also applauded by David Ehrlich.[42] Concerning the direction style, he underlines that it was "flat, purely functional." He also notices that "an ambivalence that dilutes the film's ambiguity" is uncovered in case someone watched it "on the big screen."[43] Concluding his review, Ehrlich states that "The director minimizes the fear that his subject conquers, as well as the love that he finds in the rubble" and that the movie is more interesting and agonizing through Ejiofor's presence and performance than it is through the director's point of view.[44]

Conclusion

Come Sunday portrays a present-day clergyman approaching the complex issue of faith. Textual and contextual analysis leads to the conclusion that Marston's movie is a biopic that presents the characteristics of the genre's classical form, incorporating the developments of the genre that occurred during the mid–1990s. The biopic mostly applies the genre conventions, bringing the classical aspect of the genre to the modern era of streaming services.

Netflix classifies the movie in the categories "Movies Based on Real Life, Dramas, Independent Movies." With the release of this and other "based on real life movies, Netflix has become a new platform for the film genre. With over 220 million subscribers worldwide, Netflix takes viewers inside the conventions and evolutions of one of the long-standing film genres. In this way Netflix not only "saves" indie movies but also gives the opportunity to viewers from all around the world to watch them through the popular streaming service.

Notes

1. Rick, Altman, *Film/Genre* (London: British Film Institute, 1999), 31.
2. George, F. Custen, *Bio/Pics. How Hollywood Constructed Public History* (New Brunswick, New Jersey: Rutgers University Press, 1992), 5.
3. Idid, 6.
4. Louis, Pizzitola, *Hearst Over Hollywood: Power, Passion, and Propaganda in the Movies* (New York: Columbia University Press, 2002), 87.
5. George, F. Custen, *Bio/Pics*, 6.
6. Carolyn Anderson and Jonathan, Lupo, "Hollywood Lives: The State of the Biopic at the Turn of The Century." In: Neale, S. (ed.) Genre and Contemporary Hollywood. (London: British Film Institute, 2002), p. 92.

7. Jason, Mittel, "A Cultural Approach to Television Genre Theory," In: *Cinema Journal*, Vol. 40, No. 3 (Spring, 2001), p. 3.

8. Despoina Triantafyllidou, *Το βιογραφικό Φιλμ στην Ελληνική Κινηματογραφική Παραγωγή (1926–2018) : Μια θεωρητική και ιστορική μελέτη*. PhD Thesis, Aristotle University of Thessaloniki (2019) pp. 23, 58.

9. Jason, Mittel, "A Cultural Approach to Television Genre Theory, p. 8.

10. *James* Chapman, Mark Glancy and Sue Harper(2007) "Introduction," In: Chapman, J. Mark Glancy, M. and Harper, S. (eds.) *The New Film History. Sources, Methods, Approaches*.(New York: Palgrave Macmillan, 1992), pp. 1–10.

11. "Heretics," This American Life, accessed July 15, 2020, https://www.thisamericanlife.org/304/heretics.

12. Ira Glass, "Our New Movie, "Come Sunday," accessed July 15, 2020, https://www.thisamericanlife.org/extras/our-new-movie-come-sunday.

13. Ira Glass, "Our New Movie."

14. George, F. Custen, *Bio/Pics*, 22.

15. *Ibid.*

16. *Ibid.*, 150.

17. *Ibid.*, 51.

18. *Ibid.*

19. *Ibid.*

20. Peter Debruge, " "Film Review: 'Come Sunday,'" *Variety*, January 22, 2018, https://variety.com/2018/film/reviews/come-sunday-review-1202671818/.

21. George F. Custen, *Bio/Pics*, 51.

22. *Ibid.*, 182.

23. *Ibid.*

24. *Ibid.* 67–80.

25. *Ibid.*, 154

26. *Ibid.*

27. *Ibid.*, 158.

28. *Ibid.*, 158–159.

29. *Ibid.*, 163–164.

30. *Ibid.*, 72.

31. *Ibid.*, 75.

32. *Ibid.*, 75.

33. *Ibid.*, 165

34. Peter Debruge, "Film Review: 'Come Sunday.'"

35. Tom Brueggemann, "Defending Netflix: Why the Streaming Giant May Be the Savior of Indie Film—Editorial," *IndieWire*, May 1, 2017, https://www.indiewire.com/2017/05/defending-netflix-streaming-giant-savior- indie-film-1201808694/.

36. Jamiles Lartey, "Come Sunday: how one of America's biggest preachers became a Pariah," *The Guardian*, April 12, 2018, https://www.theguardian.com/film/2018/apr/12/come-sunday-how-one-of-americas- biggest-preachers-became-a-pariah.

37. Lartey, "Come."

38. *Ibid.*

39. Glenn Kenny, "Reviews. Come Sunday," *Roger Ebert. Com*, April 13, 2018, https://www.rogerebert.com/reviews/come-sunday-2018.

40. Ben Kenigsberg, "Review: In 'Come Sunday,' Chiwetel Ejiofor Plays a Doubting Bishop," *The New York Times*, April 12, 2018, https://www.nytimes.com/2018/04/12/movies/come-sunday-review-chiwetel-ejiofor.html.

41. Tim Grierson, "'Come Sunday': Review," *Screen Daily*, April 11, 2018, https://www.screendaily.com/reviews/come-sunday-review/5128194.article.

42. David Ehrlich, "'Come Sunday' Review: Chiwetel Ejiofor Gives His Best Performance in Netflix Biopic About a Minister Afraid of God," *IndieWire*, April 12, 2018.

43. Ehrlich, "Come."

44. *Ibid.*

Works Cited

Altman, Rick. *Film/Genre*. London: British Film Institute, 1999.

Anderson, Carolyn, and Jonathan Lupo. "Hollywood Lives: The State of the Biopic at the Turn of The Century." In: Neale, S. (ed.) Genre and Contemporary Hollywood. London: British Film Institute, 2002, pp. 91–104.

Brueggemann, Tom. "Defending Netflix: Why the Streaming Giant May Be the Savior of Indie Film—Editorial." *IndieWire*, May 1, 2017. https://www.indiewire.com/2017/05/defending-netflix-streaming-giant-savior-indie-film-1201808694/.

Custen, F. George. *Bio/Pics. How Hollywood Constructed Public History*. New Brunswick, New Jersey: Rutgers University Press, 1992.

Debruge, Peter. "Film Review: 'Come Sunday.'" *Variety*, January 22, 2018. https://variety.com/2018/film/reviews/come-sunday-review-1202671818/.

Ehrlich, David. "'Come Sunday' Review: Chiwetel Ejiofor Gives His Best Performance in Netflix Biopic About a Minister Afraid of God." *IndieWire*, April 12, 2018. https://www.indiewire.com/2018/04/come-sunday-review-chiwetel-ejiofor-netflix-1201951634/.

Chapman, James, Mark Glancy and Sue Harper. "Introduction." In Chapman, J. Mark Glancy, M. and Harper, S. (eds.) *The New Film History. Sources, Methods, Approaches*. New York: Palgrave Macmillan, 1992, pp. 1–10.

Glass, Ira. "Our New Movie, "Come Sunday." accessed July 15, 2020. https://www.thisamericanlife.org/extras/our-new-movie-come-sunday.

Grierson, Tim. "'Come Sunday': Review." *Screen Daily*, April 11, 2018. https://www.screendaily.com/reviews/come-sunday-review/5128194.article.

Kenigsberg, Ben. "Review: In 'Come Sunday,' Chiwetel Ejiofor Plays a Doubting Bishop." *The New York Times*, April 12, 2018. https://www.nytimes.com/2018/04/12/movies/come-sunday-review-chiwetel-ejiofor.html.

Kenny, Glenn. "Reviews. Come Sunday." *Roger Ebert.com*, April 13, 2018. https://www.rogerebert.com/reviews/come-sunday-2018.

Lartey, Jamiles. "Come Sunday: how one of America's biggest preachers became a pariah." *The Guardian*, April 12, 2018. https://www.theguardian.com/film/2018/apr/12/come-sunday-how-one-of-americas-biggest-preachers-became-a-pariah.

Mittel, Jason. "A Cultural Approach to Television Genre Theory," In: *Cinema Journal*, Vol. 40, No. 3 (Spring, 2001), pp. 3–24.

Pizzitola, Louis. *Hearst Over Hollywood: Power, Passion, and Propaganda in the Movies*. New York: Columbia University Press, 2002.

This American Life. "Heretics." Accessed July 15, 2020. https://www.thisamericanlife.org/304/heretics.

Triantafyllidou, Despoina. *Το βιογραφικό Φιλμ στην Ελληνική Κινηματογραφική Παραγωγή (1926–2018) : Μια θεωρητική και ιστορική μελέτη*. PhD Thesis, Aristotle University of Thessaloniki (2019).

The Binge-Watch Experience and the Three-Act Structure

A Narrative Analysis of Stranger Things

Sotiris Petridis

Introduction—Netflix Originals and Binge-Watching

In recent years, audiovisual narratives started to increase due to the evolution of technology and the advent of new media. At the same time, video streaming services began to produce original content that is meant to be consumed exclusively on online platforms. Netflix is a pioneer on this field, since it was the first subscription video on demand (SVOD) platform that created original content with the intention for binge-watch consumption. In this essay, I will analyze the overarching story of *Stranger Things* (2016–present), a well-known Netflix Original series, and I will argue that the structure of the narrative works more like a long-form film, rather than a TV series. Based on theoretical tools from screenwriting and film studies, I will claim that the first season of the series works as a unified and extensive audiovisual narrative that can be compared with classical filmic texts. In order to prove this argument, I will compare the narrative structure of the first season of *Stranger Things* with the structure of *Stand by Me* (1986), a classic film that has been an inspiration to the creators of the series, and I will prove that both audiovisual works are created based on the norms of the three-act model of narration.

The circumstances of fictional storytelling have significantly altered in recent years, since the production, distribution and consumption of narrative across a range of media have become increasingly digitalized and linked to the internet.[1] In 2013, Netflix started a new digital age for television by producing *House of Cards* (2013–2018), *Hemlock Grove*

(Netflix, 2013–2015) and *Orange Is the New Black* (Netflix, 2013–2019), the first original audiovisual works created for a streaming service. The most interesting aspect that makes Netflix Original TV series stand out is that they renounce the conventions of traditional serial distribution by making available the entire seasons at once.[2] Netflix considered the new viewing habits of the audience that already had started with DVD releases or Internet streaming of older series[3] and incorporated them into the production and distribution process of its original content by building a model of individualized viewing practices and self-scheduling of TV.[4]

The new feature that became synonymous with Netflix is the binge-watch consumption of audiovisual content, a term that describes the practice of watching a television show's episodes in a row within a short-time span.[5] In an interview posted the day before Netflix released the first season of *House of Cards* in 2013, showrunner Beau Willimon stated, "Our goal is to shut down a portion of America for a whole day."[6] Netflix has produced numerous hours of original TV content and continues to maintain the same distribution pattern to the present time. As it was logical, this model of distribution influenced the structuring methods of these series, since it altered the essence of the television medium. These audiovisual texts have more in common with films than with conventional TV series.

The big difference between a conventional TV series and a film is the progression of their narratives. While a film is usually a complete story with a closed ending, a TV series is an ever-evolving narrative for both the story and the characters.[7] Since the overarching story of a conventional series can last for several seasons—and consequently years—episodes are the key elements to the communication with the audience. As Jason Mittell observes:

> American commercial television differs from much of the world in how it privileges a narrative model in which a successful series never ends, with a final episode typically regarded as a sign of commercial failure and/or creative exhaustion, and often programs end by abrupt cancellation more than planned conclusion.[8]

In order to ensure that viewers will watch the next segment, act, episode, or even season, the structuring norms of television dictate for the placement of multiple cliffhangers, leaving the viewers with all sorts of open questions, but at the same time one of the biggest challenges of a TV serial narrative is to maintain viewer comprehension. As Jeremy Butler points out, "series are based on the assumption that individual episodes may reach a certain amount of closure, but no definitive closure, which would forestall a continuation of the series."[9] But, what happens when a series is created exclusively for binge-watch consumption in an online platform like Netflix that does not have commercial breaks?

Talking about TV series made for streaming services, Veronica Innocenti and Guglielmo Pescatore note that "the single episode is now little more than a departure point for the engagement of the user, who is increasingly asked to interact with the serial product in a participatory way."[10] These audiovisual narratives have been created to be viewed all at once, hence the focus of this discourse has to change. As Kathryn VanArendonk argues, "in shows like this, the episode has become, if not a completely invisible force, then something with much less power than it used to have."[11]

With the aforementioned information, it is easily understood that Netflix Original TV series are not conceived as conventional television shows since they are meant to be consumed all at once. These series share more similarities with filmic texts that follow the classical model of narration, because they are not fragmented into pieces that broadcast each week but are concrete structures that operate as steps of a larger narrative. Of course, the question that arises is what exactly the classical model of narration is and how is adapted into a TV series.

The Three-Act Structure and the Fifteen Beats

The majority of filmic texts are part of the classical model of narration and obey some fundamental rules, while following the three-act structure, because they have a beginning (a first act), a middle (a second act), and an end (a third act).[12] The three-act structure as we know it today was introduced in 1978 by Constance Nash and Virginia Oakey[13] and became famous one year later through Syd Field.[14] Of course, there are other structuring methods on analysis of the classical narration, but the domination of this model is so concrete that many of the seemingly alternative approaches with a higher number of smaller units confirm their validity by stating how the proposed units can be fitted into the three acts.[15] Approaches of the classical narration that validate the aforementioned statement include Paul Joseph Gulino's eight sequence structure (2004),[16] Christopher Vogler's twelve stages of the hero's journey (1998),[17] and Blake Snyder's fifteen beats (2005).[18]

Each act has its own purpose and the progression of the narrative is structured in this way in order for the main conflict to come to an end. The three acts cover stable and balanced portions of narrative time (25%-50%-25%), with the first act presenting all the necessary information about the fictional world and the main characters, the second act developing the story and complicating the conflict, and the third act solving the main conflict.

Since there are several alternatives of theoretical tools that are used to analyze the classical model of narration, I will use a more detailed outline of the three-act structure in order to avoid generalizations and create more concrete results. Therefore, I will use Blake Snyder's fifteen beats approach, which keeps the three-act structure intact, but at the same time divides the narrative into fifteen units of analysis.

In his approach, Snyder breaks down the three-act structure and creates a "beat sheet" with fifteen manageable sections, each with a specific goal in service of the overall story.[19] Snyder defines the estimated time of each beat according to a 110-minute film, but it can be adjusted to the duration of any audiovisual narration. The fifteen beats and their estimated starting times are:

1. ***Opening Image*** (minute 1): The first beat has a name that is very self-explanatory, since it's the first scene that the audience sees and sets up the tone, type, and initial impression of the narrative.
2. ***Theme Stated*** (5): In this beat, the audience can detect the "heart" of the narrative, or in other words what the film is about.
3. ***Set-up*** (1-10): The beginning of the narrative is always an introduction to the fictional world, the main characters and the main antagonistic forces of the story.
4. ***Catalyst*** (12): This beat introduces an action in the narrative that attracts the viewer's attention and creates the central dramatic question and the main conflict of the film.
5. ***Debate*** (12-25): From the catalyst until the end of the first act, the main characters doubt the journey they are called to take. This call comes after the events of the catalyst.
6. ***Break into Two*** (25): This is the first plot point, or in other words the point of no return for the main characters. This is the point in which the film enters into its second act, which is the biggest part of the narrative.
7. ***B Story*** (30): After the beginning of the second act, a secondary storyline is introduced, usually in line with the theme of the main storyline and therefore, the entire narrative.
8. ***Fun and Games*** (30-55): "The promise of the premise"—From the midpoint onwards the stakes are high, so at this point the difficulties are perceived as fun and games.
9. ***Midpoint*** (55): This beat is literally the middle of the narrative, from where the stakes start to be higher than ever before and the situation is starting to get more difficult for the main characters.

10. ***Bad Guys Close In*** (55-75): After the midpoint, follows a part of the narrative in which both internally (the characters' problems) and externally (when the "bad guys" seem to win), the pressure on the main characters is higher than ever.

11. ***All Is Lost*** (75): Then, the supposed defeat of the main characters after the big pressure takes place.

12. ***Dark Night of the Soul*** (75-85): The end of the second act is the point of the narrative where the characters have lost all hope.

13. ***Break into Three*** (85): At the thirteenth beat, the narrative enters into the third and final act. This beat is the second plot point, where the characters are at their lowest point, but decide to fight back again.

14. ***Finale*** (85-110): This beat is the biggest part of the third act, in which the audience gets all the answers wanted and the narrative concludes.

15. ***Final Image*** (110): The final beat of a classical narrative is the contrasting image of the first beat (opening image) and the proof that change has taken place through the progression of the narrative.

It is clear that Snyder's approach follows the three-act structure but creates smaller units within the acts in order to provide a more detailed analysis of an audiovisual narrative. More specifically, the first five beats constitute the first act, the next seven beats are the second act, while the third act is comprised by the final three beats.

Of course, like the generalized approach of the three-act structure, this beat sheet is a powerful tool for analyzing filmic narratives. In order to better understand the three-act structure as a tool of structuring filmic narratives, I am going to analyze *Stand by Me* (1986), a classic film of the 1980s that was one of the main inspirations of *Stranger Things*.

The Fifteen Beats of Stand by Me

Stand by Me is an American coming-of-age film directed by Rob Reiner and based on Stephen King's 1982 novella *The Body*. The story is about four boys in 1959 Castle Rock, Oregon, who go on a hike in order to find the dead body of a missing boy. The film has a total duration of 84 minutes without the end credits. The film's narrative is a characteristic example of cinema's three-act structure and obeys the rules of Snyder's fifteen beats. More particularly, the fifteen beats of *Stand by Me*'s narrative are:

1. ***Opening Image*** (minute 1): The first image of the film is set in the present, in which the protagonist, as an adult, reads in the paper about the death of his childhood friend, Chris (River Phoenix). Then,

some kids with bikes pass by his car. The opening image sets the tone of the narrative and introduces the main character.

2. ***Theme Stated*** (4): Then, in a dialogue scene between the four friends, the theme of the film is stated. From this scene it is clear that the film is about friendship and more specifically about the relationship between Gordie (Wil Wheaton) and Chris.

3. ***Set-up*** (1-8): The first minutes of the film are dedicated to the set-up of the fictional world. In this beat, the audience is introduced to the main characters and the main premise of the narrative.

4. ***Catalyst*** (8): Then, at the eighth minute the catalyst occurs. In this beat, there is the establishing of the information about the dead body and the desire of the four main characters to explore the area to find it.

5. ***Debate*** (8-19): Then, the last part of the first act of the narrative that is dealing with the internal debate of the main characters is covering the fictional time between the expressed desire to find to the body and the actual beginning of their journey.

6. ***Break into Two*** (19): In the sixth beat the narrative enters its second act. The group of friends has started their journey and things are getting real for them. At this point, a train becomes a threat, something that causes tension between the four friends.

7. ***B Story*** (20): At the same time, at the beginning of the second act, a secondary storyline is starting to be developed. In this storyline, we see the whole parallel journey of the group of the bullies that will lead to the final confrontation and resolution of the main conflict between them and the main protagonists of the narrative.

8. ***Fun and Games*** (20-42): The first part of the second act is dedicated to the extension of the main conflict, but at the same time things are seemingly easy for the main characters. The journey of the group of main characters seems to be going well and all of the obstacles are manageable.

9. ***Midpoint*** (42): Then, the midpoint occurs and the stakes are getting higher. The kids continue their journey and end up on a railroad bridge. After discussion, they try to cross it, but while they are on the bridge, a train comes and puts in danger the group of friends. The obstacles are starting to get more difficult and the main characters realize the importance of their decisions.

10. ***Bad Guys Close In*** (42-53): In the tenth beat of the film, the main characters continue to face more difficult obstacles that make the antagonistic forces look more powerful than in the first part of the second act. While the night has come, the group of friends decide to sleep in the woods.

11. ***All Is Lost*** (53): While the group is sleeping in the woods, the

characters are woken by wolf sounds. It seems that the main characters are in real danger and now their trip seems a not so good idea after all.

12. ***Dark Night of the Soul*** (53-63): While there are many obstacles for the group of friends, the protagonist of the narrative has a nightmare in which he sees the funeral of his brother. He wakes up and talks with his best friend. This point of the narrative is the lowest point of the protagonist, both internally and externally. After that scene, the group of friends continue their journey.

13. ***Break into Three*** (63): Then, the narrative enters its third and final act. In the second plot point, the bullies decide to go and find the dead body themselves, something that makes it clear that eventually they will come into conflict with the main characters.

14. ***Finale*** (63-84): The rest of the narrative is the third act and therefore the fourteenth beat. In this part of the narrative, the four friends find the body, face the bullies and eventually the main conflict of the film is resolved.

15. ***Final Image*** (84): In the last image of the film, the adult version of Gordie writes this story into his computer. He finishes his writing with the phrase "I never had any friends later on like the ones I had when I was twelve. Jesus, does anyone?"

After this beat-by-beat analysis, we can clearly see that *Stand by Me* is a fine example of a three-act narrative that is structured in a manner that obeys the classical norms of narration. More specifically, the first act is 23 percent, the second act is 52 percent, and the third and final act is 25 percent—percentages that marginally match the analytical model of narration. This is not an exception, but the rule in classical cinema, since a high percentage of commercial films are following the classical model of narration. Of course, even if the three-act structure is a common option in filmic texts, TV series are long-form audiovisual narratives that are not easily capable of adapting these structuring methods.

Nevertheless, as highlighted above, Netflix has blurred the line between television and film, with Adam Hart stating that there is now a convergence of film and television on such streaming services.[20] Based on the particularities of Netflix, a fundamental question arises: can we examine original TV series produced by Netflix using the three-act structure and consider them as long form filmic texts?

The Case of Stranger Things

It is clear that the original productions of Netflix have blurred the line between television and cinema. Since Netflix is solely based on the binge-watch experience, the three-act structure can be used as a theoretical tool in order to analyze the Netflix Originals' narratives. Even if this is an innovative approach by the academic community, some creators have admitted that they have used this structure when they outlined the overarching story of a season. For example, the writers of the Netflix series *Bloodline* (2015–2017) have stated that the new aspects of the medium in the SVOD era

> allowed us to say, we're going to approach the first three episodes as the first act of our story, Episodes 4, 5, 6 and 7 is the second act of our story, and then 8 through 13 is the third act. So, we're feeling more like, we're taking advantage of this storytelling medium, meaning you can watch multiple episodes, you can watch the whole first act at once, which is very different than a network or a cable show, unless you watch it after it's already aired. And so, for us, that desire is, we can go deeper, and hopefully create a stronger bond between the audience and the characters.[21]

Even the creators of these shows admit that their work is subject to the new norms of television consumption. One of these Netflix Original TV series that work like a long form film is *Stranger Things*.

Stranger Things is an American hybrid fantasy horror TV series with science fiction elements, created by the Duffer Brothers. The series premiered on Netflix on 15 July 2016 and it already counts four seasons. Since we are talking about a series with several seasons that have not come to a conclusion yet, this analysis will be based on the first season of the show. The first season of the series has an 8-episode structure and a total duration of 383 minutes (without the end credits of each episode). The story is set in the fictional town of Hawkins, Indiana, in 1983, and focuses on the investigation of the disappearance of Will (Noah Schnapp), while supernatural events are occurring around the town, including the appearance of a girl with psychokinetic abilities, Eleven (Millie Bobby Brown), who helps the missing boy's friends in their search.

Nostalgia has a central role in *Stranger Things*, since its narrative has a lot of references to other classical films and television shows. Phillip Mlynar points out that this series "comes off like a brilliantly nostalgic ode to the '80s, as it blends horror, sci-fi and supernatural elements and affectionately nods to movies like *The Goonies*, *E.T.* and *The Thing*."[22] At the same time, *The New York Times* compared the first season of the series to Reiner's *Stand by Me*, relating their nostalgic feel by "finding that timeless moment where everything seemed tantalizingly, scarily new."[23] In this nostalgic essence of the series, even the Duffer Brothers publicly recognized *Stand by Me* as a point of reference in the whole creation process, with actors auditioning for the children roles reading lines from this film.[24]

Even if the creators of the series are referred to this film as an inspiration regarding their nostalgic tone, in this essay I will prove that the narratives of *Stranger Things* and *Stand by Me* follow the same structuring pattern that is based on the classical model of narration.

If we analyze the narrative of the first season of *Stranger Things*, it is clear that the series obeys the rules of the classical narration and the three-act structure, since it is created as a concrete narrative that is not based on episodic storytelling. Even the creators have admitted that when they created the story of the series, they structured it like a unified audiovisual narrative.[25]

Since the series is created with a nostalgic tone regarding classical Hollywood films from the 1970s and 1980s, it seemed natural to the creators to use the same techniques while creating their narrative and use similar structuring tools like the ones from the films the series pays homage to. Therefore, the narrative of the first season of *Stranger Things* can be analyzed under the three-act structure scheme, while its narrative faithfully follows the fifteen beats of Snyder's approach. More specifically, we can detect the fifteen beats of the narrative of *Stranger Things* as follows:

1. **Opening Image** (minute 1): In the first beat the audience sees a scientist getting attacked by an unidentified creature, while the four main characters are playing Dungeons & Dragons. This sequence concludes with Will's disappearance while he was going back to his house.
2. **Theme Stated** (19): The series reveals the theme of its narrative in a dialogue scene between two of its main characters. When Joyce (Winona Ryder) goes to the town's police station to see Hopper (David Harbor), they talk about the disappearance of Will. Hopper says to her that 99 percent of the kids that are disappearing are found safe and alive and Joyce responds to him "what about that 1%?" This dialogue sets the tone of the entire narrative and encompasses the theme of the first season of the series.
3. **Set-Up** (1-40): The entire first episode is dedicated to the set-up of the story, in which the audience is introduced to the main cast of characters, the premise of the narrative, and the fictional world of Hawkins.
4. **Catalyst** (46): When the group of friends wander into the woods in order to find a clue regarding Will's disappearance, they find Eleven. This point of the story is very crucial to the progression of the narrative, since the main characters that will be the subject of the whole series are met and the main conflict starts to be established.

5. **Debate** (46-100): The rest of the first act is taking place in the second episode of the series and represents the denial of the main characters regarding the metaphysical aspect of the conflict. The majority of the main characters are approaching Will's disappearance realistically and ignore the metaphysical features around it.

6. **Breaking into Two** (100): At the first plot point the audience witnesses the attack by the Demogorgon on a main character, Barb (Shannon Purser). This collision of the real world and the Upside Down starts to have real victims, while the main characters are unaware of what is coming.

7. **B Story** (110): The first plot point sets the basis for the secondary storyline that will be developed in the second act of the narrative. More specifically, since the main characters do not know about the fate of Barbara, they are starting to search for her.

8. **Fun and Games** (110-196): In the third and fourth episodes that constitute this beat, the main characters have not yet discovered the involvement of metaphysical elements in the main conflict and approach the situation in a realistic manner. Will's apparent body is found by a search party, but Joyce refuses to believe that this body is Will's.

9. **Midpoint** (196): At the midpoint of the narrative, Hopper goes to the morgue and finds out that Will's body is a plastic mannequin that is filled with cotton. Until this beat, Hooper was represented as the more realistic character of the narrative.

10. **Bad Guys Close In** (196-241): Afterwards, the narrative progresses towards the empowerment of the antagonistic forces. At this beat, Hopper is being knocked out by the lab's guards and then awakens at his house. There, he finds a hidden microphone, leading him to realize that Joyce was right the whole time. Both internally and externally, the pressure against our main characters seems more prevailing than ever before.

11. **All Is Lost** (241): At this point of the narrative, everything seems lost for the main characters. The group of friends are splitting up. Lucas (Caleb McLaughlin) blames Eleven and Mike (Finn Wolfhard), something that forces Eleven to escape from this situation immediately. Everything now seems hopeless and impossible to achieve.

12. **Dark Night of the Soul** (241-291): Nancy (Natalia Dyer) and Jonathan (Charlie Heaton) formulate a plan to kill the Demogorgon but when they find it, Nancy ends up in the Upside Down. At the same time, Mike and Dustin are ambushed by some bullies, but they are subsequently rescued by Eleven, who afterwards admits to Mike that she is responsible for allowing the Demogorgon to enter the real world.

13. **Break into Three** (291): At the second plot point reinforcements are heading towards the group of kids, while Lucas notifies them. The course of events takes a turn that changes the progression of the narrative into a new direction that resets and reinforces the main conflict, since the narrative enters into its third and final act.

14. **Finale** (291-383): The rest of the narrative is dedicated to the third act and the resolution of the main conflict. Nancy and Jonathan reveal everything they know about the Demogorgon to Joyce and Hopper. Using her telepathy, Eleven finds Barb's corpse and with Joyce's help, she finds Will alive, hiding in the Upside Down. Hopper and Joyce break into the lab, enter the Upside Down and rescue Will. Finally, Eleven sacrifices herself in order to disintegrate the Demogorgon. The struggle between the real world and the Upside Down is over (at least for now).

15. **Final Image** (383): The narrative concludes with its final image, in which the group of the kids are playing Dungeons & Dragons like in the first sequence of the narrative. Then, Will returns home and eats dinner with his family. This final beat is the proof of the big change that occurred to the fictional world, since it totally conflicts with the first sequence of the narrative. Of course, since we are talking about a series with other seasons that followed, the final image sets an unanswered cliffhanger in order to start the next season (and consequently the next three-act structured narrative).

Based on the aforementioned beat-by-beat analysis, the overarching narrative of the first season of *Stranger Things* faithfully adheres to all the norms of the three-act structure. More specifically, the first act is 26 percent, the second act is 50 percent, and the third and final act is 24 percent. This is happening because of the desirable binge-watch experience, since Netflix wants the audience to consume the content in a short period of time, just like a film. Moreover, if we closely observe the beats of the series, we can find a resemblance between its structure and *Stand by Me*'s narrative.

Of course, the two narratives have a big difference regarding their duration, since *Stranger Things* is almost five times bigger than *Stand by Me*. For this reason, if we turn the durations of each beat of the two narratives into percentages, we conclude into these data:

Beat Sheet	Snyder's Approach	*Stand by Me*	*Stranger Things*
Opening Image	1%	1%	1%

Beat Sheet	Snyder's Approach	*Stand by Me*	*Stranger Things*
Theme Stated	5%	5%	5%
Set-Up	<9%	<10%	<10%
Catalyst	11%	10%	12%
Debate	11%–25%	10%–23%	12%–26%
Break Into Two	25%	23%	26%
B Story	27%	24%	29%
Fun and Games	27%–50%	24%–50%	29%–51%
Midpoint	50%	50%	51%
Bad Guys Close In	50%–68%	50%–63%	51%–63%
All Is Lost	68%	63%	63%
Dark Night of the Soul	68%–75%	63%–75%	63%–76%
Break Into Three	75%	75%	76%
Finale	75%–100%	75%–100%	76%–100%
Final Image	100%	100%	100%

It is obvious that not only do both of the narratives follow all of the fifteen beats, but they proportionally place them into similar time points. *Stranger Things* not only relies on the nostalgic tone of the classical Hollywood of the 1970s and 1980s, but it uses the storytelling tools of this period's filmic text in order to create a unique viewing experience for its audience.

The connection between this series and *Stand by Me* is not only based on the dual homage-inspiration relationship, but it extends into a shared storytelling structuring outline. The binge-watch experience that Netflix creates through its original content pushed *Stranger Things* into adopting a more cinematic storytelling practice stimulated by nostalgic inspiration.

Conclusion

While arguing against binge-watching of conventional TV series, Jim Pagels made two valuable points: firstly, episodes have their own integrity, which is blurred by watching them in a row, while secondly cliffhangers and suspense between episodes need time to breathe.[26] These arguments are the primary foundation of the present analysis. Binge-watching has become synonymous with Netflix, while most of its original content is simultaneously releasing all its episodes at the same time. Netflix has created TV content that blurs the lines between the audiovisual media. One of these works is *Stranger Things.*

Stranger Things does not rely on an episodic narrative, a contradictory fact that defies its television nature. The structure of its narrative is solely based on the classical model of narration and the outline follows the rules of the three-act structure. The series conforms to the analytical form of the classical narration of the fifteen beats, a fact that comes in accordance with its nostalgic tone.

Stand by Me is recognized by the creators of the series as an influence that has shaped its aesthetic and the storytelling itself. With beat-by-beat analysis of the two narratives, we can clearly detect the similarity between them, since they follow the same pattern in their structures. Even if the one is part of cinema, while the other is part of television, the SVOD platform brought new conventions to the audiovisual landscape and blurred the lines between the storytelling rules in these two media.

Acknowledgment

This research is co-financed by Greece and the European Union (European Social Fund—ESF) through the Operational Programme "Human Resources Development, Education and Lifelong Learning" in the context of the project "Reinforcement of Postdoctoral Researchers–2nd Cycle" (MIS-5033021), implemented by the State Scholarships Foundation (IKY).

Works Cited

Ευρωπαϊκή Ένωση
European Social Fund

Operational Programme
Human Resources Development, Education and Lifelong Learning

Co-financed by Greece and the European Union

ΕΣΠΑ 2014-2020
ανάπτυξη - εργασία - αλληλεγγύη

Notes

1. Anthony Smith, *Storytelling Industries: Narrative Production in the 21st Century* (Cham: Palgrave Macmillan, 2018), 1.

2. Mario Klarer, "Putting television 'aside': novel narration in House of Cards," *New Review of Film and Television Studies* 12, no. 2 (2014): 205.

3. James Poniewozik, "Go Ahead, Binge-Watch That TV Show," *Time*, July 10, 2012. Accessed 23 January 2020.

4. Mareike Jenner, "Is this TVIV? On Netflix, TVIII and binge-watching," *New Media & Society* 18, no. 2 (2016): 268.

5. Sidneyeve Matrix, "The Netflix Effect: Teens, Binge Watching, and On-Demand Digital Media Trends," *Jeunesse: Young People, Texts, Cultures* 6, no. 1 (2014): 120.

6. Casey J. McCormick, "Forward Is the Battle Cry: Binge-Viewing Netflix's House of Cards," in *The Netflix Effect: Technology and Entertainment in the 21st Century*, ed. Kevin McDonald and Daniel Smith-Rowsey (New York & London: Bloomsbury Academic, 2016), 101.

7. Sotiris Petridis, "TV Mini-Series or Long-Form Film? Narrative Analysis of The Haunting of Hill House," *Journal of Screenwriting* 11, no. 2 (2020): 208.

8. Jason Mittell, *Complex TV: The Poetics of Contemporary Television Storytelling* (New York and London: New York University Press, 2015), 16.

9. Jeremy G. Butler, *Television: Critical Methods and Applications* (Belmont, CA: Wadsworth, 1994), 29.

10. Veronica Innocenti and Guglielmo Pescatore, "Changing Series: Narrative Models and the Role of the Viewer in Contemporary Television Seriality," *Between* 4, no. 8 (2015): 10.

11. Kathryn VanArendonk, "Theorizing the Television Episode," *Narrative* 27, no. 1 (2019): 66.

12. Peter Hant, *Das Drehbuch: Praktische Filmdramaturgie/The screenplay: Practical dramaturgy of the film* (Waldeck: Felicitas Hübner, 1992), 75.

13. See Constance Nash and Virginia Oakey, *The Screenwriter's Handbook: What to Write, How to Write It, Where to Sell It* (New York: Barnes & Noble, 1978).

14. See Syd Field, *Screenplay: The Foundations of Screenwriting* (New York: Dell, 1979).

15. Matthias Brütsch, "The three-act structure: Myth or magical formula?" *Journal of Screenwriting* 6, no. 3 (2015): 302.

16. See Paul Joseph Gulino, *Screenwriting: The Sequence Approach* (New York: Continuum, 2004).

17. See Christopher Vogler, *The Writer's Journey: Mythic Structure for Writers* (Studio City: Michael Wiese, 1998).

18. Blake Snyder, *Save The Cat! The Last Book on Screenwriting You'll Ever Need* (Michigan: Michael Wiese Productions, 2005).

19. *Ibid.*, 67–96.

20. Adam Hart, *Monstrous Forms: Moving Image Horror Across Media* (New York: Oxford University Press, 2019), 187.

21. Jason Lynch, "Here's the recipe Netflix uses to make bingeworthy TV," *QUARTZ*, March 20, 2015. Accessed November 7, 2019.

22. Phillip Mlynar, "Unpacking the '80s nostalgia of the 'Stranger Things' soundtrack," *Mashable*, 25 July 2016. Accessed 23 January 2020.

23. Neil Genzlinger, "Review: With 'Stranger Things,' Netflix Delivers an Eerie Nostalgia Fix," *The New York Times*, July 14, 2016. Accessed 13 January 2020.

24. Kory Grow, "'Stranger Things': How Two Brothers Created Summer's Biggest TV Hit," *Rolling Stone*, August 3, 2016. Accessed 13 January 2020.

25. Joseph M. Sirianni, "Nostalgic Things: Stranger Things and the Pervasiveness of Nostalgic Television," in *Netflix Nostalgia: Streaming the Past on Demand*, ed. Kathryn Pallister (Maryland: Lexington Books, 2019), 190.

26. Jim Pagels, "Stop Binge-Watching TV," *Slate*, July 9, 2012. Accessed November 23, 2019.

Brütsch, Matthias. "The three-act structure: Myth or magical formula?" *Journal of Screenwriting* 6, no. 3 (2015): 301–326.
Butler, Jeremy G. *Television: Critical Methods and Applications*. Belmont, CA: Wadsworth, 1994.
Field, Syd. *Screenplay: The Foundations of Screenwriting*. New York: Dell, 1979.
Genzlinger, Neil. "Review: With 'Stranger Things,' Netflix Delivers an Eerie Nostalgia Fix." *The New York Times*, July 14, 2016. Accessed 13 January 2020.
Grow, Kory. "'Stranger Things': How Two Brothers Created Summer's Biggest TV Hit." *Rolling Stone*, August 3, 2016. Accessed 13 January 2020.
Gulino, Paul Joseph. *Screenwriting: The Sequence Approach*. New York: Continuum, 2004.
Hant, Peter. *Das Drehbuch: Praktische Filmdramaturgie/The Screenplay: Practical Dramaturgy of the Film*. Waldeck: Felicitas Hübner, 1992.
Hart, Adam. *Monstrous Forms: Moving Image Horror Across Media*. New York: Oxford University Press, 2019.
Innocenti, Veronica, and Pescatore, Guglielmo. "Changing Series: Narrative Models and the Role of the Viewer in Contemporary Television Seriality." *Between* 4, no. 8 (2015): 01–15.
Jenner, Mareike. "Is this TVIV? On Netflix, TVIII and binge-watching." *New Media & Society* 18, no. 2 (2016): 257–273.
Klarer, Mario. "Putting television 'aside': novel narration in House of Cards." *New Review of Film and Television Studies* 12, no. 2 (2014): 203–220.
Lynch, Jason. "Here's the recipe Netflix uses to make bingeworthy TV." *QUARTZ*, March 20, 2015. Accessed November 7, 2019.
Matrix, Sidneyeve. "The Netflix Effect: Teens, Binge Watching, and On-Demand Digital Media Trends." *Jeunesse: Young People, Texts, Cultures* 6, no. 1 (2014): 119–138.
McCormick, Casey J. "Forward Is the Battle Cry: Binge-Viewing Netflix's House of Cards." In *The Netflix Effect: Technology and Entertainment in the 21st Century*, edited by Kevin McDonald and Daniel Smith-Rowsey. New York & London: Bloomsbury Academic, 2016.
Mittell, Jason. *Complex TV: The Poetics of Contemporary Television Storytelling*. New York and London: New York University Press, 2015.
Mlynar, Phillip. "Unpacking the '80s nostalgia of the 'Stranger Things' soundtrack." *Mashable*, 25 July, 2016. Accessed 23 January 2020.
Nash, Constance, and Virginia Oakey. *The Screenwriter's Handbook: What to Write, How to Write It, Where to Sell It*. New York: Barnes & Noble, 1978.
Pagels, Jim. "Stop Binge-Watching TV." *Slate*, July 09, 2012. Accessed November 23, 2019.
Petridis, Sotiris. "TV Mini-Series or Long-Form Film? Narrative Analysis of The Haunting of Hill House." *Journal of Screenwriting* 11, no. 2 (2020): 207–220.
Poniewozik, James. "Go Ahead, Binge-Watch That TV Show." *Time*, July 10, 2012. Accessed November 20, 2019.
Sirianni, Joseph M. "Nostalgic Things: Stranger Things and the Pervasiveness of Nostalgic Television." In *Netflix Nostalgia: Streaming the Past on Demand*, edited by Kathryn Pallister. Lanham, MD: Lexington Books, 2019.
Smith, Anthony. *Storytelling Industries: Narrative Production in the 21st Century*. Cham: Palgrave Macmillan, 2018.
Snyder, Blake. *Save The Cat! The Last Book on Screenwriting You'll Ever Need*. Michigan: Michael Wiese Productions, 2005.
VanArendonk, Kathryn. "Theorizing the Television Episode." *Narrative* 27, no. 1 (2019): 65–82.
Vogler, Christopher. *The Writer's Journey: Mythic Structure for Writers*. Studio City, CA: Michael Wiese, 1998.

Repackaging the Past

Commodification, Nostalgia and Feminist/ Queer Pleasures in Netflix Originals GLOW *(2017–2019) and* Hollywood *(2020)*

Spyridon Chairetis *and* Georgia Aitaki

Introduction

Within the current television landscape, Netflix has emerged as a primary host of nostalgic programming, serving "as both a platform for audiences to rewatch beloved content from the past, and a creator of original content with nostalgic impulses."[1] Apart from providing a library comprising "classic" films and TV series, including cult favorites, some of the most recent and popular Netflix original productions include a variety of shows reminiscent of the 1980s and 1990s pop culture. Although the relationship between television and nostalgic retromania is not new,[2] Netflix's backward glance seems to allow the continuous availability of a "media-defined past" in the here and now,[3] giving prominence to nostalgic television as a key empirical locus for the investigation of the past and its use at the present moment.

This essay contributes to the emerging debate on the potentialities and specificities of original content of streaming platforms by focusing on two Netflix original series: *GLOW* (2017–2019) and *Hollywood* (2020). Drawing from Netflix's utilization of nostalgia as a strategy to engage with multiple audiences, we argue that the above cases also offer complex entry points into feminist and queer pleasures. On the one hand, *GLOW*'s focus on a women's professional wrestling circuit problematizes gender politics in the 1980s by exposing and critiquing patriarchal culture, adopting a visual style that is simultaneously voyeuristic and empowering. *Hollywood*, on the other hand, rewrites the history of sexuality and race in post–World War II Hollywood by imagining otherwise marginalized groups of people as overly dynamic, confident, and able to position themselves beyond the boundaries of hetero and white normativity.

Placing *GLOW* and *Hollywood* within the broader smorgasbord of contemporary television's nostalgic flavors, this essay investigates the textual specificities of "repackaging" the past, alongside an interest in dimensions of production and reception, as they are expressed in television criticism. As the shows seem to adopt similar political lenses yet distinct representational strategies, our aim is to articulate functions and pleasures of nostalgia in contemporary television and to further decipher Netflix's multifaceted contributions to the present and future of entertainment.

The Feminist and Queer Politics of Television

Feminist television studies has emerged as a paradigm of research devoted to representations of women on television shows, as well as programming that has been consumed and/or created by women.[4] In a similar vein, queer television studies investigates the involvement of LGBTQIA+ individuals behind and in front of the television screen, thus advancing an agenda towards understanding how sexuality—among other identity markers—fuels and is fueled by genres, viewers' interpretations, production logics and marketing practices within the industry.[5] Recent scholarly endeavors have emphasized the connectivity between feminist and queer modes of thinking,[6] with particular emphasis being placed on eventual synergies between the two approaches and their concomitant contributions to debates in feminist and queer media studies[7]—especially when it comes to issues of representation, visibility, and empowerment of historically marginalized, misrepresented, and disserved groups.

The study of mediated representations has been one of the most prolific areas of research within television studies, especially in endeavors aiming to expose how societal inequalities shape and are shaped by media content. Viewed through the lens of feminist film and media criticism, Laura Mulvey's theory of the male gaze, concentrating on the reduction of women to the state of spectacle and "to-be-looked-at-ness," has largely defined the more general critique of television narratives as serving to sustain patriarchal relations of domination. Since then, revisions of this approach,[8] a diachronic interest in alongside an intensified examination of the ways feminism and identity politics are played out on the small screen,[9] and a more recent investigation of increasingly complex representations[10] allowed more space for nuancing the processes involved with television (viewing).[11] A characteristic illustration of such approaches includes

Charlotte Brunsdon's discussion of "heroine television,"[12] recently exemplified in a number of television texts showcasing an emphasis on female ensembles with strong feminist undertones, such as *Big Little Lies* (HBO, 2017–2019), *Insecure* (HBO, 2016–), *Orange Is the New Black* (Netflix, 2013–2019), and *The Handmaid's Tale* (Hulu, 2017–). Within this framework, the concept of pleasure(s) has been reclaimed and redefined, as rewarding emotional reactions derived from the consumption of cultural texts embodying and celebrating otherwise marginalized or invisible identities and communities. At the same time, the important roles performed by women on the production side together with the active involvement of openly queer screenwriters have revealed additional layers of pleasure associated with the power of female and queer presence at the helm of the creative process.[13]

An important dimension of this ongoing debate about representation and visibility and the pleasure potential they offer is that feminist and queer television is never adequately empowering and intersectional enough to nullify stereotypes and fully reflect all viewers (and the complexity of the identities they carry). The discussion of visibility politics is connected with the assertion that (non-dominant) categories such as women and queers "are not a homogeneous group with a unified identity, and precisely because of this diversity, what could constitute a positive or verisimilar image for some can be negative or unrealistic for others."[14] The extent to which these collective demands for improvement, both in quantitative and qualitative terms, are feasible and the question about whether feminist and queer representations can ever be deemed unanimously positive and progressive is an ongoing discussion taken up in various platforms.[15] There are some signs that television is changing. Today's television landscape has provided evidence of content diverging from the practice of incorporating women and queers as spectacles and objects to be looked at and/or ridiculed. Complex female characters in protagonistic roles, nuanced representations of female friendship, positive representations of trans characters, and non-token queer characters can be seen as some of the central ingredients of fictional television today, rendering the need to explore new visual/gendered pleasures and understandings of power hierarchies within television texts necessary and rewarding.

More Than a Feeling: The Economics and Politics of Netflix Nostalgia

The numerous ways in which Netflix has shaken up the present and future of television are continuously being registered in issues of production, distribution, and consumption as well as the content itself. In many accounts, Netflix is framed through the common trope of change and disruption in narratives of technological developments, but it is also entangled in discourses about television itself. Described as "the central force in the contemporary experience of media consumption," Netflix has been approached not only as a platform but as a defining factor in introducing a new era of relationship between media and audiences.[16] Named as a "disruptive media phenomenon," Netflix has also found its way into debates about both the death and the future of television.[17] Finally, characterized as "a powerful player in the reorganization of what television is," Netflix has been registered as the flagship of a new, reinvented television, committed to providing quality, binge-worthy, original programming.[18]

Most Netflix-centered research has focused on how the Netflix factor plays into industrial and technological changes, in tandem with a meta-discourse that continuously monitors the strength of television's heartbeat, whereas less attention has been given to in-depth investigation of the specificities of the content hosted by the platform (in the same way that AMC or HBO, for instance, have been framed as changing TV by means of differentiating their content from existing narrative and aesthetic filters). Netflix has, however, been addressed as a stream of continuity for quality television,[19] committed—together with other premium cable and streaming services such as HBO, Showtime, Amazon, and Hulu—to the production of progressive transnational programming often associated with the exploration of controversial topics.[20]

An additional lens through which Netflix's specificity has been captured concerns nostalgia, although the latter concerns a broader industrial logic and money-making strategy. Drawing from its dual role as a producer and distributor of media content, "Netflix nostalgia" has been discussed as a distinct strategy of producing intentionally nostalgic original content and as a clear-cut strategy of instigating nostalgic responses through the circulation of "older" but "beloved" content.[21] The end products of this strategy involve shows that are set in the past, such as *Cable Girls* (2017–2020), *Stranger Things* (2016–), *GLOW* (2017–), *Hollywood* (2020), revivals and sequels of fan favorites such as *The Gilmore Girls: A Year in the Life* (2016), and *Fuller House* (2016–2020), as well as distribution of "classics" such as *Friends* (1994–2004) and *Seinfeld* (1989–1998).[22] The financial logic of this practice is based on the effort to maximize audiences; popular TV shows from the 1980s and 1990s, as well as revivals, reboots, and sequels speak to both built-in audiences/fans and younger generations of viewers who take comfort in watching nostalgic TV shows,[23] while original programming with a nostalgic flavor has proven particularly popular among millennial audiences.[24]

While producing nostalgia seems to be a rather uncomplicated—albeit multifaceted—matter, the cultural politics of nostalgia are not so straightforward. Questions of decoding, popularity, and pleasure in tandem with nostalgic viewing have always been a tough code to crack, especially when placed within questions of ideology, historicity, and imagination. Theories of nostalgia, drawing from a leftist critique that sees it as an expression of lack of historicity,[25] tend to view it as "stagnating, regressive, or a reversion to outdated gender and racial politics, and the technophobic longing of a bygone era."[26] Indeed, much of the critique against nostalgic discourses, representations, and texts is based on an understanding of nostalgia as erasing the past from its lived reality and struggles, and a rebranding of the past through rose-colored glasses that tend to promote conservativism, regression, and melancholia.[27] At the same time, however, nostalgia has been conceptualized as a backward glance rather than a backward step, a turn to the past in an effort to locate resources for identity, agency, or community, all of which are felt by the nostalgic subject(s) to be lacking in the present.[28]

Nostalgia is then discussed specifically within feminist and queer studies as embracing utopian claims and an unapologetic reinvention of the past. Having been historically underrepresented, marginalized, and oppressed, gender and sexual minorities embrace nostalgia as a creative practice for identity and community, with "fantasized and fantastic pasts" playing as important a role as official pasts and narratives for identity and community empowerment.[29] Feminist nostalgia, then, should be understood as a way to reconnect to feminist pasts, struggles, and aspirations, not as a restorative but rather as a reflective practice that resonates with our (struggles and desires in the) feminist present.[30] Similarly, queer dimensions of nostalgia reveal a desire to recreate "a gay, lesbian, bisexual, and transgender heritage with its own role models, icons, symbols, emblems, and glorified imageries."[31]

This lens through which to view nostalgia seems particularly meaningful for the generation of millennials, a demographic cohort born between 1981 and 1996 (also known as Generation Y), commonly defined by their relationship with technology and access to information, as well as their ethnic/racial diversity and progressive politics.[32] In a present defined by heightened debates around the consequences of oppressive structures such as white supremacy, patriarchy, and heteronormativity, the predominance of nostalgia is to be understood as an intensified effort to understand past and current periods of societal turbulence and transition.[33] Apart from a valuable tool for coping with a difficult, complex, and disappointing present, millennial nostalgia proves surprisingly rewarding for a generation that realizes that struggles are still ongoing, that change is still to come, and that they will never get to experience a future "as good as the one their baby-boomer parents planned."[34] Drawing from the above, we argue that the phenomenon of Netflix nostalgia should not be addressed as a melancholia for a glorified long-gone past but as an imaginative attempt to wishfully reconstruct a past that was not, and, as a consequence, to cope with a present that isn't, and to look forward to a future that might still be.

"I feel different. Strong. In control": *The Feminist Nostalgia of* GLOW

GLOW tells the story of a motley group of women who become members of a wrestling show in 1980s Los Angeles. Personal aspirations for self-fulfillment blend together with professional ambitions for achievement against a background of complex female relationships and collective struggles with male characters, such as the show's director Sam Sylvia and producer Sebastian "Bash" Howard, doing their best to support the whole venture's success (but also occasionally sabotaging it). Loosely based on David B. McLane's TV wrestling show *Gorgeous Ladies of Wrestling* (INI, 1986–1990), *GLOW* revives the wrestling circuit of the 1980s, infuses it with campy pop culture aesthetics, and repackages it in a glossy feminist wrapper.

Set in a past decade, *GLOW* has been argued to fall under Netflix's profit-driven nostalgia strategy,[35] which aims to attract audiences who have lived experience of the recreated past, and relates common stories of finding oneself through collective enterprises, which resonate across generations and audiences. Similar to *Stranger Things*, *GLOW* brims with references to 1980s aesthetics, fashion, hair and make-up, soundscapes, and locations. As a decade particularly associated, especially within the U.S. context, with the birth and spread of popular culture as we know it today, *GLOW*'s nostalgic component taps into a more general longing for (and commodification of) the 1980s, characterized by an obsessive consumption of "warm and fuzzy" products and feelings that are supposed to make us feel better about our turbulent present and precarious future.[36]

Previous literature has not responded particularly positively to *GLOW*'s cultural politics, especially when it comes to the show's utilization of nostalgia as a tunnel of connection between past and present (feminist and queer) struggles and pleasures. Framed as a case of "melancholic nostalgia," *GLOW* has been dismissed with regard to whether it makes any significant contribution to television with "woke" aspirations, given that whiteness predominates and undermines questions of racism.[37] The problematic racial politics of the show have also been described as falling short, especially when compared to other contemporary television programs featuring more prominently intersectional, feminist perspectives.[38] Along the same lines, the marginalization of LGBTQIA+ characters has been argued to work against the show's claims to provide any sort of queer-friendly "alternative nostalgia," aligning instead with a case of "regressive nostalgia," thus reproducing heteropatriarchal norms.[39]

On the terrain of popular criticism, reviews communicate more mixed feelings in response to *GLOW*'s feminist agendas and pleasures. On the one hand, some responses align with the aforementioned scholarly disappointment, particularly pointing out *GLOW*'s weak feminist credentials; these are discussed on the basis of how complex and likable the character of Sam Sylvia is,[40] but also in relation to the extensive use of racial stereotypes and misogynistic moments,[41] with the overlying argument being that feminist claims are undermined and/or sacrificed for the price of a few laughs. On the other hand, spectacle and pleasure, rather than melancholia, seem to inform how some critics have read *GLOW* as a (successful) feminist text. The centrality and complexity of female characters is a consistent and iterative element that emerges in popular criticism:

> And this is where *GLOW* stands out, and truly succeeds at being different. It respects women enough to portray the messy reasons people have for doing what they do [...]. The fact that *GLOW* works to better show the human condition is what makes it a successful show, one that reminds you the women on-screen—and women, period—are nuanced, complicated and, frankly, fucked up humans.[42]

This is particularly evident in *GLOW*'s commentary of the general socio-cultural condition, but also specifically on the ideologies circulating in show business. Set against the background of contemporary debates around gender inequality, the tone of the whole show is communicated already in the pilot. In the opening sequence, aspiring actress Ruth Wilder (played by Alison Brie), who is in Los Angeles looking for her big break in show business, auditions for a film and expresses her gratitude for finally being given a chance to read for the part of a powerful female character, only to realize that she was accidentally reading the male character's lines:

> RUTH: In this world there are good guys and bad guys. And we are the good guys. You see the name on my door? That's my father's name, sonofabitch. But this isn't about him. This is about justice. This is about holding on to what is ours. This is about my firm, and my name. And I will not be bullied into submission.
>
> Can I just say—Thank you so much for bringing me in. There aren't parts like this for women right now. It's great. Really powerful.
>
> MALLORY: You were reading the man's part.

RUTH: I was? Oh. God. I'm sorry. I just thought Mel was short for Melanie. And then the other part was—okay.
MALLORY: Would you like to start again?
RUTH: Yes. I would.
CASTING ASSISTANT: This is about my firm and my name and I will not be bullied into submission.
RUTH: Sorry to interrupt. Your wife is on line 2.

For struggling actress Ruth, as for many of the female characters of the crew, such as former soap opera star (who was let go because of her pregnancy) Debbie Eagan, unemployed stuntwoman Cherry Bang, and homeless model Rhonda Richardson, the *GLOW* project becomes an opportunity to overcome rejection, to leave behind roles that society—and show business—so comfortably impose, and to co-create a safe space through which to explore empowerment and self-fulfillment:

> I've been acting pretty much my whole life, and it's always just another audition, another meeting, another year of waiting for someone to give you permission to do the thing you wanna do. But finally I'm getting to do something, and it feels different, you know? I feel different. Strong. In control [Ruth Wilder, Season 2, Episode 5].

In line with the above, the show has also been praised for its subversion of the "male gaze." The complexity and resilience of women living in a man's world are expressed in multiple textual and extratextual occasions throughout its three seasons.[43]

> It's so refreshing to see a television show about a group of scantily clad women putting on a performance specifically meant to titillate male audiences take such an empowering approach [...]. GLOW rethinks the expectations we have for women's bodies. It gives real purpose to the normal adages of body positivity. While the two main characters are fit white women, the show is motivated by the idea that the shape of a woman's body doesn't matter; it's about the confidence and training it takes to pull off a move.[44]

The feminist pleasures of GLOW are not only identifiable in popular criticism and traceable in the textual dimensions of the show, they are also associated with the lived experience of the set. Placing the show within the historical reality of its broadcast context, Betty Gilpin (playing the role of Debbie Eagan) describes the production of the show in terms of a feminist utopia, a safe and refreshing environment that distinguishes itself from the dominant sexist norms of show business:

> Being on a set with female bosses, the level of comfort and bravery I felt really made me reflect back on my whole career. My brain had taught itself to have a male gaze representative at the door, proof-reading ideas like a checkpoint: "Oh, that would make waves, don't do that" or "That choice is a little too

big...." Our set can feel like this sort of protected, feminist bubble where you get to trot out your bravest, most-empowered self for free.[45]

It can be argued that *GLOW* addresses head-on the complexities of the experience of existing in a world defined by obvious, persistent inequalities. In repackaging the past, *GLOW* makes oppressions painfully palpable but also provides some space for making people, experiences, and complexities visible. By making the past more complex, by making the non-dominant more active, and by reclaiming agency, *GLOW* provides an example of feminist nostalgia that offers diverse (textually fueled and lived) pleasures. It should, however, be stressed that the aforementioned complexities are not always sufficiently inclusive of non-hegemonic ways of being. In revisiting the past, and while attempting to offer a slice of spectacular, heart-warming, and pleasurable feminist-flavored nostalgia, *GLOW* is not in any way offering visions of an alternative past, a past that could have been. As such, it definitely does not erase structural inequalities and historical injustices. In a manner that could possibly be argued as representing the historical reality of the period it is set in (and the period during which the original show was broadcast), *GLOW* does not conceal its white, body-normative, heteropatriarchal, classist, racist, and sexist bias, nor does it erase or subvert oppressive structural inequalities. In fact, when the show was on Covid-19-related production hiatus during the summer of 2020, six of its stars sent a letter both to the streaming giant and the showrunners expressing the need for better Black, Indigenous, and People of Color (BIPOC) representation. The letter highlighted the absence of BIPOC in the writers' room and urged the production to intensify the complexity of their characters in order to explicitly address how racial hierarchies affect the characters' careers and personal lives. According to the cast, the show creators heard them loud and clear and were planning to boost the efforts for more inclusive and authentic representation, but Netflix's decision to cancel the show ahead of its fourth and final season, for reasons pinned to Covid-19 restrictions and high production costs, left the whole issue unresolved.[46]

Hollywood, *or Nostalgia for a (Queer) Past Still to Come*

Taking to the airwaves on May 1, 2020, Ryan Murphy and Ian Brennan's *Hollywood* tells the story of groups of people who are trying to break into show business. In its seven episodes, the Netflix series follows the lives of marginalized individuals who attempt to create the first major film with a black lead actress and screenwriter in a post–World War II America, a time period when racism, homophobia, and sexism constitute a reality that affects several communities in the USA, including people of color, homosexuals, and women.

Set in the 1940s, *Hollywood* can be read as a nostalgic project aiming to connect with older and younger audiences by means of resurrecting the glamor and ambiance of Hollywood's golden era. Despite reaching the number one slot in Netflix's most watched television shows within a few hours after its release,[47] *Hollywood* received mixed reviews from critics and journalists who found themselves wondering about the popular drama's use of the past and feminist and queer agenda.[48] On the one hand, a number of critical reviews, comparing the actual history of America in the 1940s with the kind of sugar-coated (hi)story that *Hollywood* brings to the fore, condemned the show, casting it as a text that "missed the opportunity to be an effective critique of institutionalized discriminatory practices in Hollywood that still exist to this day."[49] On the other hand, an equally significant number of journalists, while attesting to *Hollywood*'s distorted and unrealistic view of Hollywood itself, appreciated the creative liberties that both Ryan Murphy and Ian Brennan have endorsed.[50]

In the discussion about defining *Hollywood*'s incorporation of the past into the debate about feminism and queer politics, Ryan Murphy and Ian Brennan take a clear stand. In an interview for ABC, Murphy, creator of numerous LGBTQIA+-themed television shows, shed light on a particular segment from his past, recounting instances of exclusion experienced by black artists and also by Ryan himself, who feared being outed as gay, and thus unsuitable for the Hollywood industry. "Nothing in the world is sadder that the story of lost potential," confesses Murphy, and *Hollywood* "became sort of a love letter to Hollywood and a celebration of the best Hollywood could be."[51]

The lost potential to which Murphy refers constitutes the driving force that leads *Hollywood* to explore unknown and untaken pathways. Right from the first episode, stories of exclusion on the basis of race, color, national identity, sexual orientation, and age glide over one another, constructing Hollywood as a male-dominated and white heterosexual space. Thus, diverging from this ideal is implied as a condition that translates as invisibility from the cinematic industry or visibility under specific circumstances. For black gay writer Archie Coleman (Jeremy Pope), however, such restrictions do not prevent him from traversing hostile spaces. Ryan Murphy and Ian Brennan's script gives otherwise marginalized characters the possibility to react to white dominant culture norms through collective efforts. This idea becomes evident early on in the show, when Avis Amberg (Patti LuPone), wife of Ace Amberg, the head of Ace Studios, and a former actress takes full responsibility of the Hollywood industry and becomes the first white woman to give a black aspiring screenwriter the opportunity to work in the American film sector:

> ARCHIE COLEMAN: Look, the reason I'm here is because well, because I owe you a great deal of respect. I'm grateful because I finally feel like there's somebody in a position of power who is trying to understand me, being homosexual and a black man on top of that.
>
> AVIS AMERG: I don't think it's so hard to understand you. You and I are both outsiders. It's different, I know. I hardly know what it feels like to walk in your shoes.

Hollywood engineers an important shift in the way women, people of color, and LGBTQIA+ people negotiate the terms of their presence in Hollywood. Indeed, there are several scenes throughout the show where less privileged individuals are given voice and the possibility for agency. Archie, for instance, expresses his intention to come out as a gay black man and Rock Hudson's partner, and Avis does not impede him from doing it, despite her initial hesitations. Furthermore, when Avis has to choose who will play the female lead for *Meg*, she decides to give the role to a talented black actress and not to her own daughter. In this way, the show teases out the centrality of alliances and families of choice over family bonds with respect to forging pathways towards equality. Such stories and solutions—no matter how glamorized, oversimplified, and unreal they might seem—render *Hollywood* "an ambitious, well-crafted attempt to take control of the narrative, creating a vision of classic Hollywood that modern audiences can watch with a lot less shame and anger."[52] As Tom Reimann explains, the act of viewing *Hollywood* incites significant feminist and queer pleasures to viewers like himself[53]:

> [...] Murphy's miniseries is about using your power to raise up others, and taking chances to push for change from within. It's a wholly unique story that might not land with everyone and the show's earnestness could be mistaken for naivety. But there can be wisdom in naivety, and I found it impossible not to smile with genuine joy every time the show's many pieces fell so perfectly into place. It's an extremely satisfying watch with an invaluable message, whether you're in the entertainment industry or not—use your voice to help those whose voices aren't being heard.

The idea of standing up and allying against oppressive structures (even if not personally impacted) has been a recurrent theme in Murphy's works. Specifically, films like *The New Normal* (2014) and shows like *Pose* (FX, 2018–2021) and *Halston* (Netflix, 2021) have delved into the challenges that LGBTQI+ cultures (and subcultures) experienced in New York during the 80s-90s and documented them in a manner that was fictionalized but realistic and thought-provoking. *Hollywood*, while also exploring different times in U.S. history, brings to the fore new yet partial and unreal dimensions of the past. Under this light, *Hollywood*, in the spirit of Javier Esteban Muñoz's theory, emerges as a queer world-making project, which "hinges on the possibility to map a world where one is allowed to cast pictures of utopia and to include such pictures in any map of the social."[54] Since the past that *Hollywood* depicts is one that never actually existed, *Hollywood* does not, and could not possibly, mean to expose an authentic picture of gender and cultural politics during the chronological period it examines. What *Hollywood* does provide through this nostalgic move, however, is an expression of discontent with the strict and discriminatory social conventions of the past. Moreover, it offers glimpses of hope and the possibility to enjoy feminist and queer pleasures in a past that has yet to fully arrive.

Conclusion

The essay followed the emerging debate on the potentialities and specificities of original content of streaming platforms in an attempt to evaluate how particular Netflix productions make use of nostalgia to advance feminist and queer politics. Although *GLOW* and *Hollywood* share commonalities in terms of the political lenses they employ, the shows present significant differences in the way nostalgia is being dramatized. On the one hand, *GLOW* appears to remain as faithful as possible to the past it narrates and eager to provide realistic images that exert an in-your-face critique of the historical and structural inequalities that permeated American society in the 1980s. On the other hand, *Hollywood*, structured around the "what if" question, proffers a glittery "butterfly-effect" version of how old Hollywood (and America) could have been if homophobia, sexism, and racism had not existed. The cases of *GLOW* and *Hollywood* demonstrate the functions of nostalgia when put to use by feminist and queer agendas and the potential of entertainment when it comes to diverse and unexpected feminist and queer pleasures. Despite the controversial and often negative responses that the aforementioned shows have elicited from academia and the press, and while we share the view that we must continuously be alert to and critical of misogyny, racism, homophobia, and discrimination, we also need to contemplate what and how much a text can possibly include in its narrative. And occasionally let the scale tip towards the positives.

Notes

1. Kathryn Pallister, "Introduction," in *Netflix Nostalgia: Streaming the Past on Demand*, ed. Kathryn Pallister (Lanham, MD: Lexington Books, 2019), 1.
2. Simon Reynolds, *Retromania: Pop Culture's Addiction to Its Own Past* (New York: Faber and Faber, 2011).

3. Ryan Lizardi, "Mourning and Melancholia: Conflicting Approaches to Reviving *Gilmore Girls* One Season at a Time," *Television & New Media* 19, no. 4 (2017), 379-95.

4. Charlotte Brunsdon, Julie D'Acci, and Lynn Spigel, eds., *Feminist Television Criticism: A Reader* (Oxford: Oxford University Press, 1997).

5. Glyn Davis and Garry Needham, eds., *Queer TV: Theories, Histories, Politics* (London: Routledge, 2009).

6. Mimi Marinucci, *Feminism Is Queer: The Intimate Connection between Queer and Feminist Theory* (London: Zed Books, 2016).

7. Sarah Maddison, "'Is the Queen Dead?' Effeminacy, Homosociality, and the Post-Homophobic Queer," *A Journal of Cultural Materialism*, 4, no. 1 (2015), 1-27; Christopher Pullen, *Straight Girls and Queer Guys: The Hetero Media Gaze in Film and Television* (Edinburgh: Edinburgh University Press, 2016).

8. Laura Mulvey, "Afterthoughts on 'Visual Pleasure and Narrative Cinema': Inspired by 'Duel in the Sun,'" *Framework* 15, no. 17 (1981): 12-5; D.N. Rodowick, "The Difficulty of Difference," *Wide Angle* 5, no. 1 (1982): 4-15.

9. Michael Elasmar, Kazumi Hasegawa, and Mary Brain, "The Portrayal of Women in U.S. Prime Time Television," *Journal of Broadcasting & Electronic Media* 43, no. 1 (1999) 20-34; Svenja Hohenstein and Katharina Thalmann, "Difficult Women: Changing Representations of Female Characters in Contemporary Television Series," *Zeitschrift für Anglistik und Amerikanistik* 67, no. 2 (2019), 109-29.

10. For examples, see Jessica Ford, "Women's Indie Television: The Intimate Feminism of Women-Centric Dramedies," *Feminist Media Studies* 19, no. 7 (2019): 928-43; Claire Perkins and Michele Schreiber, "Independent Women: From Film to Television," *Feminist Media Studies* 19, no. 7 (2019): 919-27.

11. Rachel Moseley, Helen Wheatley, and Helen Wood, eds., *Television for Women: New Directions* (London and New York: Routledge, 2017).

12. Charlotte Brunsdon, "The Role of Soap Opera in the Development of Feminist Television Criticism," in *Screen Tastes*, ed. Charlotte Brunsdon (London: Routledge, 1997), 29-43.

13. Joy Press, *Stealing the Show: How Women Are Revolutionizing Television* (New York: Atria, 2019).

14. Silvia Grassi, *Gender and Sexual Dissidence on Catalan and Spanish Television Series: An Intercultural Analysis* (Newcastle upon Tyne: Cambridge Scholars Publishing, 2016), 146.

15. Apart from the work being done in the sphere of academia, organizations such as GLAAD and the Geena Davis Institute on Gender in Media are significantly active in the above-mentioned struggles.

16. Cory Barker and Myc Wiatrowski, "Introduction," in *The Age of Netflix: Critical Essays on Streaming Media, Digital Delivery and Instant Access*, eds. Cory Barker and Myc Wiatrowski (Jefferson, NC: McFarland & Company, 2017), 2.

17. Ramon Lobato, *Netflix Nations: The Geography of Digital Distribution* (New York: NYU Press, 2019), 20.

18. Mareike Jenner, *Netflix and the Re-Invention of Television* (Cham: Palgrave Macmillan, 2018), 3.

19. *Ibid.*, 141.

20. Ava Parsemain, *The Pedagogy of Queer TV* (London: Palgrave Macmillan, 2019), 15.

21. Pallister, "Introduction," 2.

22. An additional expression of this strategy could also include a number of "retro" teen dramas, such as *The End of the Fucking World* (2017-2019), *I Am Not Okay with This* (2020), *Sex Education* (2019-), and *Trinkets* (2019-2020).

23. Lizardi, "Mourning and Melancholia."

24. Lauren Friedman, "Why Nostalgia Marketing Works So Well with Millennials, and How Your Brand Can Benefit," *Forbes*, August 2, 2016, https://www.forbes.com/sites/laurenfriedman/2016/08/02/why-nostalgia-marketing-works-so-well-with-millennials-and-how-your-brand-can-benefit/.

25. Fredric Jameson, "Postmodernism and Consumer Society," in *Modern Criticism and Theory: A Reader*, eds. David Lodge and Nigel Wood (Harlow: Longman, 2008).

26. Alex Bevan, *The Aesthetics of Nostalgia TV: Production Design and the Boomer Era* (New York and London: Bloomsbury Academic, 2019), 14.

27. Amy Villarejo, *Ethereal Queer: Television, Historicity, Desire* (Edinburgh: Duke University Press, 2014).

28. Stuart Tannock,"Nostalgia Critique," *Cultural Studies* 9, no. 3 (1995): 454-64; Michelle Meagher and Roxanne Loree Runyon, "Backward Glances: Feminism, Nostalgia and Joan Braderman's *The Heretics* (2009)," *Feminist Theory* 18, no. 3 (2017), 343-56.

29. Gilad Padva, *Queer Nostalgia in Cinema and Pop Culture* (Basingstoke: Palgrave Macmillan, 2014), 8.

30. Meagher and Runyon, "Backward Glances."

31. Padva, *Queer Nostalgia in Cinema and Pop Culture*, 6.

32. Loren Saxton Coleman and Christopher, P. Campbell, "Introduction," in *Media, Myth and Millennials: Critical Perspectives on Race and Culture*, eds. Loren Saxton Coleman and Christopher P. Campbell (Lanham: Lexington Books), 2.

33. Bevan, *The Aesthetics of Nostalgia TV*, 14.

34. Lynn Spigel, "Postfeminist Nostalgia for a Prefeminist Future," *Screen* 54, no. 2 (2013), 270-78.

35. Philippe Gauthier, "Nostalgia as a Problematic Cultural Space: The Example of the Original Netflix Series GLOW (2017)," in *Netflix Nostalgia: Streaming the Past on Demand*, ed. Kathryn Pallister (Lanham, MD: Lexington Books, 2019), 82.

36. Stuart Elliott, "Warm and Fuzzy Makes a Comeback," *The New York Times*, April 6, 2009, https://www.nytimes.com/2009/04/07/business/media/07adco.html.

37. *Ibid.*, 84-5.

38. Caetlin Benson-Allott, "No Such Thing Not Yet: Questioning Television's Female Gaze," *Film Quarterly* 71, no. 2 (2017): 65–71.

39. Heather Freeman, "Shifting Nostalgic Boundaries: Archetypes and Queer Representation in *Stranger Things*, *GLOW*, and *One Day at a Time*," in *Netflix Nostalgia: Streaming the Past on Demand*, ed. Kathryn Pallister (Lanham, MD: Lexington Books, 2019), 99-101.

40. J. Fergus, "Hatewatching: GLOW (Season Two) Review," *The Medium*, July 14, 2018, https://medium.com/@NotesFromJ/hatewatching-glow-season-two-review-ca46ee4fd5dd.

41. Rachel Aroesti, "Stop! You're Hurting Me! Why *GLOW*'s Wrestling Women Aren't Just an Offence to Fashion," *The Guardian*, June 29, 2018, https://www.theguardian.com/tv-and-radio/2017/jun/29/glow-netflix-wrestling-women-arent-just-an-offence-to-fashion.

42. Sandra Song, "'GLOW' Season 2 Doesn't Pander to Your Surface-Level Feminist Rhetoric," *Nylon*, June 29, 2018, https://www.nylon.com/articles/glow-season-2-review.

43. At the time of writing this chapter, Netflix had announced the cancellation of the fourth and final season of the show, citing Covid-19's impact on production.

44. Isha Aran, "*GLOW* Is a Brilliant Subversion of the Male Gaze and a True Celebration of Women," *Splinter*, June 23, 2017, https://splinternews.com/glow-is-a-brilliant-subversion-of-the-male-gaze-and-a-t-1796363031

45. peterzt, "GLOW: Actual Feminist Filmmaking in #MeToo Hollywood," *The Artifice*, February 4, 2018, https://the-artifice.com/glow-feminism/.

46. Jordan Moreau, "'GLOW' Cast Called for Meaningful Representation, Writer of Color in Season 4 Ahead of Cancellation," *Variety*, October 20, 2020, https://variety.com/2020/tv/news/glow-season-4-inclusion-canceled-1234810596/.

47. Felicity Chain, "Ryan Murphy's 'Hollywood' Is Fashion's Favorite New Binge Watch," *L'Officiel*, June 5, 2020, https://www.lofficielusa.com/film-tv/sex-and-fashion-in-ryan-murphys-hollywood.

48. Landon Johnson, "Netflix's Hollywood: Why the Reviews Are So Mixed," *Screenrant*, May 25, 2020, https://screenrant.com/netflix-hollywood-reviews-mixed-reason-why/.

49. Courtney Dantzler, "Netflix's 'Hollywood' Is Not as Progressive as It Wants to Be," *Duke Chronicle*, June 7, 2020, https://www.dukechronicle.com/article/2020/06/dantzler-netflix-hollywood-progressive.

50. Princess Weekes, "Ryan Murphy's Hollywood Is Flawed but Left Me Longing for a

New Reality," *The Mary Sue*, May 8, 2020, https://www.themarysue.com/ryan-murphys-hollywood-a-total-mixed-bag/; Melinda Houston, "Pay TV: Hollywood," *The Age*, May 16, 2020, https://www.theage.com.au/culture/tv-and-radio/pay-tv-hollywood-20200505-p54pvd.html.

51. Lynn Elber, "Ryan Murphy's 'Hollywood' Miniseries Is a Woke '40s Fantasy," *ABC News*, April 28,2020, https://abcnews.go.com/Entertainment/wireStory/ryan-murphys-hollywood-miniseries-woke-40s-fantasy-70392281.

52. Eric Deggans, "Review: 'Hollywood' Is Ryan Murphy's Miniseries For Netflix," *NPC*, May 1, 2020, https://www.npr.org/2020/05/01/848932974/review-hollywood-is-ryan-murphys-miniseries-for-netflix?t=1602318073510.

53. Tom Reimann, "'Hollywood' Review: Ryan Murphy's Alt-History Love Letter Is an Uplifting (If Uneven) Drama," *Collider*, May 1, 2020, https://collider.com/hollywood-review-netflix-ryan-murphy/

54. Javier Esteban Muñoz, *Cruising Utopia: The Then and There of Queer Futurity* (New York: New York University Press, 2009), 96.

Works Cited

Aran, Isha. "*GLOW* Is a Brilliant Subversion of the Male Gaze and a True Celebration of Women." *Splinter*, June 23, 2017. https://splinternews.com/glow-is-a-brilliant-subversion-of-the-male-gaze-and-a-t-1796363031.

Aroesti, Rachel. "Stop! You're Hurting Me! Why *GLOW*'s Wrestling Women Aren't Just an Offence to Fashion." *The Guardian*, June 29, 2018. https://www.theguardian.com/tv-and-radio/2017/jun/29/glow-netflix-wrestling-women-arent-just-an-offence-to-fashion.

Barker, Cory, and Myc Wiatrowski. "Introduction." In *The Age of Netflix: Critical Essays on Streaming Media, Digital Delivery and Instant Access*, edited by Cory Barker and Myc Wiatrowski. Jefferson, NC: McFarland, 2017.

Benson-Allott, Caetlin. "No Such Thing Not Yet: Questioning Television's Female Gaze." *Film Quarterly* 71, no. 2 (2017): 65–71. doi.org/10.1525/fq.2017.71.2.65.

Bevan, Alex. *The Aesthetics of Nostalgia TV: Production Design and the Boomer Era*. New York and London: Bloomsbury Academic, 2019.

Brunsdon, Charlotte. "The Role of Soap Opera in the Development of Feminist Television Criticism." In *Screen Tastes*, edited by Charlotte Brunsdon. London: Routledge, 1997.

Brunsdon, Charlotte, D' Acci, Julie, and Lynn Spigel, eds. *Feminist Television Criticism: A Reader*. Oxford: Oxford University Press, 1997.

Chain, Felicity. "Ryan Murphy's 'Hollywood' Is Fashion's Favorite New Binge Watch." *L'Officiel*, June 5, 2020. https://www.lofficielusa.com/film-tv/sex-and-fashion-in-ryan-murphys-hollywood.

Dantzler, Courtney. "Netflix's 'Hollywood' Is Not as Progressive as It Wants to Be." *Duke Chronicle*, June 7, 2020. https://www.dukechronicle.com/article/2020/06/dantzler-netflix-hollywood-progressive.

Davis, Glyn, and Garry Needham, eds. *Queer TV: Theories, Histories, Politics*. London: Routledge, 2009.

Deggans, Eric. "Review: 'Hollywood' Is Ryan Murphy's Miniseries for Netflix." NPC, May 1, 2020. https://www.npr.org/2020/05/01/848932974/review-hollywood-is-ryan-murphys-miniseries-for-netflix?t=1602318073510.

Elasmar, Michael, Kazumi Hasegawa, and Mary Brain. "The Portrayal of Women in U.S. Prime Time Television." *Journal of Broadcasting & Electronic Media* 43, no. 1 (1999): 20–34. /doi.org/10.1080/08838159909364472.

Elber, Lynn. "Ryan Murphy's 'Hollywood' Miniseries Is a Woke '40s Fantasy." *ABC News*, April 28,2020. https://abcnews.go.com/Entertainment/wireStory/ryan-murphys-hollywood-miniseries-woke-40s-fantasy-70392281.

Elliot, Stuart. "Warm and Fuzzy Makes a Comeback." *The New York Times*, April 6, 2009. https://www.nytimes.com/2009/04/07/business/media/07adco.html.
Fergus, J. "Hatewatching: GLOW (Season Two) Review." *The Medium*, July 14, 2018. https://medium.com/@NotesFromJ/hatewatching-glow-season-two-review-ca46ee4fd5dd.
Ford, Jessica. "Women's Indie Television: The Intimate Feminism of Women-Centric Dramedies." *Feminist Media Studies* 19, no. 7 (2019): 928–43. 10.1080/14680777.2019.1667060.
Freeman, Heather. "Shifting Nostalgic Boundaries: Archetypes and Queer Representation in *Stranger Things*, *GLOW*, and *One Day at a Time*." In *Netflix Nostalgia: Streaming the Past on Demand*, edited by Kathryn Pallister. Lanham, MD: Lexington Books, 2019.
Friedman, Lauren. "Why Nostalgia Marketing Works So Well with Millennials, and How Your Brand Can Benefit." *Forbes*, August 2, 2016. https://www.forbes.com/sites/laurenfriedman/2016/08/02/why-nostalgia-marketing-works-so-well-with-millennials-and-how-your-brand-can-benefit/.
Gauthier, Philippe. "Nostalgia as a Problematic Cultural Space: The Example of the Original Netflix Series *GLOW* (2017)." In *Netflix Nostalgia: Streaming the Past on Demand*, edited by Kathryn Pallister. Lanham, MD: Lexington Books, 2019.
Grassi, Silvia. *Gender and Sexual Dissidence on Catalan and Spanish Television Series: An Intercultural Analysis*. Newcastle upon Tyne: Cambridge Scholars Publishing, 2016.
Hohenstein, Svenia, and Katharina Thalmann. "Difficult Women: Changing Representations of Female Characters in Contemporary Television Series." *Zeitschrift für Anglistik und Amerikanistik*, 67, no. 2 (2019): 109–129. doi.org/10.1515/zaa-2019-0012.
Houston, Melinda. "Pay TV: Hollywood." *The Age*, May 16, 2020. https://www.theage.com.au/culture/tv-and-radio/pay-tv-hollywood-20200505-p54pvd.html.
Jameson, Fredric. "Postmodernism and Consumer Society." In *Modern Criticism and Theory: A Reader*, edited by David Lodge and Nigel Wood. Harlow: Longman, 2008.
Jenner, Mareike. *Netflix and the Re-Invention of Television*. Cham: Palgrave Macmillan, 2018.
Johnson, Landon. "Netflix's *Hollywood*: Why the Reviews Are So Mixed." *Screenrant*, May 25, 2020. https://screenrant.com/netflix-hollywood-reviews-mixed-reason-why/.
Lizardi, Ryan. "Mourning and Melancholia: Conflicting Approaches to Reviving *Gilmore Girls* One Season at a Time." *Television & New Media* 19, no. 4 (2017): 379–395. doi.org/10.1177/1527476417742975.
Lobato, Ramon. *Netflix Nations: The Geography of Digital Distribution*. New York: NYU Press, 2019.
Maddison, Sarah. "'Is the Queen Dead?' Effeminacy, Homosociality, and the Post-Homophobic Queer." *A Journal of Cultural Materialism* 4, no. 1 (2015): 1–27.
Marinucci, Mimi. *Feminism Is Queer: The Intimate Connection between Queer and Feminist Theory*. London: Zed Books, 2016.
Meagher, Michelle, and Roxanne Loree Rynyon. "Backward Glances: Feminism, Nostalgia and Joan Braderman's *The Heretics* (2009)." *Feminist Theory* 18, no. 3 (2017): 343–56. doi.org/10.1177/1464700117721883.
Moreau, Jordan. "'GLOW' Cast Called for Meaningful Representation, Writer of Color in Season 4 Ahead of Cancellation." *Variety*, October 20, 2020. https://variety.com/2020/tv/news/glow-season-4-inclusion-canceled-1234810596/.
Moseley, Rachel, Helen Wheatley, and Helen Wood, eds. *Television for Women: New Directions*. London and New York: Routledge, 2017.
Mulvey, Laura. "Afterthoughts on 'Visual Pleasure and Narrative Cinema': Inspired by 'Duel in the Sun.'" *Framework* 15, no. 17 (1981): 12–15.
Muñoz, Esteban Javier. *Cruising Utopia: The Then and There of Queer Futurity*. New York: New York University Press, 2009.
Padva, Gilad. *Queer Nostalgia in Cinema and Pop Culture*. Basingstoke: Palgrave Macmillan, 2014.
Pallister, Kathryn. "Introduction." In *Netflix Nostalgia: Streaming the Past on Demand*, edited by Kathryn Pallister. Lanham: Lexington Books, 2019.
Parsemain, Ava. *The Pedagogy of Queer TV*. London: Palgrave Macmillan, 2019.
Perkins, Claire, and Michele Schreiber. "Independent Women: From Film to Television." *Feminist Media Studies* 19, no. 7 (2019): 919–27. /doi.org/10.1080/14680777.2019.1667059.

Peterzt. "GLOW: Actual Feminist Filmmaking in #MeToo Hollywood." *The Artifice*, February 4, 2018. https://the-artifice.com/glow-feminism/.
Press, Joy. *Stealing the Show: How Women Are Revolutionizing Television*. New York: Atria, 2019.
Pullen, Christopher. *Straight Girls and Queer Guys: The Hetero Media Gaze in Film and Television*. Edinburgh: Edinburgh University Press, 2016.
Reimann, Tom. "'Hollywood' Review: Ryan Murphy's Alt-History Love Letter Is an Uplifting (If Uneven) Drama." *Collider*, May 1, 2020. https://collider.com/hollywood-review-netflix-ryan-murphy/.
Reynolds, Simon. *Retromania: Pop Culture's Addiction to Its Own Past*. New York: Faber & Faber, 2011.
Rodowick, D.N. "The Difficulty of Difference." *Wide Angle* 5, no. 1 (1982): 4–15.
Saxton Coleman, Loren, and Christopher, P. Campbell. "Introduction." In *Media, Myth and Millennials: Critical Perspectives on Race and Culture*, eds. Loren Saxton Coleman and Christopher P. Campbell, 1–7. Lanham, MD: Lexington Books, 2019.
Song, Sandra. "'GLOW' Season 2 Doesn't Pander to Your Surface-Level Feminist Rhetoric." *Nylon*, June 29, 2018. https://www.nylon.com/articles/glow-season-2-review.
Spigel, Lynn. "Postfeminist Nostalgia for a Prefeminist Future." *Screen* 54, no. 2 (2013): 270–78. doi.org/10.1093/screen/hjt017.
Tannock, Stuart. "Nostalgia Critique." *Cultural Studies* 9, no. 3 (1995): 454–464.
Villarejo, Amy. *Ethereal Queer: Television, Historicity, Desire*. Edinburgh: Duke University Press, 2014.
Weekes, Princess. "Ryan Murphy's Hollywood Is Flawed but Left Me Longing for a New Reality." *The Mary Sue*, May 8, 2020. https://www.themarysue.com/ryan-murphys-hollywood-a-total-mixed-bag/.

Cats and True Crime

Empathetic Responses and Moral Consequences in On-Demand Docuseries

Jossalyn G. Larson

Though the spring of 2020 will be remembered principally for the global lockdown caused by Covid-19, another shared experience at the same time was the debut of Netflix's *Tiger King: Murder, Mayhem, and Madness.*[1] Business closures, mass unemployment, and mandatory stay-at-home orders provided the perfect conditions for binge-watching, and the seven-episode series was replete with rivalry, taboo, classism, and crime set against the backdrop of big cat sanctuaries. The structure and release date of the docuseries made conditions ideal for attracting a staggering thirty-four million unique viewers in the first ten days of its release.[2] Though the series devoted substantial attention to a number of plot points, the disappearance of Big Cat Rescue owner Carole Baskin's former husband became the dog whistle that united viewers across social media. Don Lewis, Baskin's former husband and big cat merchant, became a missing person after departing from his home in Tampa, Florida, on August 18, 1997, leaving millions of dollars in assets to his wife.[3] Though he was declared legally dead on the fifth anniversary of his disappearance in 2002, no evidence of Lewis's being killed has surfaced, and investigators believe that he had likely disappeared on his own intention.[4] Yet in spite of investigators' doubts that Lewis was murdered, the Netflix series capitalized on the true crime fervor and raised a climate of suspicion around the Big Cat Rescue owner, causing Baskin to post a refutation of allegations of her involvement in Lewis's disappearance on the sanctuary's website, in which she accused Netflix of betraying her trust and instigating a culture of harassment.[5]

Tiger King was not, however, Netflix's first cat-centric true crime success. Airing in December 2019, *Don't F*uck with Cats: Hunting an*

Internet Killer[6] followed a pair of social media sleuths who hunted down kitten-killer turned murderer Luka Magnotta. The three-part docuseries followed Deanna Thompson, a data analyst from Las Vegas, and "John Green," the alias for an armchair investigator who assisted Thompson, as they tracked the perpetrator through his posts on social media and the dark web. As the series unfolded the story of Magnotta and his internet adversaries, it maintained an air of self-awareness that was both celebratory of the efforts that brought the killer to justice, and cautionary of the agency that the true crime genre has for provoking evil deeds in the pursuit of sensationalism. Just two weeks after debuting, the series was listed as one of Netflix's top five most-watched documentaries of 2019.[7]

Cats have long been associated with the popularity of on-demand streaming, but the confluence of cats and true crime is a phenomenon that raises questions about emotional responses to media in ways that have not yet been fully understood. Studies have suggested that streaming cat content provokes empathetic responses that are generally therapeutic[8]; however, studies on true crime suggest that such responses have rhetorical power to sway the viewer's moral foundations, especially when those stories are formed around children or animals.[9] In this study, I examine cat-centric true crime through the lens of moral psychology in order to consider the manner in which the new and intense consumption behaviors enabled by on-demand platforms expedite the articulation of new moral standards, of protagonists and antagonists, and situate the viewer as a flawed crime fighter.

True Crime and Sensationalism: Agency Beyond Intent

In recent years, the true crime genre has found a wealth of new audiences through on-demand platforms like podcasts and video streaming services. The genre lends itself to the consumption habit of "binge-watching," or viewing several episodes of a series in a single sitting, primarily because of the themes of suspense and intrigue on which it is built. The genre presents evidence in a manner that allows the viewer to assume the role of pseudo-detective; the viewer gathers information across a series of episodes and casts judgment on the characters to whom the crime is connected. The on-demand platform allows the viewer to remain invested in the investigation for an amount of time that is determined by the viewer, and capitalizes on the sensationalist nature of the crime to secure the viewership from episode to episode.

Yet casting series like *Tiger King* and *Don't F*ck With Cats* as true crime can be contentious. The creators of such series occasionally push back against that designation, claiming that the work is investigatory journalism—a genre which is considered more high-brow than traditional true crime.[10] Popular culture has often ridiculed the true crime genre; even the creators of the adult animated series *South Park* have critiqued the genre's recurrent themes of softcore pornography couched in tales of murder in the show's 2013 season, with an episode titled "Investigative Murder Porn."[11] However, as critics like Ian Case Punnett have worked toward developing a more sophisticated theory of true crime narratives, the distinction between investigative journalism and true crime has begun to blur.[12] Under Punnett's analysis, true crime is not simply about gore and titillation; the genre is formed by a recurrence of themes that not only entertain, but also have agency to encourage real social change. Punnett has theorized that investigatory journalism becomes true crime when the narrative contains any combination of seven components: justice, subversion, crusaders, geographic focus, forensic investigation, vocative authority or advocacy, and folkloric instruction.[13] A narrative that features a justice component sees retribution for crimes committed against a victim as central to the story. Subversive narratives ask the audience to reconsider evidence or to be attentive to the breakdowns of the criminal justice system. Crusader narratives inspire social change, usually with regard to the treatment of marginalized groups in criminal investigations. A narrative contains a geographic component when the crime is described as intimately connected to the locality of the story—that is, the crime is considered directly related to the culture and environment which provoke the criminal's misdeeds. Forensic narratives include descriptions of case evidence and the forensic science used to evaluate that evidence, usually in vivid detail. Vocative narratives abandon impartial, journalistic tones and present the case from a perspective of authority or advocacy. Folkloric narratives focus more on the agency a crime has in shifting cultural perceptions and values. Most true crime narratives employ some combination of these features and deliver them throughout the series in a manner that provides the viewer with the experience of investigating the case through the presentation of evidence and the testimony of witnesses.

This investigatory experience is, however, complicated by significant limitations. The biases of producers and documentarians determine the manner in which the evidence is presented, and those biases are not always evident to the viewer. The subversive Netflix series *Making a Murderer*,[14] for example, inspired a cultural frenzy around Steven Avery, who is serving life in prison for the 2007 murder of photographer Teresa Halbach. Following the documentary's release in 2015, a Change.org petition asking for a presidential pardon for Avery gathered more than 530,000 signatures prior to its closing.[15] Though criticisms of the documentary's skewed details[16] and omission of key evidence[17] were widely publicized, the show's popularity caused Netflix to sign the show for a second season, which featured defense attorney Kathleen Zellner's unsuccessful attempt at exonerating Avery.[18]

Similarly, Netflix's *Tiger King* featured a series of interviews with personal and professional adversaries of Big Cat Rescue owner Carole Baskin, all of whom voiced suspicions that Baskin had murdered her husband, Don Lewis, in order to claim his land and assets and to stave off an impending divorce. The producers interviewed Don's first wife, Gladys Lewis Cross, and his daughters Donna Pettis, Lynda Sanchez, and Gale Rathbone, all of whom claimed that Don had been fearful of Baskin prior to his disappearance, that he had given them an application for a restraining order against her, and that he had asked them to deliver it to the police in the event that something were to happen to him. Baskin was unable to respond to those allegations in her brief interviews that were aired in the docuseries, but would later claim in a refutation posted to Big Cat Rescue's website:

> Don spent one week per month in Costa Rica. Don was a man who wanted to have sex daily. He would go to Costa Rica during the week I was having my menstrual cycle. I accepted this as something I had to live with. During the week he was away, I would haul off the property as much of the junk as I could. Wendell [Williams, an associate of Don's] told Don I was doing this. Don tried calling the police to get them to stop me. They told him he would need a restraining order. It is unclear if it was Don's idea that to get a restraining order he should say I threatened him or if someone like Wendell suggested that. Don filed for the order on June 20, 1997, and it was denied.[19]

Baskin goes on to refute further allegations lodged against her in the Netflix series, and points to *Joe Exotic*, a serial podcast by Wondery's Robert Moor, as an honest and fair treatment of the circumstances surrounding her husband's disappearance. In that podcast, Moor interviews the lead investigator on Lewis's case, who says about Baskin that "she was courteous and there was nothing that jumped out at me in terms of her demeanor to make me think that she was not giving us accurate information or hiding anything."[20] Nevertheless, the popularity of the Netflix series has caused Hillsborough County Sheriff Chad Chronister to reopen Lewis's missing persons case with a call for new leads.[21]

Viewers' failure to recognize biases is further complicated by an overestimation of their ability to render judgment about a case that has been dramatized for entertainment value. In her historical examination of sensationalism in true crime, Joy Wiltenburg notes that consumers of true crime media tend to have an overblown sense of crime in their communities. Wiltenburg found that increased consumption of true crime correlated with decreased objective knowledge about the prevalence of crime.[22] Despite their low or even negative informational value, Wiltenburg warns that true crime narratives have a substantial impact on the community:

The fears sparked by perceptions of crime influence decisions about where to live, how to raise children, where to invest social wealth, what punitive governmental actions to support, how to view groups perceived as likely criminals—a broad range of choices and attitudes that affect the quality of a society and its political life.[23]

Wiltenburg asserts that irrespective of the intent of producers to convey factual material in a neutral tone, true crime exerts substantial political and cultural power that can influence the audience's "lives and communities far out of proportion to the actual incidence of criminal activity."[24]

In her 2019 study on the nature of true crime podcasting, Kelli S. Boling interviewed four podcast producers in order to conduct a qualitative examination of the genre through a critical/cultural lens.[25] Boling found that a theme of education emerged across every interview she conducted. The podcasters "all felt very strongly about educating the public on the criminal justice system via podcasting," and that none of the informants "expressed any concerns regarding the likelihood that they might misinterpret the cases or manipulate audiences in a particular way."[26] Boling reports that the producers made concerted efforts to present the evidence of a case objectively, and that they "wanted to educate them [the audience] on the criminal justice system and the cases covered so that they, as an informed audience, could draw their own conclusions."[27]

Yet in spite of the intentions of true crime producers to present their cases objectively, the audience's reception of those cases and their use of that information cannot be controlled for predetermined biases. An audience's objectivity might be skewed by their reasons for consuming the material and, as Wiltenburg has noted, that lack of objectivity can impact communities significantly, especially around matters such as race and gender. Studies have found that women tend to be more attracted to true crime than men, principally because women tend to be drawn to narratives which feature female lead characters or victims, and because they believe that the information provided in those narratives can be used for their own survival.[28] In a 2018 study, Boling and her colleague Kevin Hull surveyed respondents about their motives for consuming true crime narratives and found that female respondents "were more likely to agree with statements such as, 'Listening to true crime podcasts educates me about the criminal justice system' and 'I listen to true crime podcasts so I can learn about what could happen to me.'"[29] Though the producers' intent to educate the public seems to be affirmed by the respondents' answers, the female respondents' internalization of the narrative engages a pathos which could have a significant impact on the judgment they render against the characters in the story.

Audiences: From Passive to Peeper; from Idle to Activist

Despite the visceral connection between the true crime narrative and survival, Boling and Hull's study corroborates research that suggests that true crime consumers, particularly those who consume the material via on-demand platforms like podcasts and streaming video, tend to see their consumption as passive rather than active. Boling and Hull's respondents reported that they consume true crime when they have "nothing better to do," and that this consumption activity is often used to occupy time while "doing other things like yard work or cleaning the house."[30] This affirms findings by Zizi Papacharissi and Andrew L. Mendelson, who in 2007 conveyed that audiences tend to be drawn to reality-based television most prominently as a "habitual pastime."[31] Papacharissi and Mendelson found that the realistic, non-fictional nature of story and characters in reality genres facilitated an appeal that made the consumption of those narratives a habitual component of the audience's day.[32] Particularly when consuming them via on-demand platforms, both men and women report entertainment, convenience, and boredom as the top three motivations for consuming these narratives,[33] which suggests that despite audiences' assertions that escapism is not a primary motive for consumption of true crime media,[34] the true crime genre is used as a means to escape mundane labor and to immerse oneself intellectually in the dramatic lives of other real people.

This escape from the banality of daily life is, in fact, the motivation that launches the events that form the narrative of Netflix's *Don't F*ck with Cats*. In the days following a bad breakup, Deanna Thompson (alias "Baudi Moovan") takes to Facebook for a distraction. While there, she stumbles upon a YouTube video called "1 boy 2 kittens," which had gone viral. Initially, Thompson reports that she had expected to view one of the millions of cute kitten videos that abound as distractors on the internet. Instead, she found herself watching a graphic account of a young man, known now to be porn star turned murderer Luka Magnotta, intentionally suffocating a pair of grey tabby kittens in a vacuum sealed plastic bag. Though Thompson admits that she had initially been unable to watch the full video, the content she viewed did not cause her to abandon her curiosity; rather, she dove deeper. She followed the comments, and experienced herself resonating with the outrage of the community of commenters. She joined a Facebook group, which had been linked to in a comment, called "Find the Kitten Vacuumer.... For great justice." From that group, Thompson engaged with a circuit of armchair investigators who would analyze subtle details of Magnotta's videos in order to locate and identify him, in the hope that they could bring him to justice before he unleashed his violent inclinations against another human.

Along with passive convenience and habitual distraction, studies have found that voyeurism tends to be a powerful motivation for reality-based true crime media consumption.[35] Scholars who have assessed the appeal of reality television have likened the audience's critical voyeurism to Foucault's Panopticon,[36] and have suggested that the ability to peer into the lives of real people has profound impacts on the modernization of culture and the challenging of traditional values.[37] Others have suggested that the genre represents the audience's search for the Lacanian real in an overly-digitized world,[38] and that this longing is symptomatic of a postmodern era in which everything seems constructed and reality is elusive.[39] It could be said, therefore, that the voyeuristic nature of reality-based programming is the agent that moves the audience from passive consumer to active participant in the story.

Audiences who acknowledged the voyeuristic appeal of reality narratives also expressed that they valued the companionship generated by those narratives; these audiences likewise reported low levels of interpersonal interactions in their daily lives, low personal mobility and individual agency, and high attributions of events in their lives to external forces.[40] In other words, audiences who felt repressed in their ability to engage with others on a regular basis were more likely to turn to reality-based narratives in search of human connection. Interestingly, the voyeuristic appeal of true crime seems to be strongest for women, as women were most likely to agree with statements like, "Listening to true crime podcasts allows me to get a peek into a criminal mind," "I listen to true crime podcasts because I like hearing about the personal lives of other people," and "I enjoy listening to true crime podcasts because I like hearing about the secrets or misdeeds of someone's life." The fact that women indicate stronger voyeuristic tendencies than men is a significant finding, which complicates the female viewership's dualistic motivations of identifying with the victim and of empathizing with the victimizer.

These experiences of identity and empathy serve additional psychological needs for locating one's self within group hierarchies, according to a study by Reiss and Wiltz.[41] Reiss and Wiltz discovered that the more status-oriented the audience was, the more likely they were to report that a feeling of self-importance was a significant motive for reality-narrative consumption. Because true crime ascribes social value to the lives of ordinary people, viewers who consider themselves to be ordinary could fantasize about gaining notoriety as they observe the notoriety of the characters in the narrative. Particularly for true crime viewers, the genre engages an audience that is predisposed to low mobility and social interaction, and establishes communal bonds with like-minded cohorts. In Boling and Hull's study, 63 percent of respondents indicated that they actively participate in online true crime podcast-specific communities; 41 percent reported that their level of participation with those groups is less than weekly.[42] Though the authors caution that this finding is likely related to the fact that their respondents were sourced from an online podcast community, anecdotal evidence provided by the 12.6 thousand members of Facebook's "True Crime Podcasts & Documentaries We Love ❤ Discussion Group," and the 154.7 thousand members in the series-specific "Crime Junkie Podcast Discussion Group" indicate that true crime consumers are uniquely interested in collaborating and communicating about the stories presented in this genre.

The asynchronous aspect of on-demand true crime consumption could be attributed to the establishment of communities around the genre and its narratives. Podcast hosts regularly hold in-person events and livestream Q&A sessions, they develop detailed websites with links to case files and evidence, and they regularly respond to audience questions and commentaries on social media and other web communities. New audiences discover and binge these narratives on a regular basis, giving new life to the narratives with each new engagement. Communities grow with each new consumer, and the investigative nature of true crime gives each member of the community agency to modify the narrative in intriguing ways. It could be said, then, that true crime documentarians in on-demand platforms are building interactive story templates through a variety of media, and audiences are attracted to the ability to design their own investigations that go beyond the narrative they consume. In 2003, a fledgling usability study for interactive documentaries was conducted by Marianna Nardon, Fabio Pianesi, and Massimo Zancanaro, in which users were able to track through elements of a documentary to consume information that was most interesting to that viewer.[43] The researchers found that participants preferred a structured narrative, like that in a Netflix series or podcast, with tangential components that allowed the viewer to engage beyond that narrative to create their own journey through the story.[44] This explains the agency that true crime narratives enjoy beyond the scripted episodes, and highlights the significant impact the genre can have on communities of true crime enthusiasts.

Cats, Crime and Communal Morality

Historically, sensationalism in true crime literature arose not as a commercial tactic, but as a means of promoting religious understandings of sin and punishment, of political goals for public order and authority, and for navigating cultural tensions over the changing dynamics of family life.[45] In recent years, social psychologist Jonathan Haidt and his team have developed the Moral Foundations Theory, which describes a series of foundations on which all cultures construct unique virtues and narratives. Among those foundations is the "authority/subversion" foundation, which underlies social interactions through the community's identification of legitimate authority and subversion of authorities which the community has deemed illegitimate or oppressive.[46] Haidt's concept of subversion might be marginally linked to Punnett's in the sense that true crime encourages skeptical evaluation of prejudicial beliefs, and allows the true crime community to establish new authorities based on fresh analysis of evidence. Directly connected to the authority/subversion foundation is the care/harm foundation, which Haidt says relates to evolutionary attachment systems and an ability to feel (and oppose) the pain of others.[47] When a community perceives that harm has come to a party that deserves protection, and particularly when that harm is sensationalized through vivid depictions of violence, the community establishes values around that experience and forms opinions about authority that are intended to promote care and dispense with harm.

Harm is a central theme in true crime, as the genre places much of its focus on victimhood. Victims are by nature powerless, in that the crime has caused the victims to forfeit their agency for participating actively in their own narrative. This is true whether the victim experienced power or subservience during their lifetime; however, when the victim represented a vulnerable group in life, the pathetic appeal is intensified. Wiltenburg has noted that:

> The reliance on pathos in topical reports of crime has created for many a jarring clash of genres—a sense of feelings roused in the wrong place. However, it underlies the distinctive rhetorical stance of sensationalism as a genre. Because its starting point, violent crime, is the raw material of tragedy, sensationalism operates in a mode that tends to mute the norms of ordinary debate.[48]

The sensationalistic muting of ordinary debate is represented in true crime narratives like *Tiger King* and *Don't F*uck With Cats* through the proximity of the crimes to defenseless animals. Though both narratives center on human victims—the missing Don Lewis and the murdered Jun Lin—the fact that these narratives are couched in stories of cruelty against cats has made them particularly appealing to audiences, which accounts for the popularity of both docuseries. Audiences are drawn in by the indignation of offenses against vulnerable creatures; though the audience is horrified by descriptions of violence against the cats, they are instigated by the impulse to create moral foundations around that violence that might prevent further harm from coming to those creatures.

For on-demand, multi-modal, and interactive true crime, cats are uniquely situated to activate viewers' communal response to the care and harm foundation for a number of reasons. Cats have long been internet darlings; as of 2014, there were more than two million cat videos posted on YouTube, with more than twenty-five billion total views.[49] The web has catered to felines not just as entertainers, but also as media consumers who deserve their own channels of on-demand content.[50] Because studies on pet therapy have suggested that time spent with pets can improve mood and wellbeing across a variety of populations,[51] and because research has suggested that users typically react to mediated content as if it were real,[52] Jessica Gall Myrick has posited that "mediated exposure to cats could possibly result in similar outcomes found in pet therapy studies, although perhaps to a lesser degree."[53]

Scholars have puzzled over the reasons why the internet has developed a preference for cats, though dogs have a longer history of domestication and an empirically demonstrated ability to follow and understand human social cues.[54] Particularly for true crime viewers, the answer may be related to the audience's low levels of social interaction and increased longing for connection. Cats seem to enact a judicious ability to demonstrate care for their human counterparts in a manner that dogs cannot afford. A 1999 study by Gerulf Rieger and Dennis C. Turner indicated that cats initiated more head- and flank-rubbing behaviors with human subjects who exhibited signs of depression.[55] Building on this finding, a 2017 study by a research team from Kyoto University revealed that cat owners who perceived their cats as "family members" listed "compassion" as a principal trait of their cats, leading the researchers to believe that the head- and flank-rubbing is interpreted by owners as a comforting behavior, which generates a sense of closeness.[56]

Cats are, of course, independent creatures; they display a temperament of autonomy that sets them apart from dogs behaviorally. Takumi Nagasawa, Mitsuaki Ohta, and Hidehiko Uchiyama have suggested that this autonomy is likely the result of cats' short domestication process, which may not yet be complete; the researchers posit that because domesticated cats' genes are not distinct from those of wild cats, their wild behaviors and complex relationship to human social cues could explain the mechanism underlying the benefits that cats have proven to provide to individuals on the autism spectrum.[57] Research has suggested that traits such as introversion and shyness has been linked both to greater internet usage,[58] and to a preference for cats over dogs,[59] so it is possible that introverts are drawn to streaming cat content because they identify with cats, which are often characterized as solitary and anti-social.[60] Because true crime viewers likewise exhibit traits that resemble introversion, the confluence of cats, on-demand streaming, and interactive narratives exhibited in *Tiger King* and *Don't F*ck with Cats* was the perfect recipe for sensational docuseries and a community of moral engagement.

The Feline and the Feminine

In noting that cat owners who saw their pets as family members scored their cats as significantly more compassionate than dogs, Minori Arahori and her research team recognized that pet-owner relationships often were described as similar to child-parent relationships.[61] Research has found that viewing images of cute animals promotes attention to detail and behavioral carefulness[62]; Gary D. Sherman, Jonathan Haidt, and James A. Coan have attributed this heightened focus to an evolutionary adaptation that promotes care for young children.[63] Concern for the wellbeing of children has been an emotive tool used throughout the history of the true crime genre, and generally was used to evoke the horrors of household bloodshed in order to illustrate the desperation of familial tensions caused by economic strain and threats to the familial order.[64] Historical true crime narratives often gave voice to the pleading of murdered children in order to provoke emotional responses that anchor the horror of the event.[65] Similarly, *Don't F*ck with Cats* showed clips of Magnotta's videos of tortured cats, including suffocated kittens, a cat who was served to a snake, and, perhaps most haunting, a panicked tabby who was duct taped to the end of a pole and, after uttering a soulful howl and glancing pleadingly into Magnotta's camera, is drowned in a bathroom tub. The documentary cut the videos before the graphic depictions of the torture commenced, and panned instead to viewers like Deanna Thompson, whose tearful, horrified looks were evocative enough to convey the abhorrence of the violence.

In her use of mood management theory (MMT) to explain internet users' affinity for cat videos, Gall Myrick has suggested that because viewers tend to use media to dissipate aversive emotional states or to maintain positive ones, the cute and funny nature of cat videos conveys a hedonic message feature that attracts internet users.[66] Gall Myrick also recognizes, however, that not all mood management motivations are hedonic; media consumers may also seek affective content because it promotes connections with other people.[67] Mary Beth Oliver and Arthur Raney have suggested that media choice includes not only pleasure-seeking (hedonic) motivators, but also truth-seeking (eudaimonic) motivations.[68] Oliver and Raney argue that media consumption is not just a means of experiencing enjoyment, but also for "grappling with questions such as life's purpose and human meaningfulness."[69] True crime is built on the structure of mystery and detective narratives, so truth-seeking is a principal motive for this kind of media consumption. It could also be said that, in illustrating the lives of ordinary people, the genre engages a search for meaningfulness as the narratives seek to ascribe purpose to ordinary lives that have been cut short by violence. The popularity of Netflix's cat-centric true crime docuseries, therefore, could be evidence of the true crime viewer's seeking of affective content that deeply rocks the core of their moral foundations in order to find meaning in human life and to deepen a search for connection through empathetic sufferings.

Gall Myrick has further noted that the consumption of internet cat videos is often described as a "guilty pleasure,"[70] which she connects to studies that suggest that reality media consumption is driven by voyeurism.[71] She pushes against this characterization, however, by suggesting that the role of positive emotional reactions to entertainment media could act as a moderator of the guilt-enjoyment relationship[72]; that is, the pleasure derived from viewing cat videos online can mitigate the guilt of consuming media which has little to no intellectual value. While her assessment might be true for traditional short clips of cats being cute and funny, the affective connection between cats and true crime heightens the connection to voyeuristic motivations, especially for women viewers. The appeal of cat-centric reality crime narratives is complicated by both the pleasure derived from viewing cats and the longing for human connection simulated by viewing the private lives of others.

In a paper presented for the 2012 NEPCA Conference, Leah Shafer drew attention to the feminine nature of viral cat videos. Shafer argued that "The issue of gender is central to a discussion of LOLcat memes and viral cat videos, from the way that their 'televisual' aesthetic has historically been linked to 'feminized' forms of entertainment, to the way that their ubiquity stands in as a kind of comic analogue for that other pervasive Internet obsession: the pussy."[73] Though Shafer acknowledges that this claim is built on a "kind of playful surreal logic based on wordplay," she asserts that the implications have real aesthetic, political, and affective relevance.[74] Shafer argues that the aesthetic conventions of internet cat videos mirror those of internet pornography and the manner in which the representation of bodies both distracts and conglomerates views in the internet's attention economy.[75] One link between pornography and cat videos, Shafer argues, is their international circulation: "you don't need to know Japanese to LOL at a cat video shot in Japan. Cats, like sex, are ubiquitous worldwide"[76]

Like cats and sex, depictions of crime and violence are ubiquitously capable of affecting similar emotive responses across cultures and languages. If voyeurism can be considered a principally feminine motive for consuming true crime, and if that voyeurism is linked to the dualistic motivations of identifying with the victim and empathizing with the victimizer, then it could be said that the depictions of violence against cats in *Tiger King* and *Don't F*ck with Cats* trigger not only a sensational desire to shield vulnerable, compassionate animals from harm, but also a reflection of the vulnerable and compassionate nature of the female viewer. In both docuseries, the victims—Don Lewis and Jun Lin—are male. Though *Don't F*ck with Cats* features Deanna Thompson as a leading protagonist, and *Tiger King* portrays Carole Baskin as a complicated anti-hero, it could be argued that the cats serve to ascribe a feminine quality to the victimhood portrayed in the narratives as a means to engage female viewers and to place emphasis on the "exhibition space formed around participation in the phenomenon" of watching and interacting with multi-modal, on-demand true crime.

Conclusion

As with any true crime narrative, the danger of sensationalism lies in the potential for dehumanizing the victim in order to engage fascination with the victimizer. Jun (Justin) Lin was described as a shy, kind international student from Wuhan, China. He was an undergraduate in engineering and computer science at Concordia University in Montreal, Quebec. He was a convenience store clerk, and is even noted as having a pet cat who was "like his baby."[77] Because of his connection with Luka Magnotta and the enthusiastically-binged docuseries, however, Lin's name and legacy is inseparably tied to the crimes of the notorious kitten-killer for viewers across the internet. True crime audiences who engage with the on-demand platform's new structure of multimodality can still find on the web Magnotta's video, titled "1 Lunatic 1 Icepick," of murdering, mutilating, and dismembering Lin's body.

Similarly, police and family members still do not have answers to explain the disappearance of Don Lewis. Though Lewis's personal flaws and problematic intimate relationships have been widely publicized, his loss resonates through the narrative of *Tiger King*, and unsupported allegations continue to plague his former wife. Baskin has rebounded, of course; she has even used her new notoriety to enjoy a short stint on the dance competition show *Dancing with the Stars*.[78] Yet, as with Jun Lin, Lewis's humanity has been clouded by fascination with crime and the beatification of cats who were harmed in the circumstances surrounding his disappearance.

The popularity of cat-centric crime stories in recent years has done much to bring true crime narratives into the mainstream, which has provided opportunities to analyze the genre in terms of its affect for viewers and its impact on the community. True crime viewers tend to be introverted, voyeuristic, and longing for connection. On-demand platforms, and the interactive nature of web-based multimodal narratives, have extended those narratives far beyond the intentions of their producers. Producers and audiences must be cognizant of this development in media consumption, as the limitations of the narrative and the nebulousness of the possibilities for interaction beyond the narrative can have substantial impacts on victims and their families, on viewers, and on the communities with which those viewers engage. Most assuredly, however, the unmitigated popularity of Netflix's docuseries has affirmed that when it comes to depictions crime in a digital world, Deanna Tompson's "rule zero," from which the title of her docuseries was derived, is firmly valid: *Don't F*ck with Cats.*

Notes

1. Eric Goode and Rebecca Chaiklin, dir. *Tiger King: Murder, Mayhem, and Madness.* Netflix. 2020.
2. Chan, Melissa. "'Real People Keep Getting Re-Traumatized.' The Human Cost of Binge-Watching True Crime." Time, 2020, https://time.com/5285475/true-crime-victim-families/.
3. "Disappearance on Easy Street." WTSP. November 1, 2002.
4. "Disappearance on Easy Street," 2002.
5. BCR. "Refuting Netflix Tiger King." Big Cat Rescue, 2020, https://bigcatrescue. org/refuting-netflix-tiger-king/.
6. Mark Lewis, dir. *Don't F*ck with Cats: Hunting an Internet Killer.* Netflix. 2019.
7. Oldham, Stuart. "'Don't F*ck With Cats': Deanna Thompson and Director Mark Lewis Reflect on Their Creepy Netflix Series." *Variety,* 2020, https://variety.com/2020/tv/news/dont-fuck-with-cats-netflix-luka-magnotta-deanna-thompson-1203479502/.
8. Myrick, J.G. "Emotion regulation, procrastination, and watching cat videos online: Who watches Internet cats, why, and to what effect?" *Computers in Human Behavior Vol. 52,* 2015, pp. 168–76.
9. Wiltenburg, J. "True Crime: The Origins of Modern Sensationalism." *The American Historical Review. Vol 109.5,* 2004, pp. 1377–1404.
10. Boling, Kelli S. "True crime podcasting: Journalism, justice or entertainment?" *Radio Journal: International Studies in Broadcast & Audio Media 17 (2),* 2019, pp. 161–178.
11. Trey Parker and Matt Stone, "Investigative Murder Porn," South Park, Comedy Central, October 2, 2013.

12. Punnett, Ian. *Toward a Theory of True Crime Narratives: A Textual Analysis.* New York: Routledge, 2018.

13. Punnett, Ian. "Every American Life: Understanding *Serial* as True Crime," paper presented at the 2017 meeting of Association for Education in Journalism and Mass Communication, Chicago, 9–12 August, 2017.

14. Laura Ricciardi and Moira Demos, dir. *Making a Murderer.* Netflix. 2015

15. "Free Steven Avery," Change.org, 2015. https://www.change.org/p/president-of-the-united-states-free-steven-avery.

16. Pleasance, Chris. "Key Making a Murderer evidence disputed: Puncture hole in top of a blood vial allegedly sued to frame Steven Avery 'would have been put there as standard practice,'" *Daily Mail,* January 15, 2016.

17. McBride, Jessica. "14 pieces of troubling evidence 'Making a Murderer' left out or glossed over," *On Milwaukee,* Dec. 30, 2015, https://onmilwaukee.com/articles/evidenceagainstavery.

18. Laura Ricciardi and Moira Demos, dir. *Making a Murderer 2.* Netflix. 2018.

19. BCR, "Refuting Netflix Tiger King."

20. BCR, "Refuting Netflix Tiger King."

21. McCluskey, Megan. "'Everyone Had a Different Story.' *Tiger King* Popularity Leads Sheriff to Reopen the Case of Don Lewis's Disappearance," *Time,* April 2, 2020.

22. Wiltenburg, Joy. "True Crime: The Origins of Modern Sensationalism." *The American Historical Review 109 (5),* 2004, pp. 1377–1404.

23. Wiltenburg, "True Crime."

24. Wiltenburg, "True Crime."

25. Boling, "True Crime Podcasting."

26. Boling, "True Crime Podcasting."

27. Boling, "True Crime Podcasting."

28. Boling, Kelli S., and Hull, Kevin. "Undisclosed Information—Serial Is My Favorite Murder: Examining Motivations in the True Crime Podcast Audience." *Journal of Radio & Audio Media 25 (1),* 2018, pp. 92–10.

29. Boling and Hull, "Undisclosed Information."

30. Boling and Hull, "Undisclosed Information."

31. Papacharissi, Zizi, and Mendelson, Andrew L. "An Exploratory Study of Reality Appeal: Uses and Gratifications of Reality TV Shows." *Journal of Broadcasting & Electronic Media 52 (2),* 2007, pp. 355–370.

32. Papacharissi and Mendelson, "An Exploratory Study of Reality Appeal."

33. Boling and Hull, "Undisclosed Information."

34. Boling and Hull, "Undisclosed Information."

35. Boling and Hull, "Undisclosed Information"; Papacharissi and Mendelson, "An Exploratory Study of Reality Appeal."

36. Wong, J. "Here's looking at you: Reality TV, Big Brother, and Foucault." *Canadian Journal of Communication 26,* 2001, pp. 33–501.

37. Dauncey, H. "French 'reality television': More than a matter of taste?" *European Journal of Communication, 11(1),* 1996, pp. 83–106.

38. Fetveit, A. "Reality TV in the digital era: A paradox in visual culture?" *Media, Culture Society, 21,* 1999, pp. 787–804.

39. Jagodozinki, J. "The perversity of (Real)ity TV: A symptom of our times." *Journal for the Psychoanalysis of Culture & Society, 8(2),* 2003, pp. 320–329.

40. Papacharissi and Mendelson, 2007.

41. Reiss, S. and Wiltz, J. "Why people watch reality TV." *Media Psychology, 6,* 2004, pp. 363–378.

42. Boling and Hull, "Undisclosed Information."

43. Marianna Nardon, Fabio Pianesi, and Massimo Zancanaro. "Interactive Documentaries: First Usability Studies." 2003, ITC-irst.

44. Nardon, Pianesi, and Zancanaro, "Interactive Documentaries."

45. Wiltenburg, "True Crime."

46. Jonathan Haidt. *The Righteous Mind: Why Good People are Divided by Politics and Religion*. New York: Random House, 2012.
47. Haidt, *The Righteous Mind.*
48. Wiltenburg, "True Crime."
49. Marshall, Carla. "Cat Videos on YouTube: 2 Million Uploads, 25 Billion Views," TubularInsights. October 29, 2014, https://tubularinsights.com/2-million-cat-videos-youtube/.
50. Lazzard, Slage. "Cats, Once YouTube Stars, Are Now an 'Emerging Audience,' Wired. January 22, 2020.
51. Nimer, J., and, B. Lundahl. "Animal-assisted therapy: A meta-analysis," *Anthrozoös 20*, 2007, pp. 225–238.
52. Reeves, B., and C. Nass. "The media equation: How people treat computers, television, and new media like real people and places." CSLI Publications, Stanford, CA, 1996.
53. Gall Myrick, Jessica. "Emotion regulation, procrastination, and watching cat videos online: Who watches Internet cats, why, and to what effect?" *Computers in Human Behavior 52*, 2015, pp. 168–176..
54. Cooper, J.J., C. Ashton, S. Bishop, R. West, D.S. Mills, and R.J. Young. "Clever Hounds: Social Cognition in the Domestic Dog (*Canis familiaris*)." *Applied Animal Behavioral Science, 81*, 2003, pp. 229–244.
55. Rieger, Gerulf, and Dennis C. Turner. "How Depressive Moods Affect the Behavior of Singly Living Persons Toward their Cats," *Anthrozoös, 12(4)*, 1999, pp. 224–233.
56. Arahori, Minori, Hika Kuroshima, Yusuke Hori, Saho Takagi, Hitomi Chijiwa, and Kazou Fujita. "Owners' view of their pets' emotions, intellect, and mutual relationship: Cats and dogs compared." *Behavioural Processes 141 (3)*, 2017, pp. 316–321.
57. Takumi Nagasawa, Mitsuaki Ohta, and Hidehiko Uchiyama. "Effects of the characteristic temperament of cats on the emotions and hemodynamic responses of humans." *PLoS One 15 (6)*, 2020.
58. Ebeling-Witte, Susan, Michael L. Frank, and David Lester. "Shyness, Internet Use, and Personality." *CyberPsychology & Behavior 10(5)*, https://doi.org/10.1089/ cpb.2007.9964.
59. Guastello, D., S. Braun, J. Gutierrez, K. Johnston, and, B. Olbinski. "Personality differences of self-identified canine and feline lovers." Paper presented at the Association for Psychological Science Annual Convention, San Francisco, CA, 2014.
60. Gall Myrick, "Emotion regulation, procrastination, and watching cat videos online."
61. Arahori et al., "Owner's view of their pets' emotions, intellect, and mutual relationship."
62. Nittono, Hiroshi, Michiko Fukushima, Akihiro Yano, and, Hiroki Moriya. "The Power of Kawaii: Viewing cute images promotes careful behavior and narrows attentional focus." *PLoS One, 7*, 2012, 10.1371/journal.pone.0046362.
63. Sherman, G. D., J. Haidt, and, J.A. Coan. "Viewing cute images increases behavioral carefulness." *Emotion, 9(2)*, pp. 282–286. https://doi.org/10.1037/a0014904.
64. Wiltenburg, "True Crime."
65. Wiltenburg, "True Crime."
66. Gall Myrick, "Emotion regulation, procrastination, and watching cat videos online."
67. Gall Myrick, "Emotion regulation, procrastination, and watching cat videos online."
68. Oliver, Mary Beth, and, Arthur A. Raney. "Identifying Hedonic and Eudiamonic Motivatios for Entertainment Consumption." *Journal of Communication 61(5)*, 2011, pp. 984–1004, https://doi.org/10.1111/j.1460-2466.2011.01585.x.
69. Oliver and Raney, "Identifying Hedonic and Eudaimonic Motivations for Entertainment Consumption."
70. Gall Myrick, "Emotion regulation, procrastination, and watching cat videos online."
71. Baruh, Lemi. "Mediated Voyeurism and the Guilty Pleasure of Consuming Reality Television." *Media Psychology 13(3)*, pp. 201-221.
72. Gall Myrick,"Emotion regulation, procrastination, and watching cat videos online."
73. Shafer, Leah. "I can haz an Internet aesthetic?!? LOLCats and the digital marketplace." Paper presented at the Northeast Popular/American Culture Association Conference, St. John Fisher College, Rochester, NY, 2014.
74. Shafter, "I can haz an Internet aesthetic?!?"

75. Shafer, "I can haz an Internet aesthetic?!?"
76. Shafer, "I can haz an Internet aesthetic?!?"
77. Lewis, Don't F*ck with Cats.
78. Andrew, Scottie. "Carole Baskin is eliminated from 'Dancing with the Stars,'" *CNN*, Sept. 29, 2020.

Works Cited

Andrew, Scottie, "Carole Baskin is eliminated from 'Dancing with the Stars,'" *CNN*, Sept. 29, 2020.

Arahori, Minori, Hika Kuroshima, Yusuke Hori, Saho Takagi, Hitomi Chijiwa, Kazou Fujita "Owners' view of their pets' emotions, intellect, and mutual relationship: Cats and dogs compared." *Behavioural Processes* 141 (3): (2017), 316–321.

Baruh, Lemi "Mediated Voyeurism and the Guilty Pleasure of Consuming Reality Television," *Media Psychology 13*(3) (2009), 201–221.

BCR "Refuting Netflix Tiger King." Big Cat Rescue. Last modified May 2020. https://bigcatrescue.org/refuting-netflix-tiger-king/.

Boling, Kelli S., and Hull, Kevin. "Undisclosed Information—Serial Is My Favorite Murder: Examining Motivations in the True Crime Podcast Audience." *Journal of Radio & Audio Media 25 (1)*, 2018, pp. 92–10.

Boling, Kelli S. "True crime podcasting: Journalism, justice or entertainment?" *Radio Journal: International Studies in Broadcast & Audio Media* 17 (2): 2019, 161–178.

Chan, Melissa. "'Real People Keep Getting Re-traumatized.' The Human Cost of Binge-Watching True Crime." *Time*, 2020. https://time.com/5825475/true-crime-victim-families/.

Cooper, J.J., C. Ashton, S. Bishop, R. West, D.S. Mills, and R.J. Young "Clever hounds: Social cognition in the domestic dog (Canis familiaris)" *Applied Animal Behavioral Science*, 81, 2003 229–244.

Dauncey, H. French "Reality Television: More than a matter of taste?" *European Journal of Communication*, 11(1): 1996, 83–106.

"Disappearance on Easy Street." WTSP. November 1, 2002.

Ebeling-Witte, Susan, Michael L. Frank, and David Lester, "Shyness, Internet Use, and Personality," *CyberPsychology & Behavior* 10(5), 2007 https://doi.org/10.1089/cpb.2007.9964 Fetveit, A. "Reality TV in the digital era: A paradox in visual culture?" *Media, Culture Society, 21*, 1999, pp. 787–804.

"Free Steven Avery," Change.org, 2015. https://www.change.org/p/president-of-the-united-states-free-steven-avery.

Goode, Eric, and Rebecca Chaiklin, dir. *Tiger King: Murder, Mayhem, and Madness*. Netflix. 2020.

Guastello, D., Braun, S., Gutierrez, J., Johnston, K., and Olbinski, B. *Personality Differences of Self-Identified Canine and Feline Lovers*. Paper presented at the Association for Psychological Science Annual Convention, San Francisco, CA. 2014.

Haidt, Jonathan. *The Righteous Mind: Why Good People are Divided by Politics and Religion*. New York: Random House, 2012.

Jagodozinki, J. "The perversity of (Real)ity TV: A symptom of our times." *Journal for the Psychoanalysis of Culture & Society, 8(2)*, 2003, pp. 320–329.

Lazzard, Sage. "Cats, Once YouTube Stars, Are Now an 'Emerging Audience,'" *Wired*. January 22, 2020.

Lewis, Mark, dir. *Don't F*ck with Cats: Hunting an Internet Killer*. Netflix. 2019.

Marshall, Carla. "Cat Videos on YouTube: 2 Million Uploads, 25 Billion Views," *TubularInsights*. October 29, 2014, https://tubularinsights.com/2-million-cat-videos-youtube/.

McBride, Jessica. "14 pieces of troubling evidence 'Making a Murderer' left out or glossed over," *On Milwaukee*, Dec 30, 2015, https://onmilwaukee.com/articles/evidenceagainstavery.

McCluskey, Megan, "'Everyone Had a Different Story.' *Tiger King* Popularity Leads Sheriff to Reopen the Case of Don Lewis's Disappearance," *Time*, April 2, 2020.
Myrick, J.G. "Emotion regulation, procrastination, and watching cat videos online: Who watches Internet cats, why, and to what effect?" *Computers in Human Behavior*. Vol. 52. 2015, 168–76.
Myrick, Jessica Gall, "Emotion regulation, procrastination, and watching cat videos online: Who watches Internet cats, why, and to what effect?" *Computers in Human Behavior* 52: 2015, 168–176.
Nagasawa, Takumi, Mitsuaki Ohta, and Hidehiko Uchiyama, "Effects of the characteristic temperament of cats on the emotions and hemodynamic responses of humans." *PLoS One* 15 (6), 2020.
Nardon, Marianna, Fabio Pianesi, and Massimo Zancanaro, "Interactive Documentaries: First Usability Studies." *ITC-irst*. 2003.
Nimer, J., and B. Lundahl, "Animal-assisted Therapy: A Meta-Analysis," *Anthrozoös*, 20: 2007, 225–238.
Nittono, Hiroshi, Michiko Fukushima, Akihiro Yano, Hiroki Moriya, "The power of kawaii: Viewing cute images promotes careful behavior and narrows attentional focus," *PLoS One*, 2012. 7 10.1371/journal.pone.0046362.
Oldham, Stuart. 'Don't F*ck With Cats'": Deanna Thompson and Director Mark Lewis Reflect on Their Creepy Netflix Series." *Variety*, 2020. https://variety.com/2020/tv/news/dont-fuck-with-cats-netflix-luka-magnotta-deanna-thompson-1203479502/.
Oliver, Mary Beth and Arthur A. Raney, "Identifying Hedonic and Eudiamonic Motivations for Entertainment Consumption," *Journal of Communication* 61(5) 2011, 984–1004, https://doi.org/10.1111/j.1460-2466.2011.01585.
Papacharissi, Zizi, and Andrew L. Mendelson. "An Exploratory Study of Reality Appeal: Uses and Gratifications of Reality TV Shows." *Journal of Broadcasting & Electronic Media* 52 (2): 2007, 355–370.
Parker, Trey, and Matt Stone. "Investigative Murder Porn," *South Park*, Comedy Central, October 2, 2013.
Pleasance, Chris. "Key Making a Murderer evidence disputed: Puncture hole in top of a blood vial allegedly sued to frame Steven Avery 'would have been put there as standard practice,'" *Daily Mail*, January 15, 2016.
Punnett, Ian. "Every American Life: Understanding Serial as True Crime," paper presented at the 2017 meeting of Association for Education in Journalism and Mass Communication, Chicago, August 2017. 9–12.
Punnett, Ian. *Toward a Theory of True Crime Narratives: A Textual Analysis*. New York: Routledge, 2018.
Reeves, B., and C. Nass, "The media equation: How people treat computers, television, and new media like real people and places," *CSLI Publications*, Stanford, CA, 1996.
Reiss, S. and Wiltz, J., Why people watch reality TV. *Media Psychology*, 6: 2004. 363–378.
Ricciardi, Laura and Moira Demos, dir. *Making a Murderer 2*. Netflix. 2018
Ricciardi, Laura and Moira Demos, dir. *Making a Murderer*. Netflix. 2015.
Rieger, Gerulf and Dennis C. Turner, "How Depressive Moods Affect the Behavior of Singly Living Persons Toward their Cats," *Anthrozoos*, 12(4) 1999, 224–233
Shafer, Leah, *I can haz an Internet aesthetic?!?* LOLCats and the digital marketplace. Paper presented at the Northeast Popular/American Culture Association Conference, St. John Fisher College, Rochester, NY. 2014
Sherman, G. D., Haidt, J., & Coan, J. A. "Viewing cute images increases behavioral carefulness," *Emotion*, 9(2), 282–286. 2009, https://doi.org/10.1037/a0014904
Wiltenburg, Joy. "True Crime: The Origins of Modern Sensationalism." *The American Historical Review* 109 (5): 2004, 1377–1404.
Wong, J. "Here's looking at you: Reality TV, *Big Brother*, and Foucault." *Canadian Journal of Communication*, 26: 2001. 33–501.

Super-Heroines to the Rescue (of Feminism)

She-Ra and the Princesses of Power

Christina Adamou

There are obviously different parameters to be taken into account when discussing *She-Ra and the Princesses of Power* (2018–2020) with relation to feminism: obviously feminism itself, children's television—particularly with regard to animation, genre conventions and representations, as well as children's programming on Netflix. This essay will attempt to tackle the interrelations of all these factors with reading *She-Ra and the Princesses of Power.*

As the title conveys, the serial is a remake of *She-Ra* and features representations of powerful women, who are also princesses. Although this might seem an oxymoron at first glance, I will argue that the audiovisual text works against that first impression and along with the fourth wave of feminism.

Taking into account that powerful women are the main characteristic of the program and before analyzing the representations and narratives that it offers, it is worth noting that the production and streaming of the program coincide chronologically with the Fourth Wave of Feminism. However, if we are to draw a link between a television program and a wave of feminism, it must share in its ideology, concerns and distinguishing characteristics and not just coincide chronologically.

There is a lot of discourse and debate over what distinguishes the Fourth Wave Feminism from other waves of feminism. As Chamberlain points out, "the contemporary moment of activism is hard to define. A number of waves have become rigid through the post-rationalisation of their development."[1] There is also much discourse lately about the very narrative of feminist waves, as it seems to be based upon stereotyping and dismissing earlier waves, stressing discontinuities and backlashes. As Rivers reminds us, the second wave feminists were stereotyped and dismissed by the third wave as both anti-men and masculine. The second wave has also been criticized for promoting white, middle-class and heterosexual concerns. The third wave that put emphasis on the range and right to personal choices was in turn stereotyped and dismissed as individualist.[2] Of course, the discourse that stereotypes and dismisses earlier waves of feminism tends to overlook the continuities among them and the plurality of voices, forms of activism and ideas that they have given rise to. Therefore, there is much discussion as to how we define different waves of feminism and the very usefulness of the concept of waves.[3] Although the general discussion on the concept of waves and the ways in which we define them lies outside the scope of this essay, it informs the reading of *She-Ra*, in the sense that it uses feminist theory from the second and third waves and it also points out characteristics of the fourth wave.

Although it is hard to define a contemporary and evolving wave of feminism, scholars tend to agree on some distinguishing characteristics, among which is the prominence of social media in its manifestation and forms of activism.[4] As an internet television platform, Netflix is situated within the context of the internet and therefore partakes in the feminist discourse online as well as popular culture. The fourth wave of feminism and Netflix may not always share the same ideology, yet they cohabitate within the internet and popular culture.

Another distinguishing characteristic of the fourth wave is inclusivity in terms of race, ethnicity and sexuality, allowing different women's voices to be heard and encompassing different backgrounds and experiences.[5] There also seems to be an emphasis toward criticizing political and social structures, focusing of course on patriarchy. "The fourth wave of feminism recognizes that the struggle is not just again men; it is also against women who have internalized the patriarchal ideals deeply ingrained within the fabric of the society and now act as the reinforcers of these ideas at the expense of other women's independence."[6] Thus the fourth wave of feminism breaks up gender boundaries, placing the epicenter on ideology and social structures rather than biology.

Of course, this is a continuity rather than a break with previous feminist waves, since Simone de Beauvoir—to give one example—wrote in 1949 how the sociocultural stereotypes and expectations form gender identity.[7] Inclusivity and a war against patriarchy, featuring male allies and female foes, however, are considered to be prominent characteristics both of the fourth wave and of the world of *She-Ra*, as we shall see.

Reading *She-Ra* from a feminist perspective need not and could not be limited to fourth-wave feminism. The critical analysis will also have to take into account how the serial problematizes mother-daughter relationships, while at the same time promoting classical feminist values, such as sisterhood and acting in the public domain.

This is especially important when it comes to children's television, as it has traditionally been populated by male protagonists and/or pink-clad fairies, princesses and Barbies. Some contemporary television texts that are also available on internet platforms feature strong girls as protagonists and focus on super-heroines in particular. *PJ Masks* (Disney Junior, 2015– , also available on YouTube) and *Miraculous: Tales of Ladybug & Cat Noir* (Disney, 2015– , also available on Netflix in some countries and on YouTube) both focus on male and female super-heroes/heroines. Although an overview of children's television is outside the scope of this essay, I will venture to state that many children's television series still seem to promote gender stereotypes, using unicorns, rainbows and melodramatic stories to address girls and using cars, dragons and action stories to address boys.

In fact, Dreamworks, who produces the serial, has been accused of having a patriarchal tradition. Although the serial attempts to re-create the original *She-Ra* from a feminist perspective, intertextually, it is struggling with the production company's ideological tradition. As Hassell points out, Dreamworks has a patriarchal tradition in the sense that it portrays societies that are "*male dominated, male identified, and male-centered.*"[8] She argues that Dreamworks' patriarchal tradition is exemplified by films such as *Antz, The Prince of Egypt, Madagascar* and *Chicken Run*. Even *Shrek* is criticized as patriarchal, despite portraying a dynamic female princess, because the focus remains on the male protagonist and his male sidekicks, while the film reinforces heteronormative values through the happy-ending romance between Shrek and Fiona.[9]

Both Dreamworks and Netflix, however, aim to offer a feminist television serial for children with the text at hand and perhaps redefine their identities. With regard to children's television, Netflix is in a very complex market, where production companies, networks and streaming video platforms both compete and collaborate. Many popular children's TV series are free on YouTube and/or their own official websites, such as *Peppa Pig*; public service broadcasters offer platforms for quality television programming and video games, such as CBeeBies; international television streaming platforms such as Apple TV offer children's programming as part of their services; and of course Disney has launched Disney+, which is addressed mainly to children and young audiences and offers not just Disney films and television but also National Geographic, Marvel, Pixar and *Star Wars* cinema and television content.[10] Since Netflix's premise is to offer programming that caters to different interests and tastes and is addressed to different genders, races and ages, the platform has to cater to younger audiences, thus allowing families to make the choice to subscribe solely to Netflix. In fact, studies have shown that viewers complain about missing out on sports and news, thus indicating that they expect the variety of programming that they enjoyed on broadcast television.[11] At the same time, the platform has to distinguish itself in relation to platforms specializing in children's programs, such as Disney+, offering perhaps different choices for children and guardians.

Netflix had collaborated with Disney and has moved on to distinguishing itself from Disney, partially through showcasing Dreamworks' films and original television content. Disney has a very definite and recognizable brand name and profile both with regard to traditional Walt Disney characters, such as Mickey Mouse, and with regard to Disney princesses. The deal between Netflix and Dreamworks, signed in 2013,[12] has largely shaped the platform's profile for children and family audiences, offering different choices from the Disney legacy. Also available on Netflix are quality television series for children, featuring strong girls that lead the narratives, such as *Peppa Pig* (Nick. Jr / Channel 5, 2004–), along with stereotypical "girl" cartoons, e.g., fashion-conscious Barbie, and remakes representing the struggles of young girls within patriarchal societies and families, e.g., *Heidi*.

Although we do not have the space here to explore the identity of Netflix's content for children, it becomes apparent that it offers a diversity beyond Disney. It seems to strive for popularity and technical innovations featuring brand names such as Dreamworks as well as content innovation and quality through collaboration with the BBC. Among the diverse programs, we should also discern the promotion of the platform's feminist children's programs, since it features search categories such as "girl power" in children's profiles.

She-Ra and the Princesses of Power can be found in the "girl-power" category and indeed offers both "girlie" and powerful representations of women and young girls, mainly due to its hybridity. The program is a hybrid of genres that features traditional fairy-tale and classical children's film staples, such as princesses, magical creatures and magical objects, as well as science fiction elements of an alternate world somewhere in the universe and characteristics of super-hero films, since all princesses have super-powers. Although one may consider super-powers to be a characteristic of many science fiction films and programs too, such as *Star Wars*, there are also many examples that do not feature super-powers and therefore it is helpful to consider *She-Ra* a hybrid of three genres. The program's hybridity serves to undermines stereotypes and enables feminist and positive queer representations.

Keeping the genre hybridity in mind, we will focus on the appearance of characters, their superpowers and the narrative, with regard to the plot and sub-plots, as they are all important elements of gender representations.

She-Ra, the main protagonist, follows the tradition of action-heroines and some super-heroines, as she is visibly muscular and strong, thus questioning gender-binaries. Her appearance has been altered and is no longer Barbie-like in terms of her proportions, as it was in the original series. Although the original She-Ra was a counterpart to a very muscular character, her first appearance in the 80s was hyper-sexualized and her body resembled that of Barbie. The appearance of the character in the revival of the animated serial though stresses her muscles rather that her curves. As Purse points out,

> it was the "warrior women" of the 1980s and 1990s action cinema who foregrounded their bodily exertions and their physically capable bodies in ways not witnessed previously in Hollywood. [...] In doing so, they deconstructed the notion of masculinity and femininity as "natural" categories: their bodies declared that these traditional markers of masculinity were not the exclusive preserve of men.[13]

The main protagonist's muscular appearance follows the tradition of female action heroines and highlights her super strength.

She-Ra has actually been widely criticized on the internet for its androgynous protagonist.[14] However, I would argue that she is rather too close to stereotypes of beauty. Despite the emphasis placed on her muscles and strength, She-Ra is still blonde, tall and thin. As She-Ra is the super-heroine expected to lead the princesses and save them from the Horde, she is foregrounded as an ideal that is not that different from the majority of super-heroines and ideals of beauty in western culture: white, young, blonde and blue-eyed—she only differs as to her athletic proportions. Her athletic body also does not really deviate from the norms of what is considered beautiful within western culture.

Of course, *She-Ra and the Princesses of Power* is a remake of the 1985 series and a strong counter-argument to the criticism above would be that She-Ra needed to be recognizable as the same super-heroine. Remakes capitalize on the double-appeal of many children's programs to both children and adults. Parents who may have watched or just been aware of the first *She-Ra* are likely to comment on the remake or watch it with the children and perhaps discuss it with them, due to the "intergenerational nostalgia" that revivals can evoke. As Taurino explains, "in order to create nostalgia a revival should come after a time gap and involve a historical rupture, a fracture, an interval that allows the presence of an 'intergenerational nostalgia.'"[15] Major changes to the appearance of the main protagonist might hinder the intergenerational nostalgia and/or the recognizability of the main character.

Adora, She-Ra's alter ego, is a skinny teenager. Adora changes into She-Ra through the magic of the sword, a narrative staple that foregrounds the "unreality" of her appearance and might at some level make audiences aware of her appearance as a fantasy.

However, as more and more young girls and women struggle with issues of body image, feminism needs to push for protagonists who stray even further from norms of "beauty" than just having an athletic body. Secondary characters though offer many body-positive images.

Other characters underwent more dramatic changes in relation to the original series. Bow is a dark-skin teenager who is visibly muscular, but has moved away from the body-builder's appearance of the first serial. Glimmer is a teenager with a fuller figure, very different from the young woman with Barbie's proportions that defined all female characters in the first serial. Spinnerella is a fuller-figured woman—older than most of the characters. Frosta is here designed as an Asian child, instead of the young white woman of the first serial, while Mermista has a much darker skin-color and a fuller figure than her 1986 version. Difference and inclusion are evident in the characters' appearance. The characters represent super-heroines of diverse races, ages and body-images. This diversity steps away from revisionist or postfeminist ideal images of—mostly white—women's bodies with fashion-models' proportions and falls in line with the fourth wave of feminism and the current discourse for more body-positive images and for diversity.

The diverse ensemble of princesses with super-powers is key to the feminist ideology of the serial. It allows for various roles in the narrative and different representations, as well as the development of empathy among them, in turn inviting empathy from the audience. Their appearance and powers are often intrinsic to the narrative sub-plots. The hybridity of genre also plays a big part in forming representation of active, strong women. Not only is the main protagonist known for her strength, but all princesses have super-powers. Their appearance, super-powers, genre conventions and role in the narrative are often inextricably linked and will briefly be discussed in relation to each other.

In children's films and television series, it is not uncommon for girl protagonists to have magical or super-powers. After all, Disney princesses can talk to animals, while fairies can perform magic. On the other hand, grown women who use their superpowers to take control of the narrative world are stereotypically portrayed as evil in classical narratives, e.g., the Snow Queen[16] and the evil witch in Snow-White are both dangerous for the innocent protagonist and for society and/or the natural world. There is an obvious link here to more traditional children's texts, fairy-tales, films and TV programs. The protagonists in *She-Ra* are princesses; one can turn into a mermaid and many others control natural elements like fairies. However, they follow less the traditions of princesses and magical creatures and more the traditions of super-heroines both with regard to leading the narrative and with regard to using their powers to save the world and fight villains. In *She-Ra,* the superpowers of the princesses, be they children, adolescents or adults, are not deemed dangerous for society, since they are fighting against the evil powers of the Horde to save themselves, the planet and the innocents.

Moreover, their powers are not as "girlie" as most fairy-tale and Disney princesses: As discussed, Adora, the protagonist turns into very tall, very strong She-Ra. She-Ra was initially conceived as the female counterpart of He-Man. Secondary characters also often undermine gender stereotypes. Entrapta has magical long hair, which has often been attributed to "girlie" princesses. Yet, she is a genius with technology, an attribute stereotypically masculine and she uses her hair to control objects and the technological marvels she creates, thus providing a representation of a princess that reformulates gender binaries. Although she was an ally of the Horde in the first serial, in the remake, she is captured by the Horde, helps them and develops a friendship with Lord Hordak, based on their common interest in technology, thus undermining both gender binaries and the manichaistic opposition of good and evil.

Other princesses have stereotypically feminine appearance and powers, e.g., Perfuma can grow and control plants. Apart from her "girlie" name, Perfuma is clad in pink and wears flowers. Within the narrative, she often meditates and thus her appearance, superpowers and the narrative also link her to hippie culture. Her inextricable and magical link to nature has also often been attributed to women, ranging from the ancient goddess Dimitra to the Disney princesses' ability to talk to animals. The fundamental difference here is that it is used as a weapon. Her powers are formidable and indispensable to the Princess Alliance.

Her appearance, powers and hippie connotations are in constant interplay with her character and role within the ensemble. As a character, Perfuma values friendship and trust, bringing a hippie and far from naïve notion of "sisterhood" to the forefront. She becomes friends with Scorpia, a princess with scorpion claws and tail, despite her difficulty trusting her, since Scorpia fights initially with and for the Horde. Scorpia does not expect to be accepted among the princesses, because of her appearance. The friendship with the fairy-like Perfuma signifies inclusion and diversity and seals her coalition with and inclusion in the Rebellion. Promoting diversity has been linked to the third and fourth waves of feminism. Perfuma's hippie appearance and flower-power, though, are reminiscent of the second wave. The values of friendship and of support among women transcend the waves of feminism as historical movements and permeate all.

Along with other characters in this hybrid series, Perfuma partakes in the classical and still popular fairy culture, that is so often used to address girls. Perfuma's relation to nature, Queen Angelica's wings, Glimmer's pink and magenta hair and costume, the magical sword and Swift Wing, the unicorn that becomes She-Ra's companion, are all elements of a "girlie" magical narrative world that co-exists with the sci-fi and action narrative world. All the above characters often discuss strategies that foreground their cleverness and formidability as warriors. The hybridity of genres serves to combine "girlie" traditional and popular culture with stereotypically "male" characteristics, such as cleverness and braveness. The text thus undermines binary stereotypes.

The text also uses magic to attract a young audience. As Bettelheim reminds us, "Piaget has shown that the child's thinking remains animistic until the age of puberty," attributing life, intentions and emotions to objects and animals.[17] By attributing feminist characteristics to princesses and fairy-like creatures, *She-Ra* demonstrates that audiovisual texts do not have to forgo magic in order to be feminist.

She-Ra is an audiovisual text that strives to be both magical and politically correct. The character most associated with enacting his independent will, Swift Wing, can be read as supporting animal rights while still partaking in a magical fairy and unicorn world.

She-Ra also establishes interesting links to the narrative structure of fairytales, as it refigures it from a feminist perspective. While often criticized as patriarchal, the magical world of classical fairytales has also been seen as therapeutic, enabling children to process reality. Fairies can embody the child's wishful thinking. Evil witches and voracious wolves can embody a child's fantasies and fears and help structure his/her own contradictory tendencies, as well as the contradictory behavior of parents and others.[18] Although *She-Ra* refers to fairies, princesses and evil witches, the contradictions are not represented between characters but within them. The serial uses a complex narrative that undermines binary oppositions with regard to gender, as well as oppositions such as good and evil.

The narrative supports the complex evolution of various characters. In placing women at the center of the narrative and avoiding Manichaeism, the text moves away from classical representations of women. Returning briefly to an intertextual reading, it could be noted that although *She-Ra and the Princesses of Power* focuses on princesses, it offers very different narratives and therefore different representations of Princesses from "evolved" Disney Princesses or even Fiona in the Dreamworks film franchise. Contemplating differences in Disney's more recent gender representations, *Brave*, *Frozen* and *Mulan,* Chatterjee and Bhattacharjee note that they share a common narrative pattern: "the formation of some trouble, brought about partly due to some error caused by the protagonist; a subsequent feeling of guilt and alienation; the resolution of troubles that coincide with and partly result from the protagonist's overcoming of inner dilemmas." They also note, however, two major differentiations from Disney's older princess films: the absence of a romantic climax and the focus upon self-realization that enables the resolution of problems.[19]

The self-realization of the heroine, as the core of the narrative both in Disney's more recent films and in *She-Ra*, brings to mind the Journey of the Hero, the monomyth that Joseph Campbell read in fairy-tales. The hero undertakes a journey and overcomes obstacles leading to his self-realization before taking his place in society. Campbell argued that heroines do not need to take journeys, because they were the place where the heroes wanted to go.[20] Quite tellingly, the heroines in Disney's films mentioned above as well as She-Ra and the Princesses of Power embark on journeys, both in the external physical world and on inner journeys of self-realization, rather than occupying a desired place throughout the narrative.

This stability of the desired place, also, seems to evoke Mulvey's second wave feminist critique of classical Hollywood narratives. According to Mulvey, in classical Hollywood, women are placed as the object of the gaze of the protagonist and the audience and also constitute the protagonists' award. Apart from the objectification of women, their placement in the narrative also means that the male characters are the ones leading the action, whereas women seem to stall it.[21] Although Mulvey referred to melodramas and film noirs of the 1930s–50s, these stereotypical roles can also be found in more contemporary films and genres, e.g., in the James Bond films. The classical narrative is patriarchal in that it upholds stereotypes for women, such as passivity, objectification and often weakness as well as belonging to the realm of private life.

In *She-Ra* all the above stereotypes are undermined, through the actions of female characters that take journeys, undertake missions and achieve self-realization. All the princesses of power undertake journeys of the hero (heroines in this case), leaving their kingdoms and settled lives and developing into brave warriors. The comradery and complex relations among characters support their arches of development. In order to highlight how characters interact and develop, we could look more closely into the beginning and end of the serial, as well as some character development and interaction in secondary characters and plotlines.

Adhering to the conventions of many fairy-tales, science fiction and super-hero/heroine films and television programs, *She-Ra and the Princesses of Power* starts as a fight between good and evil. In the first episode, Adora, raised by the Horde to join their army, ventures out into the magical forest and discovers the magic sword. That turns her into She-Ra when she calls upon its powers. She is captured by a princess and her best friend and she joins the Rebellion, when she discovers the devastation that the Horde causes to the lives of innocent, unarmed people. Crossing the enemy lines to fight against evil both undermines the Manichaeistic tradition of fairy-tales the as well as marks the passage to a matriarchal society.

The Horde, an evil organization with military characteristics, has taken over a large area of the planet Etheria. The Horde is patriarchal and rather fascist in that everyone fears and blindly obeys its leader, Lord Hordak. The Princesses, who have different magical powers and—more often than not—their own kingdoms, have formed a coalition out of their own free will, the Rebellion, that is led by their queen in the fight against the Horde.

Adora is the first to be introduced in the first episode, as a hungry for action Horde cadet, and we are soon introduced to her companion Catra and the evil figure of Shadow Weaver, who reminds her that she took her in as an orphan, thus entering the role of the step-mother. The Princess Glimmer, who is to become one of Adora's best friends and play a leading role in the narrative, is then introduced to the audience, also in relation to a mother-figure, her biological mother, Queen Angela. The sequence starts with Glimmer addressing her as "Your Majesty" and retreating to Mum, when Queen Angela grounds her for disobeying orders. Magic is then introduced through Adora and Catra stumbling upon the sword in the forest. The narrative then introduces Bow, Glimmer's male best friend. The audience sees Glimmer's power of teleportation and Bow states the fact that everyone in the palace is a princess—except him.

The above synopsis—just like any synopsis—might not do justice to the audiovisual text. However, the importance of multiple characters/princesses, male allies, magic and mother figures seems to come through within the first minutes. Throughout the first season, we are introduced to the majority of characters. We watch the Rebellion get stronger, as princesses join in different episodes.

Upon joining the Rebellion, She-Ra undertakes the journey of the hero, reserved for male protagonists in classical fairy-tales and classical Hollywood. Unlike female characters in many classical narratives, she drives the narrative, along with the princesses.

Friendship with men is a stable characteristic of the serial. Bow is a brave warrior and he is clever and skilled with technology, inventing and using different arrows and other devices. He introduces and upholds the idea of the "Best Friend Squad," which initially includes himself, Glimmer and Adora, but expands in the last season to include Catra. Sea Hawk, a male sea captain who joins the revolution in season one, also appears in numerous episodes. Male allies are a distinguishing characteristic of the serial as well as the fourth wave of feminism. Besides undermining binary oppositions between heterosexual genders and good vs. evil, these interpersonal relations also foreground that the fight is against patriarchy, not against men. The mother-figures and their role in the narrative are also indicative of the fight between matriarchy and patriarchy.

With regard to mother-figures, it is important to note a re-interpretation of the Oedipal complex and its role in classical fairytales. Bettelheim offers a psychoanalytic reading of evil beings in fairy tales, arguing that fairy-tales with a damsel in distress and a knight in shining armor can be read as representations of the Oedipal Complex. For boys, dragons and giants can represent the father that they want to slay. Within the narrative, they can rejoice in the adolescent innocent knight slaying the evil dragon / giant / monster without the guilt they might experience in the real world in recognizing their desire to destroy the father. For girls, the narratives and proposed reading are more complex, since girls are seen as unwilling to dispense with the mother and the care she offers. There is a dual figure of the mother: the pre–Oedipal good mother that is rendered obsolete within the narrative and the evil step-mother that is punished in the narrative with no guilt, since the love for the pre–Oedipal mother is untouched. Bettelheim goes on to argue that the parents can enjoy such fantasies with their children and encourage their daughters to seek their knight.[22]

We could notice the inherent contradiction in Bettelheim's main argument, as evil characters are seen both as a representation of the child's own destructive tendencies and as representing the parents in the Oedipus complex. Insofar as we see identification as a dynamic process rather than a stable state within a narrative though, we could consider it an interesting antithesis of roles.

She-Ra, however, steers away from heteronormative narratives and traditional roles mirroring the Oedipus complex. As has already been mentioned, it is women and girls who fight and slay evil beings. As the narrative evolves, they eventually fight robotic clones of the Horde Prime and their Otherness might indeed serve to take away the guilt of fighting against them. In their journeys of self-realization, they fulfill the role of the knight in shining armor and often save each other.

Moreover, the evil step-mother is allowed to evolve and redeem herself, thus pushing them into maturity. In the last episode, we see Adora's and Catra's evil step mother, Shadow Weaver, who has by now joined the Rebellion, sacrifice herself, in order to save them and the planet of Etheria. The gesture echoes queen Angela's earlier sacrifice, as she disappeared in a different dimension, in order to save her daughter, Glimmer, Etheria and the Rebellion. Mother figures, both good, overprotective moms and evil stepmothers, are ultimately represented as complex and brave—willing to die for their daughters. Representing the same mother figure as both bad and good, allowing her to evolve, could also stand as a resolution of the Oedipus complex, that may be much closer to reality, mirroring the journey of young girls to maturity and the acceptance of mothers as neither idealized nor evil beings.

Shadow Weaver had been a prisoner of the Rebellion that gradually joined them through a complex narrative. By developing her relationships with other characters, the evil step-mother figure turns into a protective mother, willing to sacrifice herself. This kind of narrative complexity is distinct from Jason Mittell's definition of a complex narrative, which involves a self-reflexive aesthetic that calls attention to the constructed nature of the narration, as well as to the skill of the script-writers in building and resolving the narrative.[23] However, the complex relations between characters and their evolution arch allow the serial to move beyond manichaistic traditions of absolute good and evil that are common in fairy-tales, epic melodramas and science fiction. The characters move into grey areas and evolve, allowing daughters to grow through reconciliation with their mothers.

In the last episode, Glimmer also takes part in an Oedipal drama, as she fights with her dad, who is now controlled by the ultimate evil, Lord Prime. She is thus seen fighting her father—instead of a mother figure as would be conventional in classical children's narratives. However, this sub-plot also leads to a grey area and ultimate reconciliation. Glimmer eventually manages to save him and free him from the evil Lord Prime. The daughter wins and saves the father, undertaking at the same time the male role of the knight in shining armor and the female role of the loyal daughter that takes care of her parent.

Last but not least, it should be noted that both Freud's Oedipal complex and Bettelheim's reading of classical fairytales are heteronormative. They further promote patriarchal values, by seeing girls as inherently prone to negotiation via double roles and boys as more aggressive and/or destructive. They ascribe value to heteronormative desire and posit the formation of a nuclear family as a happy ending.

As in most classic fairytales and in accordance with Bettelheim's and Freud's theories, Adora finds happiness in finding love and she is ready to enter a happy adulthood by the end of her adventure. The happy ending of the love story, though, is queer, as Catra and Adora confess their love for each other and kiss in the last episode. Along with other homosexual couples in the serial, Bow's dads and the princesses Spinnerella and Netossa who are married, the couple offers yet another non-heteronormative representation and the promise of a "happily ever after" for the lesbian heroines, who are at the epicenter of the narrative.

Inclusivity of lesbian women and anyone self-identifying as female in the LGBTQI community as well as alliance with the community and inclusivity of queer theory is a distinctive characteristic of the fourth wave of feminism. Besides offering positive representations to children who may be settling into a non-heteronormative sexuality, children's programs like *She-Ra* could also promote non-sexist attitudes amongst children tending toward heterosexuality. Having noted the above, it must also be stressed here that we cannot attribute gender identities and sexual orientation to children in the same way that we could attribute them to self-identifying adult audience.

In her seminal study of *Peter Pan*, Rose argues: "The child is sexual, but its sexuality (bisexual, polymorphous, perverse) threatens our own at its very roots. Setting up the child as innocent is not, therefore, repressing its sexuality—it is above all holding off any possible challenge to our own."[24] Adora's and Catra's kiss has been hailed on the internet as a positive lesbian representation. Following Rose's argument, it could also be read as a moment of challenge to adults' sexual identities. Keeping in mind that sexuality—in the sense of sexual desire—has largely been excluded from children's television, perhaps the very recognition and representation of sexual desire is of utmost importance here.

Along with challenging adult sexuality, *She-Ra* undermines the heteronormative gender stereotypes and narratives. The heroines in She-Ra go on quests, defeat enemies and find themselves, yet there is no simplistic Oedipal drama and the happy ending does not rely on heteronormativity and the formation of a nuclear family. The alternative representations of the Oedipus Complex serve both to undermine and question heteronormative roles but also the possible resolutions of the Oedipus Complex in a feminist context. In accordance to the Fourth Wave of Feminism, the heroines are sometimes queer, they are diverse in their appearance and roles, offer positive body-images, and have male allies. In undermining binary oppositions, being active public figures and valuing female friendship, they uphold feminist values that are largely attributed to the second wave of feminism, yet are central to all feminist waves.

Notes

1. Prudence Chamberlain, *The Feminist Fourth Wave: Affective Temporality* (London & NY: Palgrave Macmillan, 2017), 40.

2. Nicola Rivers, *Postfeminism(s) and the Arrival of the Fourth Wave: Turning Tides* (London and NY: Palgrave Macmillan, 2017), 29-31.

3. See Rivers, *Postfeminism(s),* and Chamberlain, *The Feminist Fourth Wave.*

4. Rivers, *Postfeminism(s),* 107

5. Chamberlain, *The Feminist Fourth Wave,* 88-89.

6. Ananya Chatterjee and Nisarga Bhattacharjee. "Contrivancies of Female Empowerment and the Millennial Wave in Disney Movies," in *Fourth Wave feminism in Science Fiction and Fantasy: Essays on Film Representations, 2012-2019,* Vol. 1, ed. Valerie Estelle (Jeffeson: McFarland, 2019), 129.

7. Simone de Beauvoir, *The Second Sex*, trans. Ed. H.M. Parshley (London: Vintage: 1997). First published 1949.

8. Holly Hassell. "Susan Murphy, Ginormica, and Gloria Steinem: Feminist Consciousness- Raising as Science Fiction in Monsters vs. Aliens," In *The Galaxy Is Rated G: Essays on Children's Science Fiction Film and Television,* eds. R.C. Neighbors and Sandy Rankin (31-52). (Jefferson: McFarland, 2011), 332

9. Hassell. "Susan Murphy," 33.

10. "Disney+ Launches Today—and a New Era of Disney Entertainment Begins," accessed February 2, 2021, https://thewaltdisneycompany.com/disney-launches-today-and-a-new-era-of-disney-entertainment-begins/

11. Vivi Theodoropoulou,. "From Interactive Digital Television to Internet 'Instant' Television: Netflix, Shifts in Power and Emerging Audience Practices from an Evolutionary Perspective." In *The Age of Netflix: Critical Essays on Streaming Media, Digital Delivery and Instant Access,* eds. Cory Barker and Myc Wiatrowski (Jefferson: McFarland, 2017), 583, Kindle.

12. Emily Horgan. "Netflix and DreamWorks TV Output Deal Reviewed 7 Years On," accessed January 6, 2021,
https://www.whats-on-netflix.com/news/netflix-and-dreamworks-tv-output-deal-reviewed-7-years-later/

13. Lisa Purse, *Contemporary Action Cinema* (Edinburgh: Edinburgh UP, 2011), 77.

14. Hannah Collins."TV: The Backlash over She-Ra's Redesign is Why Girls Can't Have Nice Things," last modified July 29, 2018, *Portside*, https://portside.org/2018-07-29/backlash-over-she-ras-redesign-why-girls-cant-have-nice-things

15. Giulia Taurino. "Crossing Eras: Exploring Nostalgic Reconfigurations in Media Franchises," in *Netflix Nostalgia: Streaming the Past on Demand*, ed. Kathryn Pallister (Lanham: Lexington Books, 2019), 13.

16. Disney struggled with the stereotype of the evil Snow Queen, in order to portray a strong young woman with superpowers in *Frozen.*

17. Bruno Bettelheim, *The Uses of Enchantment: The Meaning and Importance of Fairy Tales* (London: Penguin, 1976), 46.

18. Bettelheim, *Uses of Enchantment*, 65-66.

19. Chatterjee and Bhattacharjee, "Contrivancies," 128.

20. Patti McCarthry, "Jack Frost and the Heroine's Journey: Gender-Bending Back to the Goddess in *Rise of the Guardians,*" In *Fourth Wave Feminism in Science Fiction and Fantasy: Volume 1. Essays on Film Representations, 2012-2019*, ed. Valerie Estelle Frankel (Jefferson: McFarland, 2019), 149.

21. Laura Mulvey, "Visual Pleasure and Narrative Cinema," in *Film Theory and Criticism: Introductory Readings*, eds. G. Mast, M. Cohen and L. Braudy, 4th edn (746-55), Oxford: Oxford University Press, 1992.

22. Bettelheim, *Uses of Enchantment*, 111-116.

23. Elliott Logan, "Flashforwards in 'Breaking Bad': Openness, Closure and Possibility," in *Television Aesthetics and Style*, eds. Steven Peacock and Jason Jacobs (New York: Bloomsbury Academic, 2013), 220-21.

24. Jacqueline Rose, *The Case of Peter Pan, Or the Impossibility of Children's Fiction* (Pennsylvania: University of Pennsylvania Press, 1993), 4.

Works Cited

Bettelheim, Bruno. *The Uses of Enchantment: The Meaning and Importance of Fairy Tales.* London: Penguin, 1976.

Chamberlain, Prudence. *The Feminist Fourth Wave: Affective Temporality.* Palgrave Macmillan, 2017.

Chatterjee, Ananya, and Nisarga Bhattacharjee. "Contrivancies of Female Empowerment and the Millennial Wave in Disney Movies." In *Fourth Wave feminism in Science Fiction and Fantasy: Essays on Film Representations, 2012–2019,* Vol. 1, edited by Valerie Estelle Frankel (127–138). Jefferson, NC: McFarland, 2019.

Collins, Hannah. "TV: The Backlash over She-Ra's Redesign is Why Girls Can't Have Nice Things," last modified July 29, 2018, *Portside,* https://portside.org/2018-07-29/backlash-over-she-ras-redesign-why-girls-cant-have-nice-things.

De Beauvoir, Simone. *The Second Sex.* London: Vintage, 1997.

"Disney+ Launches Today—and a New Era of Disney Entertainment Begins," accessed February 2, 2021. https://thewaltdisneycompany.com/disney-launches-today-and-a-new-era-of-disney-entertainment-begins/.

Hassell, Holly. "Susan Murphy, Ginormica, and Gloria Steinem: Feminist Consciousness-Raising as Science Fiction in Monsters vs. Aliens." In *The Galaxy Is Rated G: Essays on Children's Science Fiction Film and Television,* edited by R.C. Neighbors and Sandy Rankin (31–52). Jefferson, NC: McFarland, 2011.

Horgan, Emily. "Netflix and DreamWorks TV Output Deal Reviewed 7 Years On," accessed January 6, 2021, https://www.whats-on-netflix.com/news/netflix-and-dreamworks-tv-output-deal-reviewed-7-years-later/.

Logan, Elliott. "Flashforwards in 'Breaking Bad': Openness, Closure and Possibility." In *Television Aesthetics and Style,* edited by Steven Peacock and Jason Jacobs (219–226). London, New Delhi, New York, Sydney: Bloomsbury Academic, 2013.

McCarthry, Patti. "Jack Frost and the Heroine's Journey: Gender-Bending Back to the Goddess in *Rise of the Guardians.*" In *Fourth Wave Feminism in Science Fiction and Fantasy: Volume 1. Essays on Film Representations, 2012–2019,* edited by Valerie Estelle Frankel (149–170). Jefferson, NC: McFarland, 2019.

Mittell, Jason. "The qualities of complexity: Vast versus dense seriality in contemporary television." In *Television Aesthetics and Style,* edited by Steven Peacock and Jason Jacobs (219–226). London, New Delhi, New York, Sydney: Bloomsbury Academic, 2013.

Mulvey, Laura "Visual Pleasure and Narrative Cinema." In *Film Theory and Criticism: Introductory Readings,* edited by. G. Mast, M. Cohen and L. Braudy, 4th edn (Oxford: Oxford University Press, 1992), 746–55.

Purse, Lisa. *Contemporary Action Cinema.* Edinburgh: Edinburgh University Press, 2011.

Rivers, Nicola. *Postfeminism(s) and the Arrival of the Fourth Wave: Turning Tides.* Palgrave Macmillan, 2017.

Rose, Jacqueline. *The Case of Peter Pan, Or the Impossibility of Children's Fiction.* Pennsylvania: University of Pennsylvania Press, 1993.

Taurino, Giulia. "Crossing Eras: Exploring Nostalgic Reconfigurations in Media Franchises." In *Netflix Nostalgia: Streaming the Past on Demand,* edited by Kathryn Pallister, 9–24. Lanham, MD: Lexington Books, 2019.

Theodoropoulou, Vivi. "From Interactive Digital Television to Internet 'Instant' Television: Netflix, Shifts in Power and Emerging Audience Practices from an Evolutionary Perspective." In *The Age of Netflix: Critical Essays on Streaming Media, Digital Delivery and Instant Access,* edited by Cory Barker and Myc Wiatrowski, 563–621. Jefferson, NC: McFarland, 2017, Kindle.

About the Contributors

Christina **Adamou** is an associate professor in film and television studies at the Film School, Aristotle University of Thessaloniki, Greece. She has published articles and chapters on gender representation and TV history, an edited collection on acting and a book on contemporary television studies. She is researching children's films and television with an emphasis on SVOD platforms.

Georgia **Aitaki** is a senior lecturer in media and communication studies at Karlstad University, Sweden. Her research focuses on critical approaches to television and popular culture and, specifically, on questions of inclusions/exclusions, with an empirical focus on Greek, Swedish, and U.S. media. Her work has appeared in journals such as *View: Journal of European Television History & Culture*, *Media, Culture and Society*, *Social Semiotics*, *Screen*, and in a number of anthologies.

Mayka **Castellano** is a professor at the Department of Cultural and Media Studies and at the Postgraduate Program in Communication at the Federal Fluminense University in Brazil. She is developing research on television and new media, focusing on the consumption of television serial fiction in new media platforms. She has several publications in Brazilian journals on topics such as representation, cultural consumption, fans, distinction, and video streaming services, among others.

Spyridon **Chairetis** holds a Ph.D. in media and cultural studies from the University of Oxford. He has published on Greek (LGBTQI+) cinema and television, genre studies and auto-ethnography. He is teaching television and media studies at Fårö Creative Learning in Athens, Greece. His monograph *Greek Television Comedy: Popular Texts, Queer Readings* is forthcoming.

Patrick **Gill** is a senior lecturer in the English Literature and Culture Department of Johannes Gutenberg University in Mainz, Germany. He is the author of *Origins and Effects of Poetic Ambiguity in Dylan Thomas's* Collected Poems (2014) and the coeditor of *Constructing Coherence in the British Short Story Cycle* (2018). He has lectured and published on English poetry, the contemporary novel, and British and American TV culture.

Daniel Keyes is an associate professor of English and cultural studies in the Faculty of Creative and Critical Studies at the University of British Columbia Okanagan on the unceded territory of the Sylix peoples in western Canada. He served as the founding chair of the Cultural Studies program (2007) and was the first director of Interdisciplinary Graduate Studies (2009). His research focuses on settler-whiteness in Canada and digital ephemerality.

Jossalyn G. Larson is an assistant teaching professor with the Department of English and Technical Communication at Missouri University of Science and Technology. Her research focuses on morality and rhetoric in popular culture. She has published on matters of gender and religiosity in entertainment media, cultural subsects and interest groups, as well as on issues regarding the rhetorical relationships between religious symbols and an increasingly digital world.

Andrew **Lynch** teaches cinema and screen studies in the Department of Media and Communication at Swinburne University of Technology. His research looks at the incorporation of sci-fi, horror, and fantasy genre elements by "Quality TV." His work appears in books such as *HBO's Original Voices: Race, Gender, Sexuality and Power* (2018) and journals including *Quarterly Review of Film and Video.*

Katerina **Marazi** holds a Ph.D. in intercultural studies and American pop culture. Her research interests include adaptation, brand identity theory, transmedia storytelling, and media franchise culture within the entertainment industry. She is a member of EAAS/HELAAS, the Multimodal Group, and the Hellenic Semiotic Society. She has presented at conferences both domestic and abroad, has published in peer-review journals and contributes to the *European Journal of American Studies.*

Melina **Meimaridis** is a Ph.D. candidate at the Federal Fluminense University in Brazil. Her work analyzes "comfort television series" on American TV. She is interested in the sociological ramifications of the fictionalization of social institutions in long-form television narratives. Her other areas of interest are new media, television dramas, fan studies, and spoilers. She has several publications in Brazilian journals on topics such as spoilers, Netflix, and discussions on television quality.

Sotiris **Petridis** is a postdoctorate researcher at Aristotle University of Thessaloniki. He holds a Ph.D. in film studies and two master's degrees in art, law and economy (International Hellenic University) and in film studies (Aristotle University). His research interests concern film and television genres, audiovisual rights and copyright laws, and new ways of film and television promotion. He is a member of the European Film Academy and the Greek Film Academy.

Alexa **Scarlata** is a Ph.D. student at the University of Melbourne and research assistant at RMIT University. Her research considers the achievements and constraints in the history of online television in Australia. She is the book review editor of the *Journal of Digital Media and Policy* and has published in *Communications: The European Journal of Communication Research, International Journal of Digital Television*, and *Media International Australia.*

Jason **Scott** is a senior lecturer in film studies at Leeds Trinity University. His research focuses on Disney+ and the company's shifts into streaming, as well as contemporary animation, the *Star Wars* franchise, and the Iger-era Disney company. He has also begun research on contemporary franchise adaptations in film and television. The latter relates to his continuing research on the historical development of the character-oriented franchise in film and related media.

Ahngeli **Shivam** is a dual Ph.D. candidate in American studies at the Johannes Gutenberg University Mainz, Germany, and in English (literary studies) at Georgia State University. Her interests include cross-culture communication and transnational American studies—particularly life writing, television, and gender studies. Her research focuses on contemporary multimedial representations of Asian Pacific Americans and the complexities of the pan-ethnic identity marker "Asian American."

Despoina **Triantafyllidou** holds a BA in Greek language and literature, with a specialization in Medieval and modern Greek studies from the Department of Greek Language and Literature of Aristotle University of Thessaloniki, and a Ph.D. in film studies. She is a member of the Hellenic Film Academy and the Greek Film Critics Association.

Michael L. **Wayne** is a lecturer at the Department of Media and Communication at Erasmus University Rotterdam. He holds a Ph.D. in sociology from the University of Virginia. His work has appeared in a variety of journals including *Television & New Media, Media, Culture & Society, Journal of Popular Culture,* and *Critical Studies in Television.*

Index

www.ingramcontent.com/pod-product-compliance
Ingram Content Group UK Ltd.
Pitfield, Milton Keynes, MK11 3LW, UK
UKHW041835100926
8556IPUK00018B/973

9 781476 685915